Sex, Violence and the Media

H.J.EYSENCK & D.K.B.NIAS

SEX VIOLENCE AND THE MEDIA

St. Martin's Press
New York

Contents

Figures

Introduction

This book, as the title indicates, is concerned with the possible
influence that viewing and reading overtly pornographic and
violent material may have on a person's conduct. The media –
TV, films, plays, pornographic magazines, even advertising –
have come under increased criticism because of the suspicion
that their more and more overt portrayal of scenes of violence
and sex may be responsible for changes in our civilization
which to many people are undesirable – an increase in violence,
in vandalism, in pre- and extramarital sex, in perversions, in
rape and in the sexual exploitation of minors. If these complaints are justified to any reasonable extent – and of course no
one has suggested that all the changes that have happened in
the past thirty years or so can be laid at the door of the media –
then clearly society will have to think seriously about possible
controls that ought to be instituted in order to restrain these
influences from tearing our society to pieces.

Some people have chosen to adopt an opposite point of view;
they suggest that if society is itself immoral, vicious and in-
human, then pornography and violence may provide the best
ways of bringing it to an end, and making possible the birth of a
new society. Both sides accept without question that the media
in fact have an effect on the behaviour, the outlook and the
mental climate of viewers and readers. This proposition is
doubted by many critics, including psychologists and
sociologists actually working in the field. Clearly it is important
to get the facts straight; does the evidence support the view that
the media do influence people, or does it not? Is it possible that
the evidence is so contradictory that no conclusion is possible at
the moment? These are the questions to which we have addres-
sed ourselves; the conclusions to be drawn, once the answer was
known, if only in outline, have been of much less concern to us –
if only because conclusions regarding social intervention do not
follow logically from factual material, but involve value sys-

tems which draw on sources well outside the provenance of the experimental psychologist.

Many readers will immediately ask why another book is needed in this field; there have been many such attempts to give an answer to the question. Our reply would be that none of these are satisfactory – not because we disagree with many of the conclusions, but because there are serious weaknesses which make these surveys less than useful and compelling. Our first criticism would be that while there is a very large literature relevant to the problem – books, commission reports and other types of survey – they only review this literature very partially, and with many omissions. It is clear, in reading the reports and the originals, that even when articles are referred to they have often been cited at second hand, and do not in fact represent accurately the original work, or the conclusions to be drawn from it. This is a very serious criticism to make; omission of evidence, and misquotation of evidence, make any conclusions suspect. We have a certain amount of sympathy with previous writers, in view of the difficulty we have had in getting some of the original material from the publishers; the many volumes of empirical research on which the President's Commissions on Violence and Pornography in the USA were based, in particular, were almost impossible to obtain, and it took us over a year before we were able to consult them. The details will be given later; nevertheless, such difficulties are there to be overcome, and no reliance can be placed on secondary sources, as we shall document later on.

Our second criticism must be that much of the previous work has been written by sociologists, although the problem in question, and the methods of empirical enquiry, are psychological. It will be necessary to amplify this point, as without such amplification it may simply sound a case of sour grapes, or of professional demarcation disputes. Let us take just one example. Much of the experimental work relating to pornography has dealt with the physiological effects of viewing 'blue' films, or pictures. This has often been indexed by introspective ratings of the state of arousal achieved, or by objective measurements of the degree of penile erection produced. These methods may seem adequate to the layman, or the sociologist, but the psychologist is bound to enquire whether the observed effects were indeed due to the pornographic material, or possibly to erotic fantasies stimulated by the material. The evidence, as we shall see, suggests strongly that the second alternative is the correct one, and that we may be able to distinguish the psychophysiological erection pattern made as a consequence of viewing erotic material, and fantasizing about it. Such psychological knowledge is absolutely essential if we are to interpret the meaning of much of the research in this field correctly; yet not one of the many books, reviews or commission reports in this field shows even an awareness of the problem, let alone an appreciation of the solution.

Our third criticism is related to the one just mentioned. It is concerned with the almost complete absence of psychological theory in the design of experiments or interpretation of the empirical data. As T. H. Huxley said so wisely, 'those who do not go beyond fact seldom get as far as fact'; all facts must be embedded in a theoretical framework, and the more explicit this framework, the easier it is to assess the significance of the data. As we shall see, there have been many misconceptions concerning the interpretation of follow-up data of subjects who have been shown pornographic films; these arose because, instead of using proper predictions derived from academic psychological theories based on large-scale research, the authors used some vague common-sense approach that went directly counter to our accumulated knowledge in this field. In this way the positive findings, which were as would have been predicted on the basis of theory, were neglected in favour of negative findings which also could have been predicted, but which were erroneously interpreted as showing 'no effects' of the exposure.

Another point of view which invites criticism is the one frequently heard, to the effect that there is no *decisive* evidence for the view that the media affect human conduct; this is often allied with the statement that the evidence is contradictory, and consequently that no conclusions can be drawn. As we shall see, the evidence is not really contradictory, except in the sense that a good study, properly planned, executed and analysed, may be contradicted by a bad study, carelessly planned, badly executed and improperly analysed. Too many reviewers have avoided the crucial task of looking at each study in terms of its *quality*; the conclusions drawn by the author of a study are not necessarily justified by his own results. Faulty techniques may generate faulty conclusions; one's approach must be critical, in terms of known and agreed rules of investigative procedure in the psychological sciences. Neglect of this critical appraisal is almost universal in the many books and articles which we have consulted; it is particularly apparent in the President's Commission Reports.

But even if there is much less disagreement than is usually stated, is the evidence decisive? To a scientist, this is a curious and essentially meaningless question. No scientific theory is ever completely 'true', and even if it were, there is no way in which we could prove it to be so. We judge the value of a theory on the basis of cumulative probability; the more support there is for a theory, and the more disproof there is for alternative theories, the more highly do we value the former; nevertheless all this does not guarantee that our theory is correct in all aspects. The bitter lesson of the disproof of Newton's theory of gravitation by Einstein, a theory which for 200 years had been held sacrosanct, has been well learned by scientists. All theories are plagued by anomalies of one kind or another; none are perfect or 'decisively' proven right. This is particularly so when the evidence is largely circumstantial, as it must be in the psychological field; we cannot select random samples of youths and submit them to a diet of pornographic films, or alternatively prevent them from ever seeing any. Experimental designs are complex and difficult to make fool-proof; statistical analysis often has to take care of the many unwanted variables that sneak into the experiment and may confound our data. Conclusions are probabilistic, not certain. Nevertheless, when there is such an impressive amount of agreement in studies employing different methods, different workers, and different populations investigated, we may conclude that there is sufficient evidence in favour of the theory that the media *do* influence the way people think and act and that only the most prejudiced could reject all this evidence and call the case 'unproven'.

There is still much that is not known; many aspects of the problem that require to be analysed experimentally. In particular the interaction of personality and effectiveness of exposure has hardly been touched upon; mass effects on different types of personality are almost certainly much attenuated by divergent reactions to the materials shown. If half the viewers of a pornographic film become more adventurous in their love-making as a consequence, and half are disgusted and become less so, then the overall effect may be nil. Interactions are unlikely to be so clearly marked, but there is evidence that personality plays an important part in deciding on the particular reaction that an individual will show to the presentation of acts of violence, or of perverted sex; this is one of the least explored yet most important areas in the whole field.

Throughout this book, we have used terms like 'pornography', 'erotica', 'perversion', 'deviancy', etc., and we have quoted other authors who have also used these and similar terms. No definite, clear-cut meaning attaches to words of this kind, and they are used by different authors with different implications. In quoting from the writings of others, we have simply used their own words, without interpreting them, and without necessarily agreeing with their particular usage; where a given writer wanted to use the term 'pornographic' to refer to pictures of perfectly ordinary sex practices, we did not feel obliged to censor this usage, although it would not be our own.

We have tried, in our own writings, to use the term 'erotica' and 'erotic' to denote the great variety of sexual practices, and types of fore-play, which are common in our society, without restricting ourselves to the 'missionary position' or to the dictates of religious teaching. The term 'pornography' has been used in connection with practices which are believed to be harmful either to the victims or to the people engaged in them. Thus rape, child-molestation, sadistic behaviour and bestialism would fall under this category; *fellatio* or '69' would not. There are, of course, grey areas in which the verdict would be doubtful; would fetishism, which may render its practitioners incapable of ordinary sexual reactions, or of companionate relationships, be considered sufficiently harmful to qualify for the status of 'pornography'?

The use of 'perversion' and 'deviancy' is analogous to that of 'pornography' and 'erotica'; the former word was used in connection with harmful practices, but not the latter, which was reserved for unusual but not essentially harmful types of behaviour. It proved impossible to be entirely consistent, particularly when dealing with other people's work, but we have at least made the effort.

In substance as well as in language we have tried to avoid moral judgements. It is not for us to say what is good or bad unless the activity in question can be shown to be harmful, though it is our personal belief that a society in which a variety of sexual practices is tolerated and even encouraged is better than one in which such variety is frowned upon and suppressed.

In writing this book we have tried to make it readable and intelligible to the layman, but we have also tried to make it useful to the professional psychologist, sociologist, psychiatrist or anthropologist who might be interested in the field. In thus trying to please two masters, one always runs the danger of falling between two stools; it must be left to the reader to judge to what extent we have avoided this undignified fate.

H. J. Eysenck
D. K. B. Nias
31 January 1978
Institute of Psychiatry
University of London

1   Growth of the Controversy

We are concerned in this book with the view, held by many
people, that violence, vandalism, cruelty, and undesirable sex
practices are encouraged by their representation in the media,
and that these representations may in part be responsible for
the undesirable changes in our national life which have taken
place in recent years. There is no doubt, as we shall see, that the
increase in crime, violence and vandalism, and what might be
called unorthodox or unusual sex practices, over the past
twenty or thirty years has been paralleled by an increase in the
portrayal of violence in the media, particularly films and TV,
by a similar increase in the number of pornographic
publications, films and books, and by the greater explicitness of
portrayal of sexual behaviour in the media and literary publications. The existence of such a correlation over time does not
necessarily argue a causal connection; it may be that the
changes in the cultural patterns related to violence and sex
have produced the greater permissiveness in the media, rather
than the other way about. Possibly there has been a reciprocal
interaction between these factors. Undoubtedly, even if the
media have played some role in the cultural changes that have
taken place, these cannot be the only factors that have been at
work. Nevertheless, there is disquiet in the minds of many men
and women who have observed these changes, and lived
through them, and these worries and fears may not be entirely
imaginary.

Before turning to a consideration of the facts on which these
worries are based, let us look at an individual example which
may seem to suggest that pornographic material may play a
decisive role in causing individual acts of sexual violence. Only
one case will be described in some detail; there are hundreds of
others on our files.[1] The case concerns the brutal rape of a

---

[1] Appreciation is due to the library staff of the Mirror Group Newspapers for help in
collecting these case reports.

fourteen-year-old girl. The offences connected with this case were committed by two fifteen-year-old boys and one fourteen-year-old boy; none of them knew the girl. The girl had been baby-sitting and returned home around 11.00 p.m., and the couple she was baby-sitting for gave her a lift to the street near the block of flats to which she was going. As she was walking there, a red sports car pulled up. In it were the three youths who had taken the car earlier from a nearby street. They offered her a lift but she refused.

All three followed the girl into the block of flats, where they grabbed hold of her. One of them pushed her into a dark corner and ordered her to take off her trousers, while another produced a penknife. They began fondling the girl but were interrupted by an irate resident who shouted at them. They then dragged the girl away from the flats and flung her down behind a tree near the river Lea. One of them told her, 'If you don't take all your clothes off, you'll go into the river.'

The terrified girl stripped and all three boys raped her. They called to each other: 'It's your turn,' and raped her again and again. They committed 'other horrifying sex acts'. One kicked the girl because she cried when ordered to perform a sex act.

After several minutes three men in their thirties arrived. First they watched the boys rape the girl, then they too joined in. According to the girl herself, they were friends of one of the accused. At one point the boys and the men were all engaged in some form of sex activity against the girl. When the men left the boys again had intercourse with her. Afterwards two of the youths urinated over her. Then all three left, threatening to break her neck if she told anyone. The girl, covered in mud, managed to gather some clothes together and went to her friend's flat, and the police were called. She was in a very filthy condition, and the woman doctor found bruises, scratches and teeth marks on the girl, who was also in great pain. She was so badly swollen that the police doctor was unable to examine her properly. 'The three youths were traced and all three made statements of confession. In all these lengthy statements there was not one single word or expression of remorse or care as to what the girl went through.'

The relevance of this horrifying story to the theme of this book is made clear in the words of the Prosecuting Counsel, who stated: 'At the ringleader's home, a number of pornographic photographs were found, some showing explicitly the kind of beastly sex offences that had been committed against the girl.' This suggests, but does not of course prove, that these pornographic materials were, at least in part, responsible for the crime that had been committed. Even the fact that many other, similar cases can be quoted, in which the violent or sexual activity committed against some other person was in fact a mirror image of a similar activity portrayed in a film, or a book, or a TV presentation to which the person responsible had been exposed, does not provide such proof. However, these cases raise a genuine demand for investigation, and suggest that all may not be well.

We shall later on come back to the consideration of the evidential value of single cases of this kind, and mention a few more. In this chapter, we shall first of all consider a number of acknowledged facts which have helped to persuade many people that the civilization in which we live may be in danger of being submerged under a deluge of crime, violence and sexual perversion. Consider Figure 1, which shows a 100 per cent increase in violence from 1958 to 1968 in the United States. The years since then have shown a continued rise, and it is notable that this increase applies mainly to young people. In the UK, there has been a similar pattern, with the rate of indictable crime almost doubling in the decade 1960 to 1970. Crimes of violence against the person have increased ten-fold in the quarter-century since 1951, and two out of every three known burglars are now under twenty-one years of age. Morgan (1978) summarizes the picture by saying: 'Violence, destruction, and youth, are the three distinctive features of rising crime'. Evidence of people's awareness and concern is indicated by a recent Gallup poll in which a random sample of the adult British population was asked: 'Do you consider —— to be a very serious social problem?' Top of the list came 'crimes of violence' with 85 per cent giving a clearly affirmative answer; next came 'juvenile crime' with 81 per cent, followed by 'drug taking' (71 per cent), 'bad housing' (64 per cent), and 'coloured immigration' (59 per cent).

The degree of crime and violence, of course, varies considerably from country to country; the homicide rate in the USA is four times that in Australia, six times that in Austria, and over eight times that in England and Wales. 15,000 Americans are

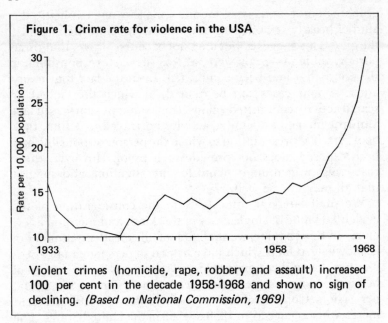

Figure 1. Crime rate for violence in the USA

Violent crimes (homicide, rape, robbery and assault) increased 100 per cent in the decade 1958-1968 and show no sign of declining. *(Based on National Commission, 1969)*

murdered annually as compared with only 150 in Great Britain. American figures for rape are 30,000, and for being violently assaulted 300,000 per annum. The statistics suggest that the murder rate would be even higher, were it not for modern medicine which succeeds in rescuing a high proportion of victims who would otherwise have died.

Regarding sex, there has been a marked increase in the number of reported rapes in most Western countries recently. Other sexual practices which are not normally subject to criminal law, or which are only reported in isolated instances, are more difficult to document; we will try to do so later on, particularly in regard to the Danish experience. One item on which there can be no doubt is the massive increase in divorce rates, which is now mounting to the 50 per cent level, suggesting that only one marriage in two will not·be disrupted by divorce. The increase in pornography and the portrayal of explicit sexual scenes in general need hardly be documented; figures are difficult to come by, particularly as much of the trade is in the grey area between ordinary business and criminal activity, and is difficult to document. Such documentation is probably unimportant, anyway, because no one familiar with the scene can doubt that the facts are as stated.

We must next turn to some consideration of the popularity and contents of TV, because many authors have made TV responsible for much of the increase in crime and violence which has taken place in the years since it appeared on the scene. Regarding the popularity of TV, there is no denying the extent to which it has become part of our lives. It is now the most widespread medium, with nearly all homes in the USA and the UK having a TV set. Reported hours of viewing have increased steadily, with people in the US watching more than the UK. In the United States, the average family has a television set in use for about forty hours each week; in England, children aged six to eleven years watch an estimated twenty-five hours a week. Other surveys indicate that lower-income families watch most TV, and children watch more than adults (National Commission, 1969).

Nias (1975) conducted a survey on the popularity of television relative to other interests. 1,152 children were asked to rate how much they liked various leisure pursuits, including the watching of TV. They were also asked to rate different types of programmes for enjoyment. The sample was aged twelve to sixteen years, and was from both comprehensive and grammar schools in the English Midlands.

Watching TV was rated as one of the more popular leisure pursuits, although both boys and girls preferred 'going on holiday', 'going camping', 'going out with boy/girl friend', and 'going to the cinema'. Among TV programmes, adventure, crime, horror, and war films, as well as cartoons, were the most popular – with only pop music programmes (for girls) getting higher ratings. Westerns, the only other type of programme involving violence, were relatively unpopular – perhaps because they are no longer novel or violent enough.

According to the latest US survey, the average child aged two to five spends a third or more of his total waking hours watching the screen. The average American watches more than 1,200 hours a year, and reads books for less than five hours a year. Although there is more TV viewing in the US than in probably any other country, these figures give some indication of the degree to which television can become a part of our lives, and the degree to which it may influence our picture of the world, and thus shape our actions.

Sex on TV has been fairly strictly controlled, with a definite relaxation in recent years; seventy-six attempted seductions (and quite a lot of them apparently successful) were noted between the early evening news and the epilogue in a recent survey of one week of British TV. In contrast to the control over more explicit sex scenes, violence has hardly been censored at all. The amount of violence shown on TV has steadily increased until just recently, when it has reached a plateau, with efforts being made to try and reduce its incidence. Even children's programmes involve violence, especially cartoons. Television officials have often promised a reduction in violence, but there is little evidence of these promises being fulfilled. Others deny or evade the problem; one producer is quoted as saying, 'There's not one-hundredth as much violence on TV as there is in the society' (Baldwin and Lewis, 1972).

A survey of the years 1967 to 1971 revealed a rate of 7.5 violent episodes per hour during prime time (Gerbner, 1972). It has been estimated that the average American child will have witnessed more than 11,000 murders on television by the time he is fourteen. The rate of violent episodes per programme hour is less in Britain, having been estimated at about 4 per hour by Halloran and Croll (1972). One reason for this national difference may be that commercial interests play a lesser part in British TV than in American; it is possible that commercial pressures lead TV producers to include more and more gratuitous violence.

The National Commission (1969) conducted a survey in 1967 which showed that 94 per cent of cartoons contained violence. In 1968, 81 per cent of prime time entertainment shows on TV in the US contained violence, and it was estimated that a child will have seen 20,000 incidents of violence on TV by the age of nineteen. There is no doubt that the most violent culture, as assessed by homicide and crime rates, in the US, whose TV programmes feature twice as much violence as those shown in the UK.

We have already referred to the difficulty of substantiating the increase in the availability of pornography, but some figures may indicate the size of the problem. At the last count, for instance, there were 264 'kiddie porn mags' of the Lolita type produced each month in the US, where child pornography is one of the fastest growing industries, 300,000 children under sixteen being involved in the commercial sex industry. The popularity of pornography magazines, generally, is indicated by their low price; only a high circulation could allow up to 150 pages of high-quality colour photography to be sold for less than a pound.

There has also, of course, been an increase in sex education, but that too is potentially dangerous. A case was recently reported in which a twelve-year-old boy attacked and killed a girl of four after having sex lessons at school. The boy said in court that the teacher had told him about intercourse, but had never mentioned marriage, love and affection. 'The teacher talked about sex, and about reproduction of animals, plants and men and women . . . The teacher never said when these things would happen or about growing up . . . I wanted to find out what intercourse was like. I thought I could do it with [a girl].' The connection between teaching emphasizing 'impersonal sex' and the action of the boy seems clear enough to serve as a warning signal.

Little is in fact known about the advantages and the dangers of sex education; as in most other fields of sexual behaviour adherents and opponents have drawn up their battle lines without waiting for the impartial scientific documentation of factual evidence without which such opinions must remain worthless. It is easy to see that sex education there must be; it is more difficult to know who is the best person to give it. It is even more difficult to know how best the programme could be carried out; there just is no empirical evidence regarding the consequences of different methods and programmes to even give us a hint. Pasteur once gave the wise advice: 'In ignorance, abstain!' Instead of rushing into new adventures, society might be better advised to carry out the needed research which alone would enable us to make sure that what we were doing was an improvement on what went before, rather than the opposite.

In the absence of experimentally ascertained facts, such as those reviewed in the remainder of the book, most people have formed their opinions on the possibly damaging effects of the portrayal of sex and violence on TV and in the pornographic literature on the basis of preconceived opinions. Even among professional psychologists familiar with the literature, differ-

ences in opinion can be observed. A few quotations may serve
to outline the range of opinions which are held by responsible
people. The first is from a standard introductory textbook in
psychology:

> What the effects are of . . . intense exposure to violence, especially
> upon children, remains, despite considerable research, a highly
> . . . debatable question. We will not attempt to summarize the data
> (often contradictory) and arguments that have been accumulated
> around this issue. At the moment we hopefully lean towards the
> view that most children (and adults) effectively insulate them-
> selves from, say, television orgies of terror and violence. It is all
> make-believe and some data suggest that it may even have a
> cathartic effect, permitting the harmless draining off of unexpres-
> sed anger. (Krech *et al.*, 1974)

Alas, as we shall see, this hopeful leaning towards optimism is
hardly justified by the data, which are less contradictory than is
suggested in this excerpt.

J. Edgar Hoover, Director of the FBI, gave voice to the
opposite view, in a much more extreme form, when he stated in
1951 that 'the increase in the number of sex crimes is due
precisely to sex literature madly presented in certain
magazines. Filthy literature is a great moral wrecker. It is
creating criminals faster than jails can be built.' This pessimis-
tic view, too, is hardly justified by the data; it expresses an
over-reaction which is just as harmful as the facile optimism
often found among the trendy.

A rather more cautious expression of the view that the media
may after all have some effect was presented by the eminent
criminologist S. Glueck, when he was asked for his view by the
Kefauver Sub-committee on Juvenile Delinquency. He said: 'A
consistent hammering-away influence of an exciting or sala-
cious crime, day-in-day-out, must have an erosive effect on the
mind of youth.' Note, however, that this view is not directly
based on evidence, but on *a priori* considerations; the truth is
probably as stated, but our views should always be based on
evidence.

Views such as these, whether justified or not, may give rise to
social action. There is evidence that judges may give severe
sentences, out of righteous indignation, to 'pornographers'
which are quite out of tune with sentences handed out to other
types of offenders. Thus in 1976 a man showing pornographic

films in a private club in Islington (London) was fined £7,000
and sent to prison for eighteen months; this seems rather
extreme when it is realized that he was showing the films in a
club, while pornographic magazines are prominently displayed
all over the West End without fear of prosecution. It also
contrasts with another court case on the same day where a man
convicted of driving without due care and attention was only
fined £100 even though he had mowed down and killed five
people. In this case the judge had considered that his guilt
would be sufficient punishment.

It may be useful, in this introductory chapter, to briefly state
some of the arguments customarily used for believing or dis-
believing in the harmful effects of the showing of violence and
explicit sex in films and in pornographic magazines. One
argument frequently made is that from advertising; TV and
magazines are successful in persuading people to buy things by
simply showing models buying and enjoying these things; why
should the same not apply to showing actions of a violent or
sexual nature which apparently are satisfying the people portraying them on the screen or in the magazines? The argument
is probably not as powerful as it seems when it is realized that
most of the things advertised on television and in magazines are
things people want anyway (motor cars, refrigerators, different
types of food and drink, holidays, etc.); it would be stretching
the facts to say that they want violence or perverted forms of sex
in the same way. The media may wake them up to the existence
of certain forms of violence or perverted satisfaction, but that is
rather a different point. It could also be argued that television
and magazine advertising is directed mainly at people already
'in the market', in an attempt to pull them towards one or other
of a number of different firms or products competing for customers. This is often suggested by cigarette firms, for instance,
to justify their advertising; unfortunately there is little empirical evidence to enable one to judge the truth or falsity of any of
these arguments.

A second argument often advanced is from the field of
socialization: TV gives a view of society, and gives repeated
examples of how to behave in different situations. Youngsters
growing up must have models set before them which they can
imitate, and from whom they can learn how to act in situations
they have never encountered before. This process of socializa-

tion is very important, and parents, teachers, peers, books, magazines, and TV all play a part, as does individual experience. If on TV the child is taught that hitting someone who deserves it is a good and accepted thing, then this will become part of the socialization programme. Similarly, cartoons may give the impression that violence is fun and does not matter – when Tom and Jerry get their fur burned off, all is well in the end! There is evidence regarding this argument, and we shall see that it is justified, at least in part.

A third type of argument frequently advanced we have already considered, namely case studies reported in the newspapers showing how TV violence and pornography may exert their influence on individual cases. Thus much was made of the fact that Ian Brady and Myra Hindley, who were convicted of murdering and torturing a ten-year-old girl, were found to have sadistic literature at home; they took a tape recording of the girl's long agony while they were torturing her. The evidential value of such cases is low, as we shall argue in Chapter 3, but they are impressive and often produce a strong emotional reaction.

Many people accept that these arguments are quite reasonable, but are not very impressed all the same. They may argue, for instance, that to eliminate violence from the screen would not cause it to go away in real life; violence has always been with us, long before the advent of TV, and the elimination of it from TV would not have any major kind of effect. This may, of course, be true but, like the opposite argument, requires proof. This argument is often supported by another, to the effect that whatever violence TV may add to the sum total of aggression and violence is negligible, compared with the many other sources of violence in our society.

Another belief, quite widespread, is that perhaps only emotionally disturbed, or otherwise vulnerable people are affected by TV violence and pornography. However, just a few violent or depraved individuals can do a great deal of harm, and furthermore it may be said that it is not an argument against the eradication of a potent source of violence in society to say that there are other sources; on that argument none of these sources would ever be eradicated.

An argument quite frequently heard is that the main effect of pornography is to stimulate the sexual appetite for normal sex, and that this is a good thing – 'make love not war'. It has also been said that people who have lost the urge to make love because they get bored with 'orthodox' practices may learn new techniques, and thus reawaken their desire for sexual unions, and thus save their marriages. Thus pornography may in fact have good effects. Some psychologists have argued for another possibly useful effect of violence and pornography on TV; they use a theory of catharsis, i.e. that fantasies satisfy a need, and are used when a delay in gratification is necessary. Broadcasters often claim that TV can discharge aggression, and so serve a useful purpose through the medium of catharsis. The evidence, as we shall see, hardly supports this optimistic view. These and many other arguments are frequently batted around by the permissive and the censorious; their value in the absence of proper scientific evidence is small, and the discussion must remain inconclusive in the absence of such evidence.

Such research is relatively recent, although we shall report some earlier studies which are of considerable interest, and suggest the necessity for many experimental controls if the results of a given piece of research are to be taken seriously. Altogether we shall find that much research reported in the literature is unimaginative, repetitive, and grossly oversimplified; conclusions are often framed without regard to possible alternatives, and may betray the *a priori* inclinations of the investigator. There are many methodological pitfalls which have not always, or even usually, been avoided.

Consider, for example, recent field studies which were designed to show that children who watched a lot of TV become more aggressive; the possibility that aggressive children might watch more TV than unaggressive children to begin with was overlooked by these investigators. Yet early studies by Cressey and Thrasher (1933) had shown that delinquents attended the cinema more frequently than other children, and Hoult (1949) had shown that they had higher exposure to comics.

Similarly, in the days before TV became prominent, Nias and Kay (1954) had shown that it would be particularly influential because of the opportunity it gave to 'dramatize' its subject matter. They found that people who listened to a half-hour dramatized feature on the radio showed a surprisingly accurate knowledge of the story when questioned afterwards.

After reviewing other work on the subject, the authors concluded that 'it would seem then that a dramatized version as compared with a talk can make a more definite and permanent impact upon listeners'. This early research has apparently been overlooked by those who argue that because TV violence is usually dramatized it will not have much effect on people.

Faults in the experimental literature, which we shall discuss in much greater detail in the following chapters, have had a considerable effect on many of the books and government reports written on the subject. We have found that conclusions agreeable to the particular author are quoted uncritically, and without drawing attention to the limitations of a given study, while those not in agreement with the author's view are rejected in a rather over-critical manner, e.g. refusing to consider acceptable parts of the evidence because the study as a whole had certain limitations. Quite frequently we have also found that authors of books and commission reports had either failed to read some of the studies they reported in the original or had misinterpreted what they had read; we have found it quite impossible to rely on secondary sources because these often misinterpret the original data, and may upon occasion quote them in exactly the opposite direction to that actually indicated by the original investigators. Readers are warned of the danger implicit in this situation because it may easily give the impression that there is far more disagreement on fact than there actually is. We have carefully read and catalogued all of the empirical evidence available to us, and have found that where contradictions and differences do exist, they can usually be explained in terms of populations being tested which differ in age and socio-economic status, different materials being used, different instructions being given, different time periods for follow-up being used, etc. It would be quite wrong to imagine that identical conclusions should be reached when parameters are varied in this way; we were in fact surprised to find how much agreement there was among different investigators, using different methods, and varying parameters of the kind mentioned. The impression of disagreement is based much more on the fact that authors have approached the field with preconceived ideas and have tried to force the evidence into a procrustean mould which it would not readily accept. We shall have occasion to document this rather severe statement in the following chapters.

It has been particularly unfortunate in this connection that the US Commissions set up to investigate the effects of TV violence and pornography were mainly manned by amateurs as far as the evaluation is concerned, and were selected expressly to represent certain interests, as we shall point out in Chapter 4. Even so, their conclusions were not necessarily incorrect, but they were expressed in such a cautious and circumscribed fashion that the wrong impression was frequently given. Thus the Commission report on TV violence declared it to be harmful, but this conclusion was couched with so many reservations that some newspapers thought the conclusion was one of 'no harm'. This is particularly sad as, in evaluating the work of these Commissions, the interested reader has a choice between studying thousands of pages of complex technical reports, or relying on unsubstantiated summaries (the final reports) produced by the Commissions, reports which gave a highly unreliable review of the actual experiments and empirical studies that had been performed. Popular accounts in newspaper articles, in turn summarizing the Commission reports, further aggravated the situation by reinterpreting the conclusions in line with their own preconceived ideas. It is small wonder that the man in the street is utterly confused, and believes that nothing is in fact known about the subject. As we shall see, this is by no means the case.

Perhaps we should here mention one particular ploy which is frequently used by those who deny 'harmful' effects of TV, against the strong evidence from empirical studies. This ploy is used particularly by sophisticated academics who wish to counter the views of most of the researchers who have investigated the effects of TV violence and of pornography, namely where these indicate potentially adverse effects. As an example, consider a book by Howitt and Cumberbatch (1975) from the Centre for Mass Communication Research at the University of Leicester in England. They did not agree with the conclusions of 'harmful' effects reached by the two American commissions on violence; instead they expressed their own view that the mass media 'do not have any significant effect on the level of violence in society'. They rightly pointed out that a reviewer cannot take the easy way out by simply accepting the statements appearing at the end of a research article; instead he 'must examine the individual worth of each study'.

They arrived at their conclusion, absolving TV of any responsibility for increased violence, by systematically finding fault with all the studies that indicated 'harmful' effects, which left only a few field studies with ambiguous results. But it does not follow that because research studies are not perfect, a conclusion of 'no effect' can be drawn. It is possible to find fault with most studies in psychology, and indeed in all science; this does not mean that a conclusion cannot be drawn even from imperfect evidence which is all that is usually available. Newton's Laws of Gravitation, to take but one example, were severely criticized because of their imperfection and their failure to account for many of the observed facts, and similarly his mathematical methods were criticized as being non-rigorous. It would have been quite wrong, however, to disregard his conclusions. Perfection is not to be found in human affairs, and every scientist is aware of the limitations of individual studies; he learns to base his conclusions on the agreed findings of many less-than-perfect studies, each having different limitations, and subject to different criticisms. To insist on 'perfect' experiments means that no conclusion can ever be reached.

It is our contention that research in this field, although not perfect, contains enough work of a high standard to arrive at a firm conclusion. As we shall see, there is important agreement between experimental laboratory studies, field studies, and 'experimental field studies' which combine some of the advantages of the former two methods of investigation. Furthermore, the results that are found are in good agreement with theoretical expectations from well-founded psychological laws and hypotheses. This network of interrelations between theory and experiment is particularly impressive, and provides sufficient evidence for certain conclusions.

We shall end this chapter with a consideration of one point which has already been adumbrated, but which it is important to be clear about; hence we will try to elaborate it into some kind of model. We have already mentioned the important suggestion that some people may be more easily influenced by TV and the other media than others; they in turn may then influence others. Cline (1974) has provided a couple of examples of how this may work. If pornography seduced only one person each year into having some sexual deviancy, and if this person yearly influenced only one other individual, who in turn affected only one other, in twenty years 1,048,575 sexually disturbed people would be the result! Cline also gives another example to illustrate the fact that even a very small percentage of people being affected by a given type of activity might add up to a sizeable number. In 1952 only 0.024 per cent of US citizens died in road accidents. But applied to the whole population of the US, this meant that 37,794 people lost their lives.

For the purpose of this model, let us take a very over-simplified view of the situation. Let us assume that predisposition to violence can be rated on a scale ranging from 0 to 100, and let us also assume that the population is distributed in the shape of a normal curve of distribution, with a mean of 50, as illustrated in Figure 2. 5 per cent of this population, as shown on the right side, are already violent; they are allocated beyond the X point which marks off the violent from the non-violent. 10 per cent are in a danger zone, meaning by that that they are near the threshold of violence, but have not quite passed it yet. Let us now assume that 1,000 people whose scores on the imaginary scale of violence have been plotted in the diagram are shown a very violent TV film which raises their scores by just one point. What effect would that have on the level of violence in this population? 5 per cent, i.e. 50 individuals, are already violent; having passed the X point they will not be further considered. However, we now have a number of people who were close to the X point, but not yet violent; these will be thrown into the violent group, i.e. beyond the X point, by the showing of the film. How many will there be?

Out of our group of 1,000, 7 people will be pushed into the 'violent' group by the hypothetical TV presentation adding just one point to each person's score. If the TV presentation had the effect of adding two points, then 15 subjects would be pushed into the 'violent' group; three points would affect 24 people, four points 34, and five points 44; in our simple model these people would all come from the 10 per cent of semi-violent or violence-prone people lying between Y and X. Shifts of this magnitude, i.e. between 1 and 5 per cent, are quite within the range of experimental findings, even with single presentations; from that point of view our model is quite a reasonable one.

The numbers involved may not seem too frightening to most

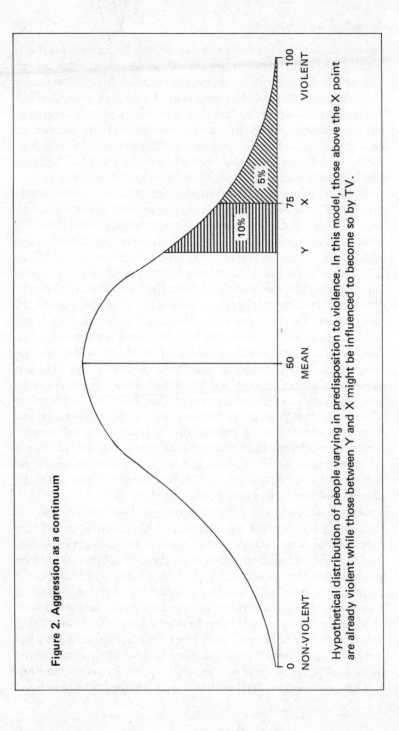

Figure 2. Aggression as a continuum

Hypothetical distribution of people varying in predisposition to violence. In this model, those above the X point are already violent while those between Y and X might be influenced to become so by TV.

readers, but of course they must be seen in a national context. The increase in the number of overtly violent people produced by just a 1 per cent shift on our scale would be 350,000 in the United Kingdom, and 1,400,000 in the United States. This surely would be a truly frightening prospect. If we took the 5 per cent increase in score, i.e. a shift of five points, then the increase in the number of explicitly and overtly violent people would be 2,250,000 in the United Kingdom, and 9,000,000 in the United States.

These figures and computations are, of course, merely illustrative, and should not be taken too seriously. The model is clearly grossly over-simplified; there are different kinds of violence which cannot easily be plotted on a single dimension, and to that extent the picture is not a realistic one. Neither is it realistic to divide the total population into those who are 'violent' and those who are not; violence is obviously a graded characteristic, and most people are violent sometimes, and to some extent, rather than never or always.

There is one further criticism one might make of such a model. It is unrealistic to expect all the people to be equally affected, and to be shifted by one point exactly. It might be that those situated between points Y and X are more easily affected, and to a larger extent, because they are already teetering on the border of violence, and need only a slight shove. Those at the other end of the scale might in fact not be affected at all, or even be pushed in the opposite direction, i.e. disliking violence even more than they did before, being brought face to face with its ugly consequences. We might also have to take into account what psychophysiologists call the 'law of initial value'; this simply states that the amount of change to be expected from a particular stimulus depends on the original state of the organism. If we measure the increase in heartbeats, or electric conductivity of the skin, or size of the pupil which is produced by a certain frightening experience (e.g. the threat of electric shock in the laboratory), then we will find that some people start the whole experiment already in a rather frightened state, with increased heartbeat, increased conductivity of the skin due to sweating, and enlarged pupils. Others are quite calm and relaxed. If we now measure the increases in psychophysiological state due to the threat of shock, we will find that the calm subjects will have more room to increase heartbeat, electric conductivity and size of pupil than those who are already nearer their maximum, and consequently will show greater increases in all these measures. This law may also apply here.

All these considerations would, of course, have to be taken into account in an actual experiment; our model was merely put forward to demonstrate in a quantitative manner that even quite small effects, so small as to be hardly measurable, may have tremendous and far-reaching consequences. To say that the media have only a minor influence, and cannot be held responsible for most of the increase in violence etc., is almost certainly true, but this should not lead us to underrate the overall size of the influence that the media may have. It is as wrong to underrate as to overrate this influence, and the studies cited in the remainder of the book will give us a chance to obtain some quantitative estimates of the possible effects on people that presentation on TV, in films, or in pornographic books may have.

In our discussions so far, we have talked about violence and pornography as if these were strictly comparable; most critics will probably feel that we are dealing here with quite different entities, and this view is fairly explicitly apparent in the reports of the two US Commissions on Violence and Pornography respectively. Violence is deplored by practically everybody; there are very few people who would defend the increase in lawlessness, violence, vandalism, etc., particularly in the urban environment, that has overtaken cities in the United States, and to a minor extent in England and the Continent also. There are some exceptions, e.g. writers like the rather absurd Frantz Fanon, whose advocacy of violence has given him a somewhat unsavoury repute, but even they would seek to justify violence in a more political context than is appropriate to ordinary muggings and rapes. Gallup polls have again and again shown the concern of the man in the street with urban violence, putting this in the top few problems that he considers to be besetting our civilization at the present time.

Pornography, on the other hand, does not seem to present anything like the same kind of problem, and indeed many people see nothing wrong in the portrayal of perfectly normal and ordinary human intercourse in the great variety of ways in which it can be achieved. Some writers and thinkers, indeed, have greeted pornography as some great liberation of the spirit, some removal of unnecessary and malevolent censorship, a rebirth of freedom and loss of inhibition and repression that ought to be welcomed rather than criticized. Whether these thinkers would include the portrayal of sex involving children or animals, the showing of films of rape, bondage and beating, or the enacting of sado-masochistic practices and necrophiliac fantasies is perhaps another question; some would seem to go that far, while others would not. What many people do question, however, is whether the portrayal of any kind of sexual activity involving consenting adults should be regarded as 'bad' in the sense that violence, which inevitably involves non-consenting adults and children, is clearly 'bad'.

There clearly is a difference, along the lines suggested, but it may not be as clear-cut as at first thought. We shall see later on that there is good evidence to show that physiologically and psychologically there is a close connection between violence and sex; some pornographic films may stimulate violence, and violent films may stimulate sexuality. It is easier to separate concepts like these in the abstract than to dissect them in the living organism; we will have to get used to the idea that to stimulate sexuality by overt representation of 'abnormal' sexual acts is likely to increase violence as well. This ineluctable fact will have to be faced by those who talk freely about the flowering of a sexually non-repressive civilization; there is a danger that setting people free to 'fuck in the streets' (in the somewhat inelegant words of the schoolgirl writing in the children's issue of *Oz* that was the cause of a famous court trial for indecency) may also set them free to beat each other up in the streets. Whether the attractions of the former might not be offset by the disadvantages of the latter is a decision that everyone must make for himself. We here simply want to draw attention to the facts of the case.

Ultimately certain decisions have to be made, and these decisions, in a democratic society, must be made by the people as a whole. We have not seen our task here as imposing our value system on the reader, and suggesting what ought to be *done*; we have been more concerned with telling the reader what is known about the effects of the explicit presentation of acts of violence and sex in the media. It is important to separate these two issues from each other; it is perfectly obvious that one issue is a factual one, concerning what actually happens, and the other is an ethical one, concerning what our actions ought to be. Unfortunately the literature shows that these two things have often been mixed up in an unholy melee, with the writer's ethical and moral preconceptions and judgements influencing his view of what the facts are. In theory it is possible to hold that the portrayal of violence and sex in the media has no effect on people, but is wrong on ethical and moral grounds, just as it is to believe that such portrayal is wrong, and also has effects on other people. Similarly, one might hold that such portrayal did have effects on other people, but was not morally wrong and should be encouraged. In actual fact the literature is almost devoid of protagonists who hold views dissociating values and effects; the great majority of those who believe that the portrayal of violence and sex is wrong also believe that it has an effect on other people, while the great majority of those who do not think it is wrong also do not think that it has an effect.

This association of value judgement and factual judgement seems to us to oversimplify greatly a very complex situation. If we start with certain moral imperatives, whether religious or anti-censorship, we are unlikely to be swayed by rational argument, or by appeal to fact, and indeed, we are likely to interpret fact in line with our preconceived ideas. The actual situation is somewhat akin to the essence of a Greek tragedy, in that perfectly good and sound principles are opposed to each other; the situation is far removed from the black-and-white contrast so beloved by the adherents of moral (or immoral) positions. The claims of artistic freedom, freedom of expression, etc., are perfectly valid in their own right; but so are claims for the protection of the individual, and for the preservation of moral and ethical values. Clearly no universally acceptable solution is possible, whatever the facts may turn out to be, but equally clearly some compromise is essential, if only to prevent the violent swing of the pendulum from utter permissiveness to large-scale repression, and back.

Mary Whitehouse and Kenneth Tynan, in their very different ways, represent the two extremes which have for long befuddled the issue. Mrs Whitehouse starts out from a Christian position which clearly prejudges the issue; if premarital and extramarital sexual activity are wrong in principle, then their portrayal on TV, in films, on the stage, or in books must also be wrong. This is perfectly true for the believer, but the great majority of people in the Western world clearly do not start out from this point of view, and consequently are unlikely to agree with Mrs Whitehouse even though much of what she has to say may be perfectly sensible and supported by the facts. The objection felt by many people seems to be similar to that voiced by Disraeli when he complained of Gladstone that he didn't mind that Gladstone always had an ace up his sleeve; what he objected to was the pretence that God had put it there!

Tynan seems to start from the point of view that freedom of artistic expression is an absolute moral imperative, and that all inhibitions and repressions, particularly sexual ones, are wrong. Belief in absolutes in this field is a sign of immaturity, and again few people would start out with this kind of imperative.

If both extremes are clearly unacceptable to the majority of people, then equally clearly some kind of compromise must be found, a compromise perhaps equally unacceptable to both extremists, but sufficiently comfortable for the majority of people to live with. We shall discuss the possibilities of such a compromise at the end of our examination of the factual evidence, but we want to emphasize that the value of the evidence should not be judged by the acceptability of our compromise. What we are competent to do is to examine the evidence, judge it, and come to some tentative conclusions. These conclusions will then have to be looked at in the light of the particular value system adopted by the reader, who will then be able to come to some conclusions of his own. Whether these will agree with ours depends on many factors, such as age, sex, marital status, personal experiences, social class, political preferences, artistic interests, and many others. There is an infinity of influences in society pushing people in various directions regarding this issue; to suggest a compromise is not to imagine that all people are alike, but merely to try and find a way of reconciling extreme differences in a way that is most acceptable to most people. We do not flatter ourselves that we have any special competence in the social–moral–ethical field, but we do believe that a psychologist who is familiar with all the varied expression of human prejudice and belief may have a better chance of reconciling these divergent prejudices and beliefs than someone who is clearly committed to one or other of them.

SUMMARY

The marked recent increase in crimes of violence and of sex, as well as the changing moral climate, the increase in divorce rates, and the growth of what are considered by many to be 'perverted' practices, have suggested to many people that perhaps the media – cinema, TV, pornographic literature, newspapers and magazines – may have played a part in producing these changes, through the overt portrayal of violence and deviant sexual activities. The concomitance of the observed changes in the behaviour of people, and in the contents of the media, suggests but does not prove the existence of a causal relation.[1] Many theories and arguments have been put forward in this connection, but serious scientific studies are of fairly recent origin, although a few pioneering studies were done twenty and thirty years ago. This book is concerned with a survey of such studies, and the theories they were designed to test. It is realized that there are many influences making for change in the social climate, and that the media may only reflect other influences, and that even where they exert an independent push, this could not be very powerful. Nevertheless, a simple model makes it clear that even quite small causes may have quite far-reaching effects in this field, and the factual question of whether the media do or do not have any influence is an important one, even though an answer in the affirmative still leaves open the additional question of whether these changes are for the better or for the worse, and also cannot tell us what we ought to do about the problem.

---

[1] This fact creates difficulties in dealing judicially with the 'copycat' syndrome, i.e. the acting-out in real life of a crime seen on stage or screen. Recently the US Supreme Court allowed Mrs V. Niemi of San Francisco to sue NBC for nearly £6 million in damages on the grounds that NBC had been negligent in portraying violence which might be imitated in real life. Mrs Niemi's nine-year-old daughter was sexually assaulted by four older girls; only four days earlier, NBC had transmitted a TV movie called *Born Innocent*, in which a female convict was raped by four other inmates. Within twenty-four hours of the Supreme Court decision, a Tacoma (Washington) probation officer reported that three inmates of a home for problem girls had raped a fourth; they had been playing *Born Innocent*, they explained! Another example is Ronnie Zamorra, a 15-year-old TV addict whose parents are suing all three major US networks for £12,500,000. Ronnie, who is serving a life sentence for shooting and killing a neighbour, is claimed by his lawyer to be unable to tell real life from the TV programmes to which he is devoted. Legal actions over 'copycat' crimes have not yet occurred in England, but they may. The difficulty is, of course, in proving that a particular film or TV show produced a particular effect in a particular person; it is not enough to show that there is general evidence for a causal connection between TV violence and acting-out of violence in viewers.

2   The Role of Theory in Science

Before considering the state of the game, it may be useful to devote some discussion to the consideration of the rules of the game: if opponents play entirely different games, it may be difficult to find the winner. The question many people are seeking to answer is an apparently simple one: do displays of pornographic and violent material in the media affect human beings in certain ways? Such a question is completely impossible to answer, and should never be asked. For one thing, its scope is far too wide to make investigation possible. Pornographic displays differ from each other in many ways and along many different dimensions; so do displays of violence and aggression. These differences may lead to entirely different consequences, and to lump all types of material together can only lead to confusion. The nature of the media may also play a powerful part in determining the effects produced; pictures, photographs, TV, films, written material all have their own peculiarities, and affect people in different ways. Last but not least, human beings differ from each other in many ways, and what may affect one person may have no effect on another, or even quite the opposite effect. Men do not necessarily behave in the same manner as women, extraverts as introverts, educated persons as uneducated persons, emotionally stable persons as neurotic persons – the number of dimensions along which people differ from each other is embarrassingly large. In addition to all these variables, we must also consider duration of exposure to the type of material under investigation; a single exposure to a short pornographic film may have quite different effects from repeated exposures to many different films.

Previous experience is also relevant; showing a pornographic film to a person who has never come across this type of material may have entirely different effects to those which follow from showing the same film to a person who has seen thousands of such films. There is a famous law in psychology (the

Weber–Fechner Law) which states in essence that perception of stimuli (visual, tactual, auditory, etc.) is a function of the amount of stimulation already present; a single candle lit in a dark room is very noticeable, while an additional candle lit in a room which already contains 100 lit candles will hardly be noticed. This law has been put in a proper quantitative form (either a logarithmic or a power function is usually preferred), but even without going into such detail it obviously is likely to apply in this field also. Age and sexual experience generally also come into the picture, along similar lines; a middle-aged and sexually experienced person will react differently to the showing of a pornographic film than would a young and inexperienced person.

Considerations such as these suggest that we would be well advised not to draw too far-reaching conclusions from empirical studies using highly selected populations, one particular type of material, a small number of exposures to that material (frequently only a single exposure), and a short time of follow-up – effects may be of the kind sometimes called 'sleepers', i.e. they do not become apparent immediately, but may only emerge after some time has elapsed. Negative conclusions have sometimes been reached about the effectiveness of representations of erotic and violent behaviour where the population consisted of such unrepresentative people as university students, where no effort was made to test their personality characteristics, where no account was taken of their previous sexual experience, or their previous exposure to pornography, where the availability of sex partners after exposure was not considered, and where follow-up was confined to a single week or less. The consideration of 'availability' is of crucial importance; a young man who sees oral sex performed in an erotic film may be only too keen to practise this new technique, but may fail to do so because there is no suitable partner of the opposite sex, or because he feels she would not agree, or for other related reasons; this does not mean that when occasions arise where he can put into practice what he has learned, he will not do so. Similarly violence in the media may arouse a desire on the part of a given viewer to practise the techniques he has seen on the screen, but this may have to await an occasion where such practices can be safely indulged in. For all these reasons, the likelihood of obtaining positive results from the studies to be reported is not high, even though pornographic exhibitions and demonstrations of violence in the media may in the aggregate have a powerful effect on many people. Negative results do not tell us very much, and should certainly not be interpreted as whitewashing material of the kind under discussion; positive results, on the other hand, precisely because the dice are loaded against them, are much more impressive, and deserve careful scrutiny.

One further point must be considered in some detail. We shall be describing a large number of experiments in this book, and discussing their results; it should be made clear right from the start that the term 'experiment' has two meanings which must be kept carefully separate. In the popular language, which means the way politicians talk as much as the way the man in the street does, 'experiment' simply means 'trying out something new'. We may introduce a new method of teaching French, or proclaim a new law of labour relations, or try giving suspended sentences to large numbers of miscreants; all these would popularly be called 'experiments'. To the scientist, however, there are two important features missing without which he would withhold the approbation which the term is meant to inspire. In the first place, there should be a proper theory which predicts what the expected results are; such a prediction should preferably be quantitative. And in the second place, the 'experiment' should be arranged in such a manner that we can actually test the outcome in a proper manner. It is not enough to look at the number of successes reported by our French teachers, or the number of strikes subsequent to the introduction of our law, or the number of persons with suspended sentences who fall foul of the law again. These figures must be compared with some other figure, namely a figure resulting from not introducing the new methods in question; only in this way can they acquire some meaning. In the case of the new method of teaching French, we would have to compare the classes using this method with other classes following in the older tradition; and we would have to be careful to make sure that the pupils in both types of class were equally intelligent, had equal numbers of boys and girls in them, came from similar social status groups, and were matched in many other ways. In other words, we need a properly set-up control group; without such a group the 'experiment' will not give us any information of scientific relevance. This is often difficult to do, but it is an indispensable precaution, the absence of which makes our 'experiment' meaningless. Most social 'experiments' unfortunately fall into this category.

The need for control groups will be obvious to most people; this is simply an application of common sense. But why do we need a theory? The most obvious answer is that only the possession of a good theory will tell us where to look in our search for results. Consider an experiment in which a number of young students are shown a series of erotic films depicting, say, *cunnilingus* and *fellatio*, and let us suppose that hitherto they have not come across these practices. We now ask them to keep a diary of their sexual activities for a week, and compare the results with the information contained in a similar diary kept during the preceding week. What would we expect to find? The man in the street (and unfortunately also the authors of some papers reporting just such experiments) apparently expected that 'effects' of such exposure should be that the subjects of the experiment now indulged in the activities shown in the films. If no such behaviour is found, the conclusion is arrived at that there was no effect of the films. What kind of prediction would psychological theory make?

Keeping the discussion at a very elementary and simple level, we may say that psychological theory would first of all point to the importance of distinguishing between *drive* variables and *habit* variables. Drive concerns such factors as hunger, sexual excitement, thirst, etc., while habit concerns established ways of acting and perceiving. A widely accepted formula reads: $P = D \times H$, which means that performance (i.e. what a person does in a given situation) is determined by his established habits, multiplied by his state of drive. Suppose the subjects in our experiments habitually act out their sexual drives by having intercourse on the lines of the technique known as the 'missionary position' (i.e. with the man above the woman), then seeing the films in question should increase their drive, but should not alter their habits. Our expectation would therefore be that they would have intercourse in the habitual manner, only more so – and this is precisely what has in fact been found. The expectation that these students would immediately imitate the film exploits and practise *cunnilingus* and *fellatio* is naive, and counter to psychological theory; it would require a lengthy period of learning before we could expect a change in *habit*. What is even more surprising is that the increase in drive produced by viewing the film should make such change-over *more* difficult, because the original habit, powered by a strongly increased drive, issues ever more strongly in the habitual pattern of behaviour. This point has been made very powerfully by Spence and Spence (1966), and their theory has received much experimental support in the laboratory, in connection with learning and conditioning work of all kinds (Eysenck, 1973).

Much of the work which we shall review in this book is naive in the sense of paying no attention to well-established psychological theories, and rather taking a point of view characteristic of the uninstructed layman. Worse, the official committees set up to look into this problem have consisted almost entirely of lawyers, politicians, theologians, artists and other eminently worthy citizens unfortunately lacking entirely any competence in the only field of knowledge relevant to the issue in question, namely psychology. When we add to this unfortunate state of affairs the ideological preconceptions which have always affected this field of enquiry, it will not come as a surprise to anyone that the outcome of the vast research undertaking documented in hundreds of books and articles has been, not a mountain, but a mouse. Even this mouse has been variously described as either non-existent, or else as a raging tiger – partisans have been hypnotized by their preconceived opinions, and have interpreted reality in line with their preconceptions. This is not a useful way to approach a scientific problem. As the German aphorist Lichtenberg once said, 'I do not mind prejudice [pre-judgement], as long as judgement follows'. Such judgement is the purpose of this book.

It is sometimes suggested that there are no psychological theories which deserve our attention. This is not so; there are theories (which we shall discuss presently) which deserve careful attention because they have been successful in promoting extensive experimental laboratory work which has provided powerful support in their favour. Others have given rise to equally successful clinical methods of treatment, e.g. behaviour therapy. To disregard reasonably well established theories of this kind seems to go counter to the spirit of science, which has always insisted on the primacy of good theories. One or two examples, taken from the history of science, may make this point clear. Consider the shape of the earth. The ancient Greeks already knew that the Earth is spherical, and Eratosthenes, in the third century BC, succeeded in measuring its circumference with considerable accuracy. This notion was widely accepted, but in 1687, in one of the finest of the many brilliant analyses in his *Principia Mathematica*, Newton deduced that the Earth must be flattened, i.e. that the equatorial diameter is greater than the polar diameter. He came up with the numerical answer that the flattening should be one part in 230. (The true value is now known to be 1 part in 298. Newton, as he himself realized, did not allow for the increased density of the Earth's interior.) Many attempts were made to test this deduction, with rather poor results. Expeditions were mounted, and much money spent, on these measurements. Jacques Cassini in 1720 announced that he had discovered, not a flattening, but an elongation of the Earth at the poles. Ten years later, the French Academy of Sciences sent out two expeditions, one to Lapland, the other to Peru. Both suffered great hardships; the members of the Peru expedition quarrelled over their results, and in any case the estimates of flattening, which was observed, were less accurate than Newton's deduction. Between 1750 and 1950, many other estimates were made on an observational basis, and by then the results were pretty well known, using altogether four different methods of measurement. The most widely accepted result was reported by Sir Harold Jeffreys in 1948, using all four methods; his estimate was a flattening of 1 part in 297.1 – a result challenged when the putting in space of satellites enabled physicists to use a fifth and even more accurate method, which gave the value of 1 part in 298.25.

The point of this story is that a good theory is often more reliable than empirical determinations; these may require a lengthy process of refinement before they can be taken very seriously. Another example is the heliocentric theory, according to which the Earth and the other planets circle round the Sun; this theory also was known to the ancient Greeks, but was rejected because they could not observe any parallax, i.e. the hypothetical alteration in the appearance of the stellar positions which should follow from the fact that today we observe them from one side of the sun, and six months later from the other side. The lack of parallax was used as a criticism of

Copernicus and Galileo when they revived the heliocentric theory, and it was not till the nineteenth century that stellar parallax was in fact observed – the stars are much more distant from the Earth than used to be thought, and it needs refined instruments to observe the very tiny changes that take place in stellar positions. Thus a good theory may be rejected because measuring instruments are not refined enough to provide the required evidence. It would be sad if a similar mistake were to be made in the field with which this book is concerned. It is well known that the observational instruments we are using, and the experimental designs on which we rely, are extremely primitive; failure to discover results may easily be the result of faulty instruments and designs. This danger should be ever-present to our minds.

Kurt Lewin, a famous social psychologist of the between-war years, used to say that a good theory is the most practical thing of all; with that we would entirely concur. Such theories usually emanate from laboratory studies, and this is true even of theories in the field of social science – contrary to widely held views that such studies are so lacking in 'naturalness' that they are irrelevant. The same view used to be held quite widely in physics; a good example is the famous story of Sir Oliver Lodge and his fight against the Post Office engineers. The engineers, a very practical-minded group, held the view that lightning consisted of a single stroke which decended from the cloud to the earth; this view was based on observation of actual lightning flashes. Sir Oliver Lodge was asked his opinion for the purpose of taking part in a meeting of the British Association for the Advancement of Science in the latter part of the nineteenth century, and he hurriedly rigged up some Leiden jars in his laboratory, photographed the sparks that resulted, and came to the conclusion that lightning consisted of repeated strokes going in both directions. The engineers laughed him out of court, ridiculing the notion that laboratory observations of tiny sparks from Leiden jars could be used to decide such a question, but of course Lodge was right, and they were wrong. To take another example, methods for treating neurotic patients were derived by Freud from extensive observation of actual patients, and by modern behaviour therapists from laboratory experiments with animals; the outcome of comparing the effectiveness of the two methods has been quite clear-cut. Freud's methods still lack any empirical support, and do not seem to work any better than no treatment at all (spontaneous remission), while behaviour therapy works not only well, but also very quickly (Eysenck, 1977a). The endless jokes about psychologists and their pet rats may be mistaken, after all, if they are taken to imply that nothing useful can be learned from rat experiments.

Relevant theories are of three major kinds. First in order of importance are theories using the concepts of Pavlovian *conditioning*, such as the set of theories on which the processes of desensitization are based. Second are *social* theories, such as those involved in modelling and imitation. And third are the so-called *cognitive* theories, giving rise to concepts of identification and the like. Most readers will readily accept the social and congitive types of theories, and consequently we shall not devote much space to a discussion of their underlying principles. The position is slightly different for conditioning, however, and a few words of introduction may be useful here.

We may begin by stating one of those obvious truths which nevertheless are often neglected in practice. *Man is a bio-social organism*; in other words, man is a *biological* organism on whose natural and instinctive equipment *social rules* of a very complex kind have been superimposed. Neither nativists, with an eye entirely on the biological side, nor environmentalists, with an eye entirely on the role of social influences, are capable of doing justice to the dual nature of man. Through the processes of evolution, man's primitive paleocortex or lower brain, narrowly concerned with emotions and other elemental feelings, was enveloped by the neocortex, the burgeoning organ of rational thought, intelligence, and infinitely flexible adaptability. It is easy to overrate the importance of the neocortex, just because it is this that separates us most clearly from other animals; our emotions and more primitive ('animal') reactions are still governed by the paleocortex, the brain-stem and the visceral brain.

Each of the two reaction systems, the primitive, emotional, and the modern, rational, needs to adapt to circumstances, and to foresee likely sources of danger and satisfaction. The neocortex can do this by thinking, by reason, by cognitive foresight; the paleocortex, being much more primitive, also developed a system which, though much less complex and much less satisfactory, has worked well for hundreds of millions of years, from the most primitive forms of life right up to and including man. This is the system of what Pavlov designated 'conditional' or conditioned responses. Pavlov's defining experiments are too well known to describe in detail; by pairing the sound of a bell (the conditioned stimulus, to which the dog did not salivate) with the sight of food (the unconditioned stimulus, to which the dog did salivate), Pavlov was able to make the dog salivate to the bell after a number of pairings, even though no food might be produced for the dog to see. In this way the dog was able to prepare for the food expected to come once the warning bell had sounded.

Conditioning of this kind has been demonstrated in man as much as in other animals, and it primarily concerns emotional reactions. These are mediated by a semi-separate nervous system, the autonomic system; voluntary activity is mediated by the central nervous system. Just as the voluntary activities of man are organized and controlled by the neocortex, so his emotional reactions are controlled by the 'visceral brain', situated in the limbic system. We thus have two largely separate and independent systems controlling behaviour, the old-fashioned, primitive, but very powerful emotional-conditioned system, and the new-fangled, recent, cognitive system. Often these two systems are in opposition; neurosis is a typical and very widespread condition which exemplifies this opposition (Eysenck, 1977a). However, even in perfectly normal people there may be strong opposition between the primitive demands of the visceral brain, often responding to conditioned stimuli, and the socialized demands of the neocortex, often reflecting the mores of the society in which the organism was brought up. The relevance to our main theme will be plain: both sexual activity, and aggression and violence, are deeply rooted in the more primitive system of the paleocortex, and become attached to certain objects or situations through processes of conditioning which may defy rational thought and cognitive control. Sexual behaviour, such as tumescence and detumescence, are directly governed by the autonomic system; so are rage and other emotions leading to violence. A great deal of knowledge has been acquired about the precise details of these processes, but it would go beyond the confines of this book were we to discuss this knowledge in any detail.

Given that this is a true, if somewhat dogmatic and inadequate, account of the origins of sexual and aggressive behaviour, we can see at once that the usual habit of many writers in this field of treating the influence of the media in strictly rational and cognitive terms, i.e. assuming that the neocortex is all that matters, is strictly inadmissible. Films like *The Blue Angel* have given powerful portrayals of the losing fight waged by the neocortex against the temptations and conditioned responses of the visceral brain. Reason might side with Lord Chesterfield, when he said of sexual intercourse: 'The pleasure is momentary, the position ridiculous and the expense damnable'; the paleocortex will see to it that rational objections come to naught in the long run. Similar rational objections to the use of violence, to vandalism, and to other courses of action which may threaten to destroy civilization, are equally unacceptable to our unreasoning, primitive visceral brain; not sweet reason, but proper methods of conditioning have any chance of changing our conduct. Such a change may be for better or for worse; we shall argue that the media produce their effects on human conduct through the use of conditioning mechanisms.

One further point requires mention. Sexual behaviour in particular has been found to be strongly susceptible to methods of conditioning; examples will presently be given. There are reasons why this should be so (Eysenck, 1977a), but they are too technical to be discussed here in detail. Most conditioned responses extinguish when the reinforcement (the unconditioned stimulus) is withheld for a number of presentations; ring the bell without showing the dog the food, and he will eventually cease to salivate to the bell alone. Two kinds of responses do not seem to show this extinction response: anxiety and sexual behaviour. Instead they may show incubation, or positive feedback; in other words, they will become stronger and stronger on repetitions of the conditioned stimulus, in spite of the absence of the unconditioned stimulus. The reason for this is probably that anxiety and sex responses themselves have drive properties; a conditioned anxiety is almost as real as an unconditioned one, and a conditioned sexual response almost as real as an unconditioned one. Small wonder that most if not all neuroses embody anxiety and sexual responses of a conditioned kind which are inappropriate to the situation in which the patient finds himself.

People differ considerably in the degree to which they respond with strong emotions to anxiety-provoking situations; they also differ markedly in the degree to which they form conditioned responses. Some condition quickly and strongly, others slowly and weakly. This suggests that different people will react differently to displays of sex and violence in the media, and as we shall see in Chapter 10 this is indeed so. These differences in conditioning and in emotionality are tied to personality, and without taking these personality differences into account no sensible summary of the evidence in this field is possible.

Many critics of the way in which the media may influence people are concerned, not only with overt actions, but also with changes in attitudes, in values, and in general cognitive appraisals of situations, members of the other sex, etc. There is much evidence that such attitudes and values, too, can be conditioned; Martin and Levey (1978) have used the term 'evaluative conditioning' to characterize this type of effect, and a full account of the kind of experiments done in this field can be found in their monograph. They prefer this extension of the conditioning model to the field of 'evaluation' to alternative models, such as the social or the cognitive, on grounds of simplicity, and because of our knowledge of the general laws followed by conditioned responses. In principle we agree with this view, but as other workers in the field have frequently presented their data and hypotheses in terms of such alternative theories, we find it essential to present these theories in this chapter, in order to evaluate them later on in connection with the experiments to which they have given rise.

Conditioning not only establishes behavioural patterns, whether neurotic or otherwise; conditioning theory also predicts in what way we can decondition these unwanted behaviour patterns, or otherwise remove them. The complex of methods used for this purpose has received the name of *behaviour therapy*, and a brief consideration of some of its applications is appropriate, not only because it illustrates the importance of experimentation in developing theories of human conduct, and in applying these to practical problems, but also because these theories are very relevant to a consideration of the effects of exposure to sex and violence in the media. It would not be possible to discuss in any detail the applicability of the whole range of methods used in behaviour therapy to this problem; we have concentrated here on two such methods (desensitization, and 'modelling' or imitation), and even these will have to be dealt with in short compass.

Let us begin with desensitization. This is a method of treatment which is widely used, with considerable success, to cure neurotic patients of anxieties, fears, phobias, obsessive-compulsive neuroses, and other disorders of the emotions involving inappropriate feelings, too strong for the occasion and too long-lasting to be easily coped with. Sometimes these emotions have a single point of reference (as in simple phobic fears of spiders, cats, snakes, open spaces, heights, etc.), or, more frequently, fears may be widespread and refer to many objects or situations. Sometimes these fears seem so all-embracing that there seems to be no fixed anchor point which can be blamed for producing the fear (so-called free-floating anxiety). Most of these fears are conditioned in the manner which Pavlov was the first to demonstrate experimentally; a neurotic fear can arise through the pairing of any neutral object or event with a fear-producing happening or object. Thus one patient developed a phobic fear of traffic (particularly oncoming traffic) by being involved in an accident; she was so afraid of cars that she could not drive any longer, and finally did not dare leave her house. Here cars and traffic are the conditioned stimuli (CS), and the events involved in her accident are the unconditioned stimuli (UCS). The development of neurotic illness does not always involve such traumatic events (indeed these are not all that usual); sub-traumatic events can lead to a positive feedback system in which anxiety, once started, begins to spiral until it is totally out of control (Eysenck, 1977a).

Desensitization is a method of treatment designed to counteract such fears, and literally to 'desensitize' the person to the appearance of the feared objects and situations. As an example, take the case of a woman with a strong spider phobia. (For the sake of simplicity we are here taking a very clear-cut and unusually specific example; much more complex anxieties and their treatment are found in the more typical cases treated in the clinic (Eysenck, 1974; Poser, 1977).) How can we combat these fears, which are so strong that they prevent the woman from leaving her house, for fear of encountering spiders, thus making her life a misery, and preventing her from going out to work, from shopping, and from visiting cinemas, theatres, etc.? It is well known that fear and anxiety involve tension; muscles literally tense up as part of the neurotic response. Thus relaxation is opposed to anxiety, physiologically as well as psychologically, and treatment begins by training the patient to relax her muscles properly – a process which may take several hours. Then begins the counter-conditioning treatment. The fear of spiders is a conditioned emotional response (or it may even be innate to some extent; it does not matter much for the purpose of the example). We now wish to condition another response to the CS (the spider), namely relaxation. We do this by constructing first of all a hierarchy of fears for the patient, ranging from the lowest fear-producing situation – say, a very small spider, seen at a great distance, and with a window between spider and patient – to the most fear-producing of all – say, a very large and hairy spider scuttling across the patient's body while she is lying in bed. We then get her to relax completely, and when completely relaxed ask her to imagine the lowest-ranking item in her hierarchy. She will usually be able to do this without losing her relaxed posture – thus associating relaxation responses with the feared object, and building up a conditioned response (relaxation) to the spider, cancelling out a little bit of the conditioned fear which constitutes her symptom.

Once this is accomplished, we can go up the scale, following the lowest item in the hierarchy with the second-lowest, then the third-lowest, and continue this method until we reach the highest item – always taking care that at no point is the patient unduly stressed, i.e. stressed to such an extent that actual anxiety is evoked. The usual finding is that patients reach the top level after a few weeks, and are then ready to cope with actual encounters with the feared objects – also graded, of course, in the same way as the imaginary encounters were graded. In this way the great majority of neurotic fears and anxieties can be overcome speedily, lastingly, and economically. This method of desensitization has perfectly general validity; it is often applied by mothers to their children's fears, without any knowledge that the method has the blessing of academic psychology. A mother whose baby daughter is afraid of the bath, and screams when she lets in the water, will gradually desensitize the girl by first of all relaxing her (usually by playing with her, reading to her, etc.), then gradually get her used to water in the small basin in the bathroom, then wash her feet in the bath-tub, with very little water in it, and then gradually work her up to having a proper bath. This is little more than common sense, but it can work just as well for the mother as it works for the professional psychologist.

How does this general theoretical-experimental-therapeutic system apply to the topic of this book? The answer is very simple (Eysenck, 1961). Civilized man everywhere has erected barriers to the simple expression of sexual and violent impulses in direct action – rape and murder are universally prohibited, and punished by law. These barriers are internalized, probably through some form of conditioning (Eysenck, 1977b), although it is quite possible and even likely that innate factors also play some part – even animals tend to act out their intraspecific conflicts in a more or less symbolic way. Lions seldom kill lions, nor do gorillas normally kill gorillas. Humans are almost unique in having ritualized murder by inventing 'war', but even so humans tend on the whole to have some seemingly innate aversion to taking human life. It seems probable that these innate tendencies are strengthened by a process of conditioning, but for the purpose of this book it is not really vital to know the precise provenance of the very obvious barriers to the direct expression of primitive impulses which characterize civilized man (and even primitive man).

Let us now consider how we could weaken these barriers, supposing that we wanted to. Clearly it could be done by using the methods of desensitization. What would be required would be the portrayal, at second hand (i.e. through the written word, or in pictures, or film, or on TV) of acts of violence or abnormal sex which, had they occurred normally in our presence, would have aroused strong negative emotions of disgust, dislike and fear. By viewing them in this second-hand, indirect form we immediately reduce the impact and relegate the images to the lower ranks of our hierarchy. At the same time we view them under conditions of relaxation – in our own homes in the case of TV, or in a comfortable seat in the cinema, in the case of films. Thus the situation combines all the vital elements of desensitization – relaxation and exposure to low-ranking items in the hierarchy of fears and anxieties. We are in fact free to select for ourselves the precise images which are low enough in our own, individual hierarchy to make the viewing tolerable, and not excite too much anxiety – we usually have some information about the film or play to be seen, or the TV series to be viewed. And if we are wrong in our choice, we can always walk out of the cinema, or turn off the TV, to reduce anxiety. It would not be too much to say that if the Martians had in mind the brutalization of our civilization by incitement to violence and sexual exploitation, they could not have hit upon a better method than making use of the media in their present form to achieve their aims.

Desensitization, then, is a method of changing conduct and emotional reactions which is well documented experimentally, both in animals and in humans; it has been widely used, with considerable success, to cure neurotic fears and anxieties; it seems highly unlikely that under the conditions under which pornographic and violent materials are shown these should have no effect on the viewer whatsoever. Desensitization in this case is the technical term for what many critics of the media call 'brutalization'; the idea is the same. It would need a very powerful argument indeed to persuade anyone familiar with the extensive literature on desensitization (Bergin and Garfield, 1971) to take seriously the proposition that viewing large numbers of scenes of explicit sex and violence on film or TV would leave the viewers completely unaffected. Most writers who favour the view that such scenes have no effect do not in fact argue the point; they simply disregard the evidence and the theory, as if it did not exist. This is a simple way of dealing with the difficulty, but it does not impress the unbiased critic as a good way of disposing of an inconvenient argument. It is true that the conditions of viewing are not scientifically prearranged to produce optimum effects, as could only be done in individual therapy; it is the large number of people exposed to the 'treatment', and the large number of exposures, which create the effect.

Some readers may object that Pavlovian conditioning is a very primitive method which surely does not apply to human beings in the same manner as to dogs, rats and other mammals. The evidence is strong that this is not true; humans follow the same laws of conditioning as do animals. Sexual preferences, in particular, may develop partly as a result of conditioning. McGuire *et al.* (1965) advanced the theory that repeated masturbation accompanied by the memory of an erotic incident is the mechanism by which a deviation is formed and shaped. This theory was arrived at after interviewing forty-five sexual deviants who were receiving treatment.

Appearance of a patient's aberrant sexual preference seemed to take place after an initial experience, which was seen as playing a part only in supplying a fantasy for later masturbation. With the passage of time the original memory often changed and its sexual significance may or may not have been appreciated at the time. The deviants reported having regularly imagined a certain scene before orgasm, and in their case this scene happened to be of a deviant nature. They appeared to have chosen an aberrant fantasy because the precipitating incident constituted their first real sexual experience (this applied to three-quarters of the patients). Consistent with this, the deviations tended to start at puberty.

This theory is consistent with findings from conditioning experiments. An image which regularly precedes orgasm by the correct time interval should become more and more sexually stimulating. If the fantasy image is of a deviant nature, then normal sexual preferences will be extinguished through lack of reinforcement. A possible reason why deviants are unlikely to deliberately develop normal fantasies is that they believe a normal sex life is not possible for them. Half the patients reported early aversive experiences or feelings of social inadequacy which led them to believe that their chances of a normal sex life were low. It was noted that this belief usually predated the deviation, although it naturally tended to increase after development of their deviation.

Male predominance in deviations can be explained in terms of masturbation to a fantasy as the main sexual outlet being more characteristic of men than women. The theory allows for a person having several deviations (which often happens in practice) since he may choose to masturbate to a variety of fantasies. Because this conditioning may take place thousands of times, and because the reward from sexual excitement and orgasm is so strong, people such as psychopaths or sociopaths who normally condition only with difficulty are also susceptible. The choice of a fantasy may arise from an accidental experience or it may be deliberate. This provides a rationale for treatment, which can be carried out by aversion therapy to the deviant fantasies (deconditioning) and by instructing the patients to deliberately imagine normal sex in the critical seconds before orgasm. The success of this treatment provides support for the theory. To illustrate this theory case histories are provided by McGuire *et al.*, of which the following is an example.

> A 28-year-old patient, married at the age of 24, had had normal sexual interests. However, his wife proved to be totally frigid so that the marriage was never consummated. In the early months of his marriage, while sexually frustrated, he observed that a young lady in the opposite flat was in the habit of stripping in a lighted room with the curtains open. (The patient's wife confirmed this story.) The patient found this very stimulating sexually. The marriage had not been consummated when the couple moved house. In his new environment the patient sought opportunities of seeing women undressing and developed the habit of masturbating on these occasions. It is interesting to note that the patient retained all the circumstances of the early stimulus and had no interest in nudist films or strip-tease shows. He came to our notice after his fourth conviction for a 'Peeping Tom' offence.

McGuire *et al.* do not consider the role of pornography in their theory, but there seems no reason why it should not serve to provide material for sexually exciting fantasies. Any stimulus that arouses the viewer, or one that is linked with the sexual response, is probably capable of being developed along the lines described. Looking at pin-ups and scenes of petting or intercourse can probably do little but good, unless the vicarious pleasure so gained comes to be valued more than real-life sex. This would seem unlikely with the availability of a partner, although cases are reported of married men who become addicted to pornography in this way. In contrast to material portraying 'normal' sex, exposure to scenes of rape, torture and sex with children and animals does appear to be potentially dangerous. Even if such material is not arousing, it can still be incorporated into a person's fantasies immediately before orgasm, in which case a new sexual preference could well develop. Associating novel or 'abnormal' sex with material that is arousing may also be sufficient to lead to the conditioning of new preferences.

Consider the following experiment, carried out originally to demonstrate that fetishism could be produced by means of a conditioning experiment (Rachman, 1966). Male subjects were shown slides of boots (the CS); these were not found to be sexually exciting (as indicated by a failure of the penis to show an erection, measured by an instrument called a 'penis plethysmograph'.) Slides of nude women (the UCS) were found to be exciting, in that they produced an erection. Pairing slides of boots and nudes soon produced a conditioned reflex, such that the sight of the boots by themselves (i.e. not paired with nude slides) produced an erection. Along similar lines have been experiments demonstrating that opinions about other people, including likes and dislikes, could be manipulated without the affected person's knowledge, through a process of conditioning. Conditioning is far more powerful, and far more closely integrated with the rest of our personality and conduct, than most people realize; we are part animal, part socialized human being, and the process of socialization itself is in part based on conditioning paradigms testifying to our animal origin.

Desensitization is not a new idea or method; a classical statement of the principles underlying it is given by the Stoic philosopher Epictetus, when he said: 'Begin with a torn robe or a broken cup, and say, "I don't care." Go on to the death of a pet dog or horse and say, "I don't care." In the end you will come to the stage where you can stand beside the bed of your loved one and see that loved one die, and say, "I don't care." ' Two thousand years later Alexander Pope enshrined the same idea in his poetic statement about vice:

> Vice is a monster of so frightful mien,
> As to be hated needs but to be seen;
> Yet seen too oft, familiar with her face,
> We first endure, then pity, then embrace.

'Familiarity breeds contempt' is another well-known expression for the same fact. Whitehouse (1977) gives some interesting examples of the deliberate use of desensitization in breaking down the resistances of children and students to explicit sex. She quotes a professor at the University of Minnesota in whose sex education classes the young male and female students ritually intone the Latin names of the genitals, and are then directed to address one another by saying 'sexual intercourse', or 'clitoris', etc. 'It is necessary', the professor is quoted as saying, 'to desensitize my students.'

This particular use is ridiculous rather than impressive; it gives more insight into the nature of some American professors of psychology than into the mechanisms of desensitization. Rather more relevant is the use of films by the US Army to desensitize troops sent out on combat missions. The object of the training is to desensitize the viewers' reaction to pain and suffering in others, so that in the end they will inflict pain and death without qualms. Physiological reactions are monitored to the explicit exposure of the viewer to harrowing scenes involving loss of limbs, torture, etc., and at first these reactions are quite marked, and indicate severe emotional upheaval. Gradually these reactions become less severe, until finally there is almost no reaction of an emotional kind to the sight of such scenes. The programme next enters a further stage, entitled 'Dehumanization of the Enemy', in which the potential target is presented as belonging to some inferior form of human life; in this way desensitization is coupled to a more positive kind of conditioning in which the target is more closely identified. In a more primitive way these same steps were gone through, with what success we know only too well, by the Nazis (and indeed by most Army sergeants as well), with the exception that they used *in vivo* techniques; the use of films and polygraph psychophysiological recording constitutes a refinement which links it up with the question of the effectiveness of modern media in desensitizing emotional reactions, and makes the whole process more easily subject to scientific control and evaluation.

What sort of predictions could we make from the theory of desensitization, with special reference to the sort of experiments that have been carried out in this field, and that will be reviewed in later chapters? By making expectations explicit, we can all the better evaluate the actual findings, and pinpoint weaknesses in the design of experiments. In the first place, desensitization takes time; many repetitions are involved. It follows that the usual single exposure to explicit sex or violence, or even a small number of closely packed exposures, would not be expected to have much of an effect; if any effects are observed, this would betoken the power of the method. In the second place, desensitization has to work up the hierarchy; if the first few steps are too steep (i.e. if actual anxieties are aroused at any stage, too strong to be counterbalanced by the relaxation into which the patient has been trained) then the whole process becomes ineffective and may be counterproductive. In most experiments no attention has been paid to this principle, so that again we would expect very variable results depending on the initial status of the subjects. In the third place, there are considerable individual differences in responsiveness to desensitization; there is some evidence, for instance, that patients who condition easily respond better than those who do not. There should always be available a measure of relevant individual differences; as we shall see, this rule has not been observed by the great majority of studies in this field. If one were to characterize the majority of published studies, one would not go far wrong in saying that they seem to have been perversely designed, not to get the maximum effect of exposure on behaviour, but rather that the design completely ignores major rules deriving from experimental study and clinical experience. It is remarkable that, in spite of this, measurable consequences have usually followed upon exposure, although mostly of a rather weak and evanescent kind. This is what we would expect, on the basis of the theory, if effects under better controlled and designed experimental conditions were likely to be strong and lasting.

Desensitization is only one of the many techniques used, for therapeutic purposes, by behaviour therapists, but which can equally well be used for destructive and inhumane purposes – like most scientific discoveries, the recent improvements in psychological techniques of 'behaviour modification' can be used for good and bad ends. Of equal importance, both in behaviour therapy and in the production of evil effects through exposure to explicit and perverted films, TV programmes, etc., is 'modelling'.

New behaviour is partly acquired by copying others; an obvious example is the imitation of a TV character such as Batman by children. In one study, 71 per cent of parents reported that their children imitated TV characters by, for example, using their slang expressions and accents (Woodrick *et al.*, 1977). Similarly in a survey among children, 60 per cent admitted having spontaneously imitated TV characters (Lyle and Hoffman, 1972). Sometimes this can have tragic consequences. After watching *The Good, the Bad, and the Ugly*, a twelve-year-old boy re-created the hanging scenes in his garden shed.

But the make-believe went wrong, when a cardboard box on which he was standing crumpled, and he was found unconscious hanging from a wooden beam. Another example concerns a sixteen-year-old who armed himself with a knife, broke into a neighbouring house and attacked a sleeping woman in her bedroom. The crime was almost a replica of a *Starsky and Hutch* episode which the boy had been watching only hours before. Numerous experiments have demonstrated the tendency for novel acts to be imitated. Typically a filmed model will be shown hitting, kicking and threatening a large inflated clown doll, and most children when observed in a playroom will be found to imitate these acts if there happens to be a similar doll handy (Bandura, 1973).

Although the research has usually been with children, imitation probably also occurs in adults. A cinema projectionist was obsessed with Kung Fu and American 'devil' films, and began turning his fantasies into action. After learning the martial arts, and adopting an American accent, he started to prey on young women. After his arrest it was reported in court that while trying to rape a woman he was making the guttural sounds he had heard in *The Exorcist*. A more conscious decision to imitate is illustrated by the annoying tendency for crime prevention films to be followed by a wave of crime. *Break-in* was a TV programme in which a former burglar showed in detail how to enter property. The aim was to advise people on how to stop housebreaking, but within hours of the programme going out, 'carbon copy' burglaries were being reported.

Critics of imitation theory point out that it merely 'shapes' the form that the inevitable occurrence of aggressive and antisocial acts will take. A youth who was carrying a Chinese flail when stopped by a policeman claimed it was only for hitting people in self-defence. Clearly, the boy had got the idea from a Kung Fu film, but without this film he might instead have been carrying a knife or bicycle chain. In other words, without the prompting provided by modelled examples, crimes will still be committed even if in a different way and at a different time. Another criticism concerns the rational element of choice in imitation. For example, children are noted to be far too sensible to copy the aggressive acts of Tom and Jerry. Similarly, the acts of imitative aggression demonstrated under experimental conditions are dismissed as merely 'play', being likened to the

playful 'fighting' of young animals. Nevertheless, even if imitation involved no more than this, there would always be the
chance that use would one day be made of the aggression
learned and if it happened to be particularly dangerous then
someone would suffer. Basically, it is all a question of prob-
abilities. Even if a film increases only slightly the tendency for
people to imitate, then as we saw in the last chapter the consequences can be very far reaching.

There is no apparent reason why imitation cannot occur
along with desensitization effects; a multiplicity of causes and
effects is the rule rather than the exception in psychology.
Modelling is often used in conjunction with desensitization
methods with apparent success in therapy. An intense fear of
dogs in children has been overcome by repeatedly showing
them films of a boy happily playing with dogs which progressively increase in size and fearfulness (e.g. Bandura and
Menlove, 1968). In fact, it is usually in conjunction with
desensitization-like methods that TV provides viewers with
examples of new forms of aggression. This circumvents another
criticism of imitation theory to the effect that crime is likely only
if there is a change in attitude as well as the tendency to imitate.
The screening of films portraying criminal acts carried out in
various ways, and with various motives, appears to facilitate
both attitude change and the realization that such acts can be
successfully accomplished.

Closely related to imitation is the theory of 'identification' or
'wanting to be like'. It is argued that we tend to 'identify' with
people whom we respect and admire, and that consequently we
are likely to be influenced by their actions as a result. This is a
psychoanalytic concept but is really little more than a
common-sense notion. The BBC implies acceptance of the
theory since one of its recommendations to producers is to
avoid portraying bad habits, such as smoking, in 'good' characters. The complement of this tends to occur with American TV
since tobacco companies often veto smoking in any 'undesirable' characters who appear in the programmes which they are
sponsoring. Copying the hairstyle and clothing of a film star or
pop singer is often given as an example of the effect of identification. The potential dangers of this tendency to imitate
heroes may be illustrated by reference to the 'cold-blooded'
killers who become cult figures and are idolized by many

people. Examples would include William F. Bonney who as Billy the Kid supposedly killed twenty-two men before he was himself shot at the age of twenty-one by a sheriff, and Bonnie Parker and Clyde Barrow, the much glamorized 'public enemies' of the 1930s. Attempts to test the theory of identification have not been very fruitful because, as we shall see, there is the confounding problem that people tend to like others who are like themselves to begin with.

While imitation is concerned with the acquisition of new behaviours, 'disinhibition' theory makes the assumption that certain responses already exist but that their expression is inhibited (Berkowitz, 1962). In everyday life, there are certainly constraints on acting aggressively even when we are strongly provoked. Viewing violence is claimed to have the effect of weakening such inhibitions, thus making the expression of aggression more likely. How this might work is not clear, but seeing aggression in others appears in some way to make the actions less unthinkable than before. In a sense a deviant act is legitimized by its very portrayal, especially if it is done in a way that conveys permissiveness or acceptability. As we shall see, there is considerable support for the 'disinhibition' of aggression after witnessing even a single act of violence. In order to demonstrate the effect, it is not necessary for the violent act to be reproduced as it would have to be in the case of imitation. Indeed, the witnessing of fairly extreme forms of aggression may be necessary in order to 'disinhibit' the expression of much milder forms; for example, hitting someone instead of using a gun or knife.

Rather similar to disinhibition is the 'stimulation' or 'triggering' theory so beloved by the newspapers. The stimulation provided by rock 'n roll music was claimed to have triggered the 'rock' riots of the 1950s. More frequently the theory is applied to the effects of pornography. Sexual excitement aroused by pornography is claimed to stimulate certain people into action – to act out their fantasies. Nevertheless, if the resulting actions are modelled on those portrayed in the pornography then this would appear to be an example of imitation, and if the actions indulged in are already part of a person's repertoire then it would seem to be a case of disinhibition. For obvious reasons it is only the latter effect which has been observed, or rather reported, under experimental conditions.

Some theories predict effects opposite in nature to those from the above, and one of these is 'sensitization'. Because of its shock value, the witnessing of extreme violence may actually result in an inhibition of aggression. After seeing horrifying acts of cruelty, a person's attitude against aggression may 'harden'. It has been argued that film producers should concentrate less on the excitement and glamour of violence and more on its consequences, such as the damage that can be done and the suffering involved. The following is an extract from the justification offered for publishing Hurwood's (1969) book *Torture Through the Ages*.

> From ancient times to the Twentieth Century, this is the complete, factual record of the infinite varieties of pain inflicted by man on his fellow man. . . . A book such as this, one that draws in graphic detail his brutal aggressions, will perhaps stir man's conscience . . . Frankly, the book is meant to shock! For mankind must be shocked into recognizing its capacity for cruelty. We must be shocked out of our self-righteous assumption that torture is just another way of passing sentence: We must be shocked into recognizing its essential abnormality, its expression as one of man's most sickening perversions of spirit and sexuality. Once we have seen the infinite terrors of torture, perhaps we can turn away from it, damn it and discard it.

The shock value provided by pornography is claimed to have a similar effect on some people by causing them to reject it. In fact, the position is rather more complex than this. There is also believed to be a 'polarization' effect with prevailing attitudes being held more strongly after sudden exposure to pornography. Thus while exposure may result in a change of attitude towards greater permissiveness for the sexually experienced, the opposite effect is claimed for the inexperienced. As we shall see, there is some evidence for this view, although for the majority of students, at least, the so-called 'liberating' effects of pornography appear to outweigh the 'restrictive'.

Gerbner and Gross (1976) have developed a similar theory along the lines that excessive TV violence, by painting a picture of the dangers that might exist in the outside world, is likely to arouse anxiety and so lead to a paranoid attitude and a mistrust of others. They point out that the world of TV drama is indeed a violent one in which, during prime-time viewing, more than half the main characters are involved in violence, and at least a tenth of them in killing. Because for many people TV, with its implicit acceptance of violence as a social reality, provides a 'window' to the real world, a heightened sense of danger and insecurity is felt to develop. It is argued that if people accept the distorted, violent picture of modern society presented on TV, then this will 'make them more compliant, more malleable, more hopeless, and more fearful'. The warning is given that acceptance of violence, and passivity in the face of injustice, may be consequences of far greater social concern than occasional displays of aggression.

There is plenty of anecdotal evidence that even adults 'believe' what they see on TV. A probably exaggerated account was reported in the newspapers of an actor who was flagged down by a police car and made to pull into the kerb. He had appeared as a blind man in a TV programme, and so convincing was his performance that the police waved their hands in front of his face to make sure he could really see; 'jolly good acting' was their only remark. Rather better documented is the account of what happened when the novel *War of the Worlds* by H. G. Wells was broadcast as a radio play. The acting was seen as reality by many adult listeners who came out into the streets to escape from the invading Martians.

Gerbner and Gross point out that TV teaches the role of the victim, and raise the interesting possibility that viewers may identify not with the aggressors but with the victims. While this may be true for some people, it is interesting to note that it is directly counter to the theory that we identify with people we respect and admire. The second part of their theory, to the effect that by witnessing violence we become 'scared' rather than aggressive, sounds plausible and there may be an element of truth in it, but they have completely overlooked the counterbalancing effects of desensitization. In view of this it will perhaps not be surprising to learn that the theory is hardly supported by the evidence.

A beneficial effect from witnessing sex and violence is suggested by the theory of 'catharsis'. Catharsis is derived from the Greek work for purgation, meaning to dissipate or purge an emotion. Dramatic art on the stage has always been thought to provide the audience with an opportunity to release strong emotions harmlessly through identification with the actors and events depicted in the play. Aristotle wrote in *The Art of Poetry* that drama is 'a representation . . . in the form of actions directly presented, not narrated; with incidents arousing pity and fear in such a way as to accomplish a purgation of such emotions'. The producer of *Daddy*, a film about incest which is banned in almost all countries, expressed a similar opinion during a panel discussion at London's Institute of Contemporary Arts. He claimed that we all need doses of visual violence and explicit sex to prevent us from repressing our own aggressive and sensual urges. Similarly, producers often defend the portrayal of TV violence by arguing that it can have beneficial effects by allowing the viewer to purge himself of aggressive tendencies.

The popularity of sport, James Bond thrillers, and aggressive humour have all been claimed to attest to the need for 'outlets' of aggression. After being frustrated, people often daydream about getting revenge. The story of Papillon describes how a man in solitary confinement spent his time planning revenge; he did nòt think he could have survived without this 'outlet'. Upon his release after escaping he did not find it necessary to act out the plans. After watching a violent film some people report feeling more relaxed than before. If true, this could be due to catharsis. But equally well it could be due to the distracting effects of the film, with the viewer being carried away by the excitement, which may stop him thinking about his troubles, and so produce relaxation.

There are many other claims for catharsis. The finding that aggressive people tend to watch a lot of violent programmes has been explained in terms of their need to drain off aggressive impulses. Similarly, after acting aggressively it is claimed that people report feeling satisfied. Nevertheless, there is very little evidence that catharsis is responsible for these effects, and the majority of experiments point to a tendency for people to be more rather than less aggressive after watching or even participating in violence. An extreme example of the latter is the phenomenon of 'overkill'. Violent criminals tend to become more and more aggressive with repetition of their acts; in the famous case of Jack the Ripper it was reported that his later victims were increasingly mutilated. There is in fact experimental support for the tendency for aggression to escalate if repeated (see Chapter 9). In spite of the fact that catharsis has been largely discredited, it is a very popular theory and is still widely believed; for this reason we shall have occasion to refer to it again in later chapters.

Similar to catharsis is the 'safety-valve' or 'substitution' theory, which is usually applied in the case of pornography. It is argued that pent-up sexual desires, if they cannot be expressed in the normal way, may be satisfied by just looking at pornography. If so, then pornography offers a very useful and beneficial outlet for such people, and especially for the sexual pervert with illegal or socially unacceptable desires. But, equally well, exposure to pornography may further increase the strength of the unacceptable urges, and there seems no reason why sooner or later the person will not want to act out his fantasies. To suggest that pornography might serve instead of the deviant act could possibly apply in the case of minor sexual variations such as voyeurism, but hardly for the more 'active' and involved sex crimes such as rape and sadism. Unfortunately, on the evidence available there is little support for the belief that pornography can serve a useful purpose as an alternative to sexual behaviour.

Another theory concerned with the effects of pornography is that of 'satiation'. It is argued that if pornography were freely available then it would lose much of its appeal, which at present is largely dependent upon its 'novelty' value and the fact that it is a 'forbidden fruit'. In the US Commission (1970) report, Lipton and Greenwood suggest that exposure to obscenity is an inevitable part of growing up and that it may even serve a purpose: 'Although . . . somewhat far-fetched, it seems possible that graded exposure may immunize in somewhat the same fashion that exposure to bacteria and viruses builds resistance.' Nevertheless, the question arises as to why people should be required to immunize themselves against the 'harmful' effects of pornography and how this can be separated from the potentially beneficial effects. This issue will be dealt with in connection with the treatment applications of pornography in Chapter 8. Having outlined the theories that are relevant to media effects we must now turn to a consideration of the methods by which theories are investigated.

SUMMARY

Psychological theory and scientific methodology indicate ways in which evidence on the effects of TV violence and of pornography might be collected. Research to date has usually proceeded without much regard to theory, and has often used methodologies which are inherently weak. This has resulted in apparently contradictory results and much confusion, with people merely selecting those interpretations of the evidence which support their own preconceptions. In many cases, important and socially relevant conclusions have been based on quite inadequate studies. In spite of this, if the available evidence is interpreted in terms of well-founded psychological theories, and if the limitations of the methodologies employed are recognized, then a fairly consistent picture begins to emerge. The media can be shown to have many different effects, depending on such factors as the type of material and the conditions of viewing. As well as reviewing the theories relevant to the issue of media violence and pornography, this chapter discusses the important part that theory has to play in the development of a science.

3 Methods of Investigation

Having reviewed some theoretical expectations, we must now turn to a consideration of the possible empirical sources of evidence. These are additional to much experimental work which is of indirect relevance, in that it supports general theories such as those of desensitization or modelling; in so far as these methods of behaviour modification have been found effective in many situations, and with many subjects, it must be assumed that they would be equally effective in relation to exposure to sexual and violent content. We would be prepared to argue that such laboratory evidence, linked with well-developed psychological theory, provides the best evidence in this field. It may seem curious to non-scientists that theory is given such a powerful position, as compared with direct empirical study; the history of physics has shown many examples, as we have already noted, where the theory has triumphed over what were alleged to be facts contradictory to it, but which were later found to be faulty in one way or another. Fortunately no such opposition arises in this field; as we shall see, the effectiveness of exposure to sex and violence is not really put in doubt by the direct evidence, which is strongly supportive.

There are four major ways in which this association has been investigated; the first of these, oddly enough, is popularly regarded as the most convincing and impressive, but is scientifically of least interest, and probably largely lacking in power of proof. We have consequently not given a detailed discussion of what might appeal most to many people, namely the discussion of individual case histories illustrating the effects of specific acts or habits of viewing. As *illustrations* such cases (of which we shall briefly mention a few) are of course of considerable interest, and they are also quite suggestive of research that might with advantage be undertaken. But they do not provide scientific proof for the theories they illustrate; in each specific case we cannot disentangle what in fact are or were the causal factors, what preceded what, and what came after what. Some people who agree with our proposition that the media do influence people's views, attitudes and actions profoundly are somewhat impatient with detailed, scientific proof, and demands for exclusion of all extraneous influences that might produce the observed effect (e.g. Whitehouse, 1977); we cannot agree. To be crucial, proof must be able to exclude alternative hypotheses; individual case histories, however convincing they may appear, can never do this. Once the general scientific proof is available (as it now is through the use of the other three methods of investigation discussed in detail in later chapters), illustrative case histories may be of use in giving more concrete body to the findings, and in demonstrating the sort of thing that is happening in the real world, and outside the psychologist's laboratory. More than that they cannot do.

With this caveat in mind, we may look briefly at some well-documented court cases. The first concerns the trial for murder of a young British schoolboy in July 1973. He had viciously battered to death a harmless old tramp, acting out in considerable detail in real life scenes from the film *A Clockwork Orange*. The boy had become fascinated with the film, then turned into a killer, using the content of the film to give direction to his murderous impulses thus excited. Defence counsel, prosecuting counsel, and the psychiatrist who examined the boy agreed that the film played a prominent part in the murder. The boy was not drunk, had not taken drugs, and was not suffering from any form of mental disease. The ferocity and cruelty of the attack are almost beyond belief; so is the utter lack of emotion or guilt on the part of the boy after the murder. His action beautifully illustrates the combination of desensitization and modelling which jointly accompany the viewing of appropriate films. This particular film left behind a rich harvest of similar crimes; in May 1976, Herbert S. Kerrigan, one of Scotland's leading advocates, spoke of three murder trials in the previous year similarly 'triggered off by seeing *A Clockwork Orange*'.

A trail of tragedies and mental breakdowns followed the showing of *The Exorcist* in Britain. In Lowestoft, to take but one example, a man admitted to sexually assaulting an eleven-year-old girl, just a few hours after leaving a cinema showing the film; it was suggested in court that his behaviour towards the girl reflected some of the scenes shown in the film. A more direct influence from a film was suggested in a case concerning *The Omen*, which includes a gory scene in which a child's nurse gets stabbed in the throat. Half an hour after the presentation of this film at a cinema, the manager of a local betting shop lay dead having been stabbed through the throat. A man who had been watching the film had robbed him of the day's takings and knifed him in a very similar way to that shown in the film.

Other court cases have indicated the role played by TV in precipitating crime. *The Brothers Karamazov* involves a scene of a father being battered to death by one of his sons. After watching this film on TV, a seventeen-year-old boy used a meat cleaver to attack his sleeping father. Only after hours of neurosurgery was the father's life saved. The boy is reported to have told police: 'It's just that when I watch television I sometimes imagine myself committing murders and thinking I can get away with it.'

A fifteen-year-old girl attempted to murder her parents by cutting the brake pipes of the family car after getting the idea from *Starsky and Hutch*. The attempt went wrong when she came out of school and was horrified to find her parents waiting to drive her home! In the week before the murder attempt, the girl was reported to have become immersed in crime fiction, reading novels by Agatha Christie and Alfred Hitchcock.

A burglary on a TV programme looked so easy that two viewers decided to have a go themselves. They went out after the programme had ended to carry out a 'carbon copy' break-in. They found an empty house by noting a newspaper in the letterbox and then got in through a back window. But something went wrong. Unlike what happened in the programme, the householder turned up while they were still inside. In court one of them was reported to have told police: 'We saw how it was done on "Z-Cars" and decided to have a go. It looked so easy.'

Many psychiatrists (of widely differing persuasions) have examined actual cases before the court, or in their private practice, or in hospitals, and have come to the conclusion that a direct causal link existed between pornography and violent crime. In an interview on the BBC Radio 4 programme, Dr Arthur Hyatt Williams, a consultant psychiatrist who had worked in one of Britain's prisons, was asked precisely this question, and answered: 'Yes . . . [he had come across] at least three murders, a case of grievous bodily harm, rape with sadistic sexuality and several homosexual assaults with sadism, followed by murder.' Dr Williams also took up the point that pornography might be beneficial therapeutically, in leading to inoffensive masturbation rather than to acting-out. He answered, basing himself on his clinical experience: 'Masturbation may protect for a time by keeping the perverse and criminal impulses within the self, but there is a time in most people who practise perverse masturbation when the fantasy and the masturbatic private act no longer satisfies them. And at that point they go out and commit a crime; and I've met it in at least fifty cases.'

It would be equally idle to dismiss the views of experienced psychiatrists, who have made a special study of cases of this kind, as it would be to accept them without corroborative proof. When Whitehouse (1977) says, recalling the Hindley/Brady trial, 'that no one cares or even remembers any more, that we get hung up on cold clinical arguments about what *proof* there is that pornography affects behaviour is a measure of how coldly indifferent we have become', we must answer that one's moral, social and ethical attitudes are one thing, scientific proof is another, and that asking for proper proof is not necessarily an indication of lack of concern. The cause of those who advocate a greater degree of censorship is in our view correct, but it requires proper factual support; concern is not enough. The cases mentioned, which could be multiplied a hundredfold, are sufficient to cause massive anger, fury, even despair; they do not establish beyond cavil that the hypothesized causal link actually exists – even though they do make it seem likely. Nevertheless, all this material is best seen in the light of the total sum of existing evidence, rather than as enforcing a premature decision. Ultimately the weighing of the evidence must be left to the individual; others may disagree with our estimation of the respective merits of the different methods used.

The first of these methods to consider is the so-called *field study*. The essential characteristic of the field study approach is that naturally occurring behaviour is being studied. People are assessed without artificially manipulating or influencing them in any way, and as a result it can be assumed that their behaviour is 'natural'. The method encompasses naturalistic or sociological observations, surveys and *in situ* comparisons of groups of people. It is argued that results obtained in the 'real world' are somehow more genuine than those obtained in a laboratory. A second claimed advantage is that any effects, in this case of media sex and violence, can be assessed relative to the many other factors that influence behaviour in real life. If effects are not apparent, then it is usually assumed that they are absent or of negligible importance. A third, and perhaps the most telling advantage offered in defence of the field study, is that the results obtained are likely to be believed and taken seriously. Laymen in particular feel better equipped in evaluating a field study than a laboratory experiment. For these reasons, field studies have been very popular and are often seen as a crucial test for the effects of TV and pornography.

There are many problems associated with the field study approach. Basically, the method lacks the precision of laboratory work and so is unsuited for testing complex theoretical issues. The biggest disadvantage is that subjects cannot be randomly assigned to the conditions being compared. This means that any differences discovered between the groups might be due to any one or more of an infinite variety of reasons. For example, if a group of TV viewers are found to be more aggressive than a group of non-viewers, this could be due to the influence of TV violence on the viewers. But equally well it could be that aggressive people choose to watch TV while unaggressive people choose instead to join clubs, visit friends, help with charities, etc. The point is that having found a difference between the groups, we still do not know the reason for this difference.

Researchers attempt to get round this problem by 'matching' subjects in the two groups. Suppose that the viewing of TV violence is more common in men than women, young rather than old, and in working-class people rather than middle-class. A random sample of violence-viewers would include a surplus of young, working-class men, and a control group of non-violence-viewers would include a surplus of old, middle-class women. To discover a higher incidence of aggression in the former group would tell us nothing about the effects of TV. Such a field study would not of course be conducted, although some studies have come rather close to it! What is done is to select two groups, not on a purely random basis, but in such a way as to ensure that men and women are equally represented in the two groups, as too are young and old, and working-class and middle-class. This is known as matching in terms of sex, age and social class, and is a fairly standard procedure.

Unfortunately the above matching is unlikely to be sufficient. Suppose that people with low intelligence are more aggressive and also more likely to watch violence on TV than people with high intelligence, and there is some evidence for believing this to be the case, then it is necessary to match the two groups in terms of this variable. Administering a proper intelligence test to a large sample of subjects can be a time-consuming procedure, and has been done in few of the studies with which we are concerned. Therefore it is possible to argue that any tendency for violence-viewers to be more aggressive than non-violence-viewers is due to differences in intelligence rather than to the effects of TV violence. Nevertheless, even if the groups were matched for intelligence, it is still possible for other variables to be distorting the results. Personality would be just one possible example. If people with an aggressive type of personality have a particular liking for violent programmes, then any tendency for them to be more aggressive than non-violence-viewers cannot be accounted for in terms of the influence of TV violence.

Another way of illustrating the problem is in terms of the limitations that are attached to the correlation coefficient. A field study might lead to the discovery that amount of violence-viewing is 'correlated' with the tendency to be aggressive. However, an association between two variables does not necessarily mean that the two are causally related. To find that violence-viewing is related to aggression could mean that TV violence 'encourages' aggression, or it could equally well mean that aggressive people choose to watch a lot of violent programmes. Alternatively, it could also mean that a third variable is causing both aggression and a preference for violent programmes. For example, people who are physically strong may, as a result of this attribute, tend towards aggressive acts and to enjoy watching violent programmes. While each of these alternative interpretations could possibly be discounted by further research, or else controlled by appropriate matching, the point is that the list of possibilities is almost endless.

A few more examples may help to substantiate the problems

involved in interpreting the results of a field study. People who tend not to watch TV may be more likely than those who do to attend cinemas and so be exposed to violence in that way. Alternatively they might be profoundly influenced, as a sort of contrast effect, by the few violent programmes they do happen to see. This effect might well apply in the case of pornography. Even a single exposure to pornography may have a lasting effect on sexual attitudes and behaviour. Because of the powers of memory, it is possible for such experiences to be repeatedly recalled and, according to the conditioning theory described in the last chapter, this may be sufficient for the development of a sexual deviation. The quality or nature of the experience may be more important than the quantity. It is even possible that excessive exposure to pornography has a sort of immunizing effect. In view of these possibilities, it makes little sense to compare heavy with light TV viewers or people with high and low exposure to pornography. In the case of TV, it would help to assess subjects in terms of the violence to which they have been exposed, rather than the amount of TV as such. Similarly in the case of pornography, it would help to know about the nature of the materials to which they have been exposed. Pornography depicting 'abnormal' or illegal acts is of fairly recent origin, and if the nature of the act depicted is important, then it would be necessary to compare people who have had exposure to this type of material with those who have not. Needless to say, most of the studies in this area have been concerned solely with amount of exposure.

In spite of all the objections to the field study method and the difficulties involved, it is a very popular method, with many large-scale projects being mounted and whole books devoted to a discussion of them. As one might have expected, however, the results vary from study to study and are generally inconclusive. Critics of the hypothesis that TV violence can encourage aggression, and that pornography can encourage sexual deviancy, have used the results to argue that the evidence is contradictory and only slightly, if at all, in favour of the hypothesis. But if the method is faulty or inappropriate, then this is the very outcome that would have been predicted. Rather more promising is the method of the *experimental field study*.

Laboratory investigations are criticized as being artificial, and field studies are always open to the criticism that the groups to be compared are not appropriately matched. The experimental field study is a compromise solution which circumvents at least the latter criticism. Its essential characteristic is controlled manipulation in a naturalistic setting. The people to be studied are randomly assigned to groups and their real-life behaviour is then observed. Because the assignment is random, any significant differences detected can be attributed to the differential effects of the conditions imposed. Ideally, these conditions should not appear contrived, and the observation of effects should be on behaviour that is genuinely spontaneous.

The main limitation of the experimental field study is that only rarely is it possible to assign people to different conditions without it appearing contrived, artificial or unfair. If it is obvious to the subjects that they are in an experiment, then their behaviour may be affected as a result. An example concerns the assignment of children to a regime that includes violent TV or one that does not. Those deprived of their usual programmes may resent this and so become aggressive. As we shall see, this appeared to happen in just such a study. The research was designed to show that children who watch violent programmes on TV will, through catharsis, become less aggressive than children who are only allowed to watch non-violent programmes. The hypothesis was partly supported but, because of the possibility that the control children were aggressive merely on account of their resentment at being restricted to non-violent programmes, any interpretation of the results must be only tentative.

There is also the ethical problem of deliberately interfering with people's lives for the purposes of an experiment. To expose a group of students to hard-core pornography, suspecting that it may have subtle effects on their attitudes to sex and maybe even cause sexual deviancy, is difficult to justify. In the event, researchers have not done this but have instead limited the exposure to fairly brief sessions of erotica or mild pornography. Their results, which have at best indicated a temporary increase in some of the activities portrayed, have been claimed to support the argument that exposure to pornography does not lead to sex crime. But if it is only with exposure to material portraying sex crimes that such an effect might be demonstrated, then such a conclusion would be unjustified and misleading.

The problems arising in an experimental field study may be illustrated by reference to the testing of new treatments. Suppose it is decided to test the effectiveness of a new drug which has been found to be effective and safe in the laboratory. To administer this drug to some needy patients and not to others would be unethical, especially if the control group were led to believe that they were receiving treatment. In practice, the drug would be compared with the existing method of treatment or the patients would be told that they may be given a placebo and their consent obtained. It would only be fair, however, to ask for this consent if the patient was unlikely to suffer as a result of treatment being withheld. Moreover, if they are told that they may be receiving only a placebo, then by looking for side effects they will be trying to discover which group they are in. In the case of such experiments, patients do tend to discover what they are receiving and this knowledge probably influences their progress. Similarly in the case of exposure to violence or pornography, any results obtained may be due to 'psychological' effects rather than the exposure as such. If subjects expect exposure to violent films to make them more aggressive, then they may become so because of this expectation or, equally well, they might resist this supposed effect by deliberately making an effort to be unaggressive.

As with the experimental field study approach, the main advantage of the *laboratory method* is that subjects can be randomly assigned to the conditions being compared. This effectively allows an interpretation of the results in terms of cause and effect. Another advantage is that conditions can be arranged to maximize the chances of detecting effects. In the case of aggressive behaviour, any increase as a result of exposure to a violent film may be very small and so not manifested in overt behaviour – such as a direct attack on someone. Among the techniques adopted to detect small increases in aggression is that of assessing attitudes or mood changes. Another way is to encourage the expression of aggression by providing the subject with an opportunity. One way is to invite him to administer electric shocks to an apparent volunteer participating a study on the effects of punishment. Yet another technique is to annoy or frustrate the subject so as to increase the chances of aggression occurring.

The main criticism of the laboratory method is that the

typical situation is too far removed from real life to give useful results. It is felt that subjects do not behave in their normal fashion and that this can lead to distorted results. For example, in an experiment where the expression of aggression is being encouraged, a subject may feel safe in giving vent to such urges, knowing it will not get him into trouble. Critics talk of the 'demand' characteristics of the experimental situation such that subjects will behave in accordance with what they see as expected of them. In claiming that people in the laboratory 'are subjected to the demands of the experimenter and thus respond in a different way in research studies than they do in everyday life', Noble (1975) gives the example of a four-year-old girl who was heard to say on her first visit to a modelling laboratory: 'Look, Mummy, there's the doll we'll have to hit'.

A partial answer to the above criticism is that the demand characteristics apply to the control subjects as well as to the experimental. In the case of the little girl, her attitude to the doll may result in her hitting it, but since she has an equal chance of being assigned to the control as to the experimental condition it is not a problem. The relevant question is whether the laboratory situation in some way elicits behaviour from the experimental group that would not be elicited in everyday life. Stein and Friedrich (1975) expressed this limitation, along with some others, as follows:

> The fact that a permissive adult has exposed the child to the model in the laboratory may be an important disinhibitor that is not present in 'real life'. Most behavioral observations are conducted immediately after exposure in situations very similar to the ones in which the models were observed. Therefore, these studies do not indicate how durable the behavioral changes are nor how much disinhibition would generalize to other situations. They also provide no information about generalization to other types of aggressive behavior, particularly behavior that is more serious and potentially harmful than the play activities measured in most studies.

The complaint about the measurement of play activities rather than serious aggression is inevitable because of the ethical difficulties involved in eliciting the latter. Nevertheless, there seems no reason why mild forms of aggression, such as giving shocks to another person, should not be subject to the same laws as more extreme forms. We do not have one set of theories for mild aggression and another set for serious. The complaint that laboratory experiments usually involve observations made immediately after exposure is probably because of the assumption that the effects will not be long-lasting. In the case of modelling, however, it has been found that much the same effect is apparent in children whether they are tested immediately after seeing the model or one week later. A more serious limitation is that exposure to violence has to be of relatively short duration if the subject is not to be deprived of a normal life. It is not, for example, possible to study the effects of years of exposure to TV under laboratory conditions. One compromise is to assess the effects of repeated doses of shortterm exposure, and another to investigate theories, such as desensitization, that are relevant to long-term effects.

New aircraft are first tested in wind tunnels and heat chambers so that on the basis of these laboratory results, the designers can be reasonably confident that they will not crash when eventually tested on a real flight. In the same way, when the problems of media sex and violence are reasonably well understood, researchers will be in a better position to design a field study controlling for relevant variables that might have been overlooked without the preliminary laboratory work.

The experimental approach must be the method of choice because of the obvious limitations of field studies. The laboratory method, in particular, allows the investigation of detailed theoretical issues that would not be possible in a naturalistic setting. In contrast to results from field studies, those from the laboratory have tended to be consistent and, in general, in accord with predictions from well-established theories. To a lesser degree the same can be said for the better-designed of the experimental field studies.

Noble (1975) asked: 'Do we want to know with certainty what will happen in a highly specific set of circumstances, or do we want to know what is more or less likely to happen when media violence is seen "in natural, everyday viewing situations"?' The answer seems to be that only by investigating the issue in a highly specific set of circumstances will we ever be in a position to understand what probably happens in everyday life.

Laymen are often impatient with the sustained critical doubts which scientists express when dealing with their various problems, and with published experiments. They often feel that the answer is obvious, and does not require all the careful experimental designs and multiple safeguards the scientist tries to build into his researches. Medical people and psychiatrists often share this 'let's get on with it' spirit, but the evidence shows that this impatience is likely to be counter-productive. Two examples may serve to illustrate the need for care. The first comes from the field of coronary heart disease. When intensive care units for this disease were introduced, the suggestion that the efficacy of these units needed proof was opposed on the grounds that the answer was obvious, and that it was unethical to deprive patients of these new facilities. When trials were instituted, however, using a control group of patients who were treated in their own homes, it turned out that the patients in the control group in fact got better quicker than those in the intensive care units.

Another example comes from the field of electroshock (ECT) treatment for psychiatric disorders. This is widely used, but has little proper research background (and no theoretical justification at all). Nevertheless, many psychiatrists believe that their experience, coupled with common sense, amply proves the usefulness of the treatment, without proper scientific trials. Recently, an ECT machine was installed in a British mental hospital and used for six months; it was only after a routine overhaul that it was discovered that through a wiring fault the machine had not been delivering any current! The doctors using the machine had not noticed that it was not functioning, nor had they noticed any difference in the effects of the treatment on their patients from that expected from a properly functioning machine.

This lack of concern also pervades many of the articles and books written in the field this book is concerned with; writers and commentators seem to know *a priori* what the answer to the problems posed should be, and are impatient to get on with it. Critical discussions of methodology, and of theories, are rare, and usually of low quality; the Presidential Commissions and their reports present a low which it would be difficult to surpass. We have carefully noted in conjunction with each type of experiment, and often with each experiment, just what are the major strengths and weaknesses; this may not make for joyful reading, or for definitive conclusions, but we feel that it comes closer to the spirit of science than would a more journalistic approach.

Given that all methods have weaknesses, and make assumptions, how can we ever come to any conclusions, however carefully worded, and however guarded? The answer must be in terms of agreement between workers using different methods; when similar conclusions are presented by experimentalists employing designs which have compensating faults and virtues, then we may reasonably assume that these conclusions are more firmly based than when we have to rely on just one method of investigation. If we also find that the conclusions are in good accord with predictions from well-established theories, then our confidence may justifiably be higher still. This, as we shall try to show, is the position in this field; there are still some anomalies, but this is so in all scientific theories and research. Complex situations are not easily reduced to scientific order, and the many parameters which determine the observed effects can seldom all be specified and controlled. Partial control is the most we can hope for, and occasional departures from expectation are to be regretted, but cannot be avoided. What is important is to base conclusions on the total sum of evidence available, not on selected and possibly non-representative studies alone. We believe that all three methods mentioned here have a contribution to make, although our order of importance would be the reverse of that the layman would probably choose. We believe that the experimental laboratory method gives the most clear-cut and reliable results, followed by the experimental field study. The field study method is the least reliable, owing to the difficulties of controlling variables. The method of single cases, so attractive to journalists, has no scientific value, and can be used only to illustrate, never to prove, any points about the effects of the media; we shall not consider it a scientific method of investigation at all.

SUMMARY

Four methods of investigation have been widely used, of which only three can be regarded as of scientific interest. *Single-case studies* of individuals who apparently were pushed into committing crimes of a violent or sexual nature by the portrayal of such crimes in the media are of interest in suggesting causal links, and may be used to illustrate scientific findings using methodologies having a better factual basis, but they can never furnish us with proof. *Field studies* have a wider basis than single-case studies, and may furnish us with acceptable evidence provided they are properly designed. Unfortunately the possibilities of control in these studies are very limited, and this makes the drawing of conclusions difficult and hazardous. *Experimental field studies* avoid some of these difficulties, and are therefore preferable in many ways; they tend to lead to more certain conclusions. From the point of view of testing scientific theories in a rigorous manner, however, *experimental laboratory studies* are without doubt the method of choice, in spite of the allegedly 'unnatural' nature of such studies. Proper controls can be designed to take care of this undesirable feature of the experiment, and in all other ways laboratory studies are clearly superior to field studies, however carefully planned and executed. Many people wonder why psychologists are so concerned with small details of design of experiments, with complexities of statistical analysis, and with random allocation of subjects. The answer is that the whole value of an experiment depends on such 'quality control'; a single design error, or fault in the analysis, can destroy completely the evidential value of the study. Experiments will be quoted to illustrate this important point in later chapters.

4 The American Commissions

That part of social psychology which is concerned with violence and pornography has the honour of having been the subject of three specially appointed commissions in the United States. The first of two violence commissions was concerned with the problem of violence generally, and consisted of reviews of social policies and existing research and the formulation of a set of recommendations. The other violence commission was specifically concerned with TV violence and its effect on children, and was unusual in that it sponsored a substantial amount of new research. The pornography commission also sponsored new research as well as considering previous work in attempting to decide whether or not pornography is 'harmful'. This chapter describes how these commissions were organized and, in evaluating the content of the three reports, attempts to gain some insights into the usefulness of this manner of enquiry.

The Pornography volumes carry a foreword which says: 'We expect and invite critical examination and appraisal of these reports, for we have only begun the task of interpreting the wealth of information they contain.' It might be thought that they would be readily available for examination, and so it may be of interest to relate some of the difficulties we met in originally trying to obtain the reports. It took over a year and six letters to obtain the first batch, by which time several of the others were out of print.[1] While waiting for the reports to arrive we tried to borrow copies from the British Lending Library, which organizes an inter-library loan system. Unfortunately, none of the participating libraries had copies of the reports. The only public copies were held by the British Museum, and even these are kept 'in store' at a depot. The original publishers

[1] Thanks are due to Frank Ochberg and Ben Dean of the National Institute of Mental Health for providing us with 'out of print' copies of the technical reports of the US Commissions on Violence and on Pornography.

apparently did not reply to enquiries from the London purchasing agent, H. K. Lewis & Co. Ltd. Subsequently an order sent to the official suppliers, the US Government Printing Office, a request for such information as a complete list of titles, and then enquiries after several months had passed as to why the order had not materialized, did not yield helpful answers. Rather than replying to letters, the Office adopts the practice of returning them with comments pencilled in the margin. Rarely were these comments relevant or of much help, although a few of the technical volumes did eventually arrive. We are now informed that clients who order books from the Government Printing Office should expect a delay of at least six months. Unfortunately, this story is only too typical of the problems that researchers have to overcome in seeking information.

The assassinations of John and Robert Kennedy and Martin Luther King prompted President Lyndon Johnson to set up the first violence commission. Thirteen committee members were appointed and included lawyers, politicians and a solitary psychiatrist. Their brief was to investigate the problem of violence in all its aspects, and they were assisted in this by experts who reviewed their specialist fields. Within eighteen months a final 'summary' report was produced that reflected the deliberations of the committee (National Commission on the Causes and Prevention of Violence, 1969). This was accompanied by some fifteen volumes of detailed essays and reviews referred to as the 'task force reports' and subsequent discussions or 'hearings'. Most of these volumes were concerned with such aspects of violence as terrorism and gun laws, but two were concerned with TV violence and its effects (Baker and Ball, 1969; Briand, 1969).

The summary report gave an overview of existing research and presented the conclusions and recommendations agreed on by the thirteen committee members. It was noted that violent crime, defined as encompassing homicide, rape, robbery and assault, had increased 100 per cent in the previous decade. With respect to the nature of TV programmes, the excessive amount of violence was illustrated in terms of a survey finding that 94 per cent of children's cartoons contained violence, as did 81 per cent of entertainment programmes presented during prime-time viewing. Perhaps even more relevant was the observation that leading characters or heroes often inflict violence upon others, and that violence is often portrayed as a successful means of attaining a desired end.

With respect to the effects of TV, a theoretical position taken by the committee was that TV is a primary source of socialization, and that children begin to absorb the lessons of TV before they can read or write. In this way, TV is seen as helping to create what children expect of themselves and others, and of what constitutes the standards of civilized society. The committee similarly observed that we often learn by vicarious reinforcement, and that there seems no reason why TV should not be included among the sources of such reinforcement. The parodox of advertising did not go unmentioned. It was noted that firms spend millions of dollars in the belief that TV advertisements can influence human behaviour, and that while the TV industry enthusiastically agrees with them, it nonetheless contends that programmes of violence have no such influence.

The TV industry has often taken the position that the research evidence on the effects of TV violence is wholly inconclusive. After reviewing this evidence, the committee did not agree and stated their own conclusion in various ways, for example: 'The preponderance of the available research evidence strongly suggests . . . that violence in TV programs can and does have adverse effects upon audiences – particularly child audiences.' The committee also concluded that catharsis theory is hardly supported since the research shows that violent film content stimulates aggression rather than the opposite. Their conclusions were tempered by a few qualifications. For example, while accepting that fictional violence by dulling emotional reactions can desensitize viewers to violence in real life, so making them feel less inhibited about engaging in aggression when provoked, it was suggested that exposure to particularly horrifying episodes could have just the opposite effect. In particular, focusing on the painful results of violence could sensitize viewers to the potential harm that it can inflict. Another qualification was to suggest that TV is more likely to be a contributing factor than a principal cause of violence in society.

On the basis of the conclusion that TV violence is potentially harmful, four main recommendations were made. First, 'the broadcasting of children's cartoons containing serious, non-comic violence should be abandoned'. Second, 'the amount of time devoted to the broadcast of crime, western and action-adventure programs containing violent episodes should be reduced'. Third, 'more effective efforts should be made to alter the basic context in which violence is presented in TV dramas'. In particular, it was recommended that producers should avoid depicting violence as the routine method of solving problems. Fourth, 'the members of the TV industry should become more actively and seriously involved in research on the effects of violent TV programs, and their future policies, standards and practices with regard to entertainment programs should be more responsive to the best evidence provided by social scientists, psychologists, and communications researchers'.

All this might seem clear-cut and fairly obvious, but it was not enough to convince the authorities. In fact, the conclusions of this commission were very much over-shadowed by the second violence commission that was now under way. The reported conclusions of the second commission were not expressed in quite such clear terms and this, together with inaccurate press coverage, seems to have led to a 'contrast' effect with many people gaining the impression that TV violence was perhaps after all of little consequence. We will now turn to an examination of this second commission.

The second violence commission was specifically concerned with TV violence, especially its effect on children, and was initiated by Senator John Pastore. It was organized under the auspices of the Surgeon General and the National Institute of Mental Health. The purpose was not just to review the literature but to fund and evaluate further research, this being one of the recommendations of the previous commission. More than $1 million was made available and of 46 submitted proposals, 23 projects involving 60 researchers were selected by a panel of full-time staff. The results of these projects, together with literature reviews and critiques, were presented in five volumes of technical reports. Appendix reports were also produced consisting of a bibliography of 550 articles relevant to the subject of TV violence, and various subcommittee hearings. The results and reviews presented in the technical reports were evaluated by an advisory committee for the final 'summary' report (Surgeon General's Scientific Advisory Committee on Television and Social Behavior, 1972).

Boffey and Walsh (1970) and Bogart (1972) describe how the

advisory committee was appointed. The Surgeon General sent letters to various professional organizations, such as the American Psychological Association, describing the nature of the enquiry and requesting nominations for the committee. Forty people were selected as qualified to evaluate the research evidence, and their names were sent to three major TV networks with the invitation to identify any whom they considered 'would not be appropriate for an impartial scientific investigation of this nature'. To his credit, Frank Stanton of CBS declined the opportunity, saying, 'I know you seek to construct the most objective study possible, and I would be most reluctant to introduce even a suggestion of bias into the selection of the investigators'. The other network representatives took the chance to veto seven individuals known to have previously interpreted research findings as indicating adverse effects. These men were subsequently dropped from the list; they included eminent researchers such as Bandura and Berkowitz, penalized it seems because of the outcome of their experiments. All but one of the twelve members for the committee were chosen from the remaining thirty-three names. Various disciplines were represented but five were employed by, or had close links with, the TV networks.

The above by any standards appears a rather odd selection procedure in that the broadcasting industry was allowed to veto the appointment of potentially hostile critics, while no provision was made for allowing the rejection of men committed to an opposite point of view. The appointment of a committee, so obviously 'loaded' in favour of the broadcasting industry, happened in spite of the Secretary of Health, Education and Welfare publicly proclaiming that the government 'was looking for individuals without a previous commitment to one side of the controversy or another'. The matter, although kept quiet at the time, did not go unchallenged. Fifteen fellows at the Center for Advanced Study in the Behavioral Sciences at Stanford sent an open letter urging 'procedures to ensure that . . . scientific advisory committees include all major relevant viewpoints', and adding: 'We find particularly objectionable procedures that exclude one side of a controversy'. But all protests were to no avail and led to one of the committee members conceding that 'the scientific independence of this study has obviously been subverted to some kind of political consideration'. This sentiment was echoed by the full-time staff who were quoted as being in the habit of referring to the committee as 'the network five, the naive four, and the scientific three'. In its summary report, the committee was forced to admit that the procedure by which well-known researchers were vetoed was 'a serious error'.

The role of the committee was to evaluate the research results and reviews and to produce the summary report. The more basic job of defining research needs, soliciting and select-ing research projects, and editing the technical volumes, needed to be carried out by appropriately qualified full-time staff. Cater and Strickland (1975) describe the difficulties encountered in finding competent staff to handle this responsi-bility. Academics are usually involved in their own research and are naturally reluctant to upset their schedules by taking on new responsibilities at short notice. In the event, there were no fewer than thirty-eight refusals before a senior research coordinator was found, and then it was a person holding a comparatively junior position as assistant professor of jour-nalism at Berkeley. There were similar problems in finding well-qualified social scientists to do the actual research, with many declining the invitation to submit proposals. Neverthe-less, the whole undertaking went ahead on the scale planned.

Senator Pastore had hoped that the committee would come to a definite conclusion that would have an impact on the TV industry. This hope was not realized since the conclusions in the summary report were hedged with various qualifications and reservations. There were positive conclusions such as statements that 'violence depicted on TV can immediately or shortly thereafter induce mimicking or copying by children', and that 'under certain circumstances TV violence can insti-gate an increase in aggressive acts'. There were also more general conclusions such as noting that 'the data, while not wholly consistent or conclusive, do indicate that a modest relationship exists between the viewing of violence and aggres-sive behavior'. But these conclusions were invariably followed by words of caution.

Many instances could be given of how a conclusion was immediately qualified, for example: 'We have noted in the studies at hand a modest association between viewing of vio-lence and aggression among at least some children, and we

have noted some data which are consonant with the interpretation that violence-viewing produces the aggression; this evidence is not conclusive, however, and some of the data are also
consonant with other interpretations.' Similarly, when evaluating the status of the catharsis theory the conclusion was expressed as follows: 'As matters now stand, the weight of the experimental evidence from the present series of studies, as well as
from prior research, suggests that viewing filmed violence has
an observable effect on some children in the direction of
increasing their aggressive behavior. Many of the findings,
however, fail to show any statistically significant effects in
either direction.'

Apart from the above qualifications, the strength of the
findings was further attenuated in various ways, such as point-
ing out that 'TV is only one of the many factors which in time
may precede aggressive behavior'. There was also the ever-
present call for more research with the inevitable implication
that the present findings were suspect. For example, in noting
the convergence of experimental and field study evidence of a
link between TV violence and aggressiveness, the report concluded that this 'constitutes some preliminary indication of a
causal relationship, but a good deal of research remains to be
done before one can have confidence in these conclusions'. The
point here is that such qualifications and reservations can be
made of most psychological, or indeed any kind of scientific,
research. It is rare to find an area in which the evidence allows
much more than a tentative conclusion. It is against this background that the present body of research should have been
evaluated.

The conclusions reached by the committee were unanimous,
in contrast to those reached by the pornography commission.
This appears to be the key to the over-cautious nature of the
conclusions and to the excessive number of qualifications
expressed in the report. In order to satisfy all its members, the
committee had to arrive at a consensus report. Because of the
different viewpoints and academic backgrounds of the members, this proved to be very difficult. John Murray, one of the
full-time staff, noted: 'There was a lot of anger, the meetings
were extremely tense with the warring factions sitting at either
end of the table, glaring at each other, particularly towards the
end.' Against this background it is perhaps not surprising that

the summary report reflects not so much the research evidence but a compromise summary of the views of the 'opposing factions' making up the committee. Bogart (1972) describes how the network representatives played a very active part in the drafting of the report. They would allow certain research findings to be described only if various qualifying clauses were stressed. They also insisted on including obvious conclusions, such as: 'The accumulated evidence . . . does not warrant the conclusion that televised violence has a uniformly adverse effect nor the conclusion that it has an adverse effect on the majority of children. It cannot even be said that the majority of the children in the various studies we have reviewed showed an increase in aggressive behaviour in response to the violent fare to which they were exposed.' All this acted to obscure the actual findings and to make the text almost incomprehensible to the layman, as the following quotation may illustrate: 'The experimental findings are weak in various . . . ways and not wholly consistent from one study to another. Nevertheless, they provide suggestive evidence in favor of the interpretation that viewing violence on TV is conducive to an increase in aggressive behavior, although it must be emphasized that the causal sequence is very likely applicable only to some children who are predisposed in this direction.'

Evidence that the summary report was misleading and contained various distortions came from a survey carried out by Paisley (1972). Most of the researchers involved were sent a questionnaire, with twenty-three of them providing usable returns. Their initial reaction to the report was rated as somewhat unfavourable, but it was not as bad as some of them had expected, given the composition of the committee. More seriously, half of them felt that the conclusions from their own research had not been accurately covered in the report. Regardless of their own work, 70 per cent were of the opinion that viewing TV violence increases aggressiveness, none felt that there was no effect, and the remaining 30 per cent were unwilling to commit themselves.

It might seem unjust to assume that the research was misrepresented because of biases in the committee members. The technical reports upon which they had to rely in preparing their summary were, with few exceptions, far from easy to read. They had been written under pressure of time, and were not subject to competitive selection and careful editing as they would be in the normal course of submission to a learned journal. Worse than this, the quality of the work itself was open to question. Douglas Fuchs, the senior research coordinator who had been found with such difficulty, wrote: 'With few exceptions ... the surveys are superficial, ungeneralizable, myopic exercises in opportunistic grantmanship for the sake of political expedience.' His dissatisfaction probably resulted in his leaving the commission after a year, his place being taken by George Comstock. Anyway, the quality of the work coupled with poor presentation in the technical volumes might well account for any misrepresentations that appeared in the summary report. On the other hand, the committee members were acquainted with research that existed prior to the specially commissioned projects as well as with the previous summary report. The new research did not change the picture of a link between media violence and subsequent aggression; it merely strengthened and extended the evidence that already existed. So it seems that the most likely alternative to the charge of bias in the committee members is that of incompetence at evaluating research evidence. For this they could be excused since the academics who would have been most suited for the job were not represented on the committee.

Further distortion of the research evidence occurred later as a result of inaccurate press coverage. The summary report was published before the technical volumes and attracted a good deal of publicity. This was unfortunate because the accuracy of the conclusions could not be checked against the more factual information contained in the technical volumes. Press reports began to appear a week before the summary report was published, with the *New York Times* being first off the mark. Having obtained leaked copies of the report from sources it would not reveal, its story was printed under the front-page headline 'TV violence held unharmful to youth'. The text of the article was less extreme, containing conclusions similar to those expressed by the committee, such as: 'The office of the United States Surgeon General has found that violence in TV programming does not have an adverse effect on the majority of the nation's youth but may influence small groups of youngsters predisposed by many factors to aggressive behavior.' Other press accounts varied widely. Similar to the *New York Times* was that of the *Washington Evening Star* which wrote: 'A government-funded study cautiously concludes that televised crime and violence contribute in only a small way to violence in America.' Rather different was the story in the *Chicago Daily News* which opened: 'Dynamite is hidden in the Surgeon General's report on children and TV violence, for the report reveals that most children are definitely and adversely affected by televised mayhem.'

Similar press coverage appeared in England, with most papers drawing attention to the claim that the link between media violence and aggression is weak. The *Guardian* wrote: 'Contrary to popular belief, violence depicted on TV has little effect on the young, according to a government report . . . A group of psychologists found only a "modest" relationship between watching violence on TV and aggressive behaviour – after 2½ years of research.' Likewise *The Times* wrote: 'A panel of scientific experts concluded that there appeared to be a tentative link between TV violence and delinquency among children already predisposed towards violence.' In fairness, both papers went on to say that at a press conference the Surgeon General, Jesse Steinfeld, denied that the report condoned TV violence and that he tried to clarify the picture by emphasizing that 'the study shows for the first time a causal connection between violence shown on TV and subsequent [aggressive] behavior by children'.

It may be noted from the above press reports that psychologists or scientists were thought to have arrived at the conclusions expressed in the summary report. In fact, as we know, this report had been written by the committee members rather than the scientists who had done the research. Attention was drawn to this misunderstanding, a month after publication of the report, by the magazine *Newsweek*. They accused the five network committee members of influencing the summary report, saying that they 'tried to rig the Surgeon General's study in their favor' and that 'to a considerable extent they succeeded'. The article went on to record how 'they managed to obfuscate and dilute most key findings that were detrimental to TV's image', and finally that 'the Advisory Committee misrepresented some of the data, ignored some of it and buried all of it alive in prose that was obviously meant to be unreadable and unread'.

Further clarification of the report came two months after publication from 'hearings' held before the US Senate Subcommittee on Communications. Senator Pastore, who had initiated the enquiry three years earlier, asked the Surgeon General to spell out as simply as possible what the conclusions were. Dr Steinfeld responded by expressing his views as follows: 'The overwhelming consensus and the unanimous Scientific Advisory Committee's report indicates that TV violence, indeed, does have an adverse effect on certain members of our society.' Perhaps attempting to redress the balance upset by the media coverage, he went on: 'While the Committee report is carefully phrased and qualified in language acceptable to social scientists, it is clear to me that the causal relationship between televised violence and anti-social behavior is sufficient to warrant appropriate and immediate remedial action.' Other witnesses were asked the same question and each gave a similar reply. For example, a political studies member of the committee, Ithiel Pool, noted: 'Twelve scientists of widely different views unanimously agreed that scientific evidence indicates that the viewing of TV violence by young people causes them to behave more aggressively.' The committee members, it seems, were more convinced of the 'harmful' effects of TV violence than were many readers of their report.

The conclusion that TV violence has harmful effects still left the problem of what to do, and this was discussed at the hearings. It was recognized that the research had not been designed to answer this question and that, anyway, views on censorship depend on personal values rather than scientific evidence. The many problems of introducing censorship were discussed, as were alternatives such as finding ways of encouraging the producers to take a more responsible line. Nicholas Johnson, a Federal Communications Commission member, highlighted the economic problem involved here with a colourful example: 'If you do it [molest a child] during the week, on the school playground, to one child, you are driven off to prison in a police car. But if you do it on Saturday morning, in the living room, to millions of young children, you are just driven home, by a chauffeur, in a long, black limousine'. It was also recognized that those who write programmes for TV are unlikely to be familiar with the relevant evidence, there being a large communication gap between TV writers and research scientists. Perhaps because of these problems the only tangible result of the discussions was the agreement to monitor the amount of TV violence over the next few years.

An unfortunate effect of the second violence commission has been to counteract the conclusions of the first commission. Subsequent clarification of the commissioners' position has not been sufficient to overcome the initial impression that a conclusion of 'little harm' had been reached. Even today it is commonly supposed that the evidence on media violence is ambiguous with indications of both good and bad effects. A recent report of the BBC Advisory Group on the Effects of TV stated: 'In the absence of any persuasive evidence to the contrary from properly conducted research, we are not convinced that the BBC's quantity and treatment in programmes of various kinds of violence is irresponsible or dangerous.' Similarly in the 1976 report of the Independent Broadcasting Authority, Stephen Murphy, who had been Secretary of the British Board of Film Censors, claimed that there is no proof that violence in the media has undesirable social consequences.

How can a special investigation have the effect of obscuring an issue that it was designed to clarify? Many reasons can be given. Some of the researchers themselves can be faulted for not presenting their findings in a clear and concise fashion. This, together with the appointment of an industry-biased committee, allowed the publication of an ambiguous summary report. This in turn allowed the *New York Times* to publish its story that TV violence had been found to be unharmful. The 'primacy' effect of this premature press report probably had an effect that subsequent statements to the contrary could not completely eradicate.

All we can do now, apart from studying original research reports, is to learn from the mistakes apparent in the functioning of this commission. It is clear that future enquiries of this type will have to be organized somewhat differently. Albert Bandura, who had been excluded from the list of experts considered for the Advisory Committee, was called before the hearings as a witness. He commented: 'The Surgeon General's Report demonstrates that the TV industry is sufficiently powerful to control how research bearing on the psychological effects of televised violence is officially evaluated and reported to the general public.' He went on to say: 'This sorry case further illustrates the need for procedures to ensure that in the future scientific advisory panels will not be controlled by the very industries whose practices they are supposed to evaluate.' But even this safeguard is unlikely to be enough, as we shall now see in evaluating the pornography commission, where the 'industry' itself was not represented.

President Lyndon Johnson initiated the Pornography Commission in 1967 in response to public concern. Congressmen were receiving more letters from their constituents about unsolicited pornography sent through the mail than they were about the war in Vietnam. The commission was similar to the second violence commission in that new research was funded and that a committee, rather than the researchers themselves, evaluated the results and produced a 'summary' report (US Commission on Obscenity and Pornography, 1970). In this case it was particularly appropriate to sponsor new research as very little existed at the time. As with the other commission, the summary report was published before the accompanying technical volumes, which appeared over the course of the next two years. This delay was to allow the completion of more detailed analyses required in some of the research projects. There were nine technical volumes in all, of which two were specifically concerned with the effects of erotica (Volumes 7 and 8).

In an attempt at balanced representation, an eighteen-man committee was appointed from such different fields as law, sociology, religion, psychiatry and publishing. Cline (1974) describes the characteristics of these members. While most of them had impeccable reputations, it was also notable that most held very liberal attitudes and, in particular, were anti-censorship. Even the Chairman, William Lockhart, was known to have previously defended pornography on 'free-speech' grounds. Being anti-censorship is not, of course, incompatible with believing that pornography can have harmful effects, but in the event these two issues appear to have been confounded. It is noticeable that the conclusions arrived at by the individual members tend to correspond with their own attitudes to censorship.

In order to investigate separate issues, such as legal matters and the effects of erotica, the committee members were subdivided into four study groups or panels. Five members were involved in the important 'effects' panel, and all appear to have been anti-censorship to begin with. They consisted of three sociologists, a psychiatrist, and a PhD student in communications. One of the sociologists, Joseph Klapper, was employed by the CBS network and was also a prominent member of the violence commission. The PhD student, William Jones, had already written an anti-censorship book. These five men had been chosen for the 'effects' panel because, of the eighteen, they were the only ones with any formal knowledge of behavioural science (but not necessarily of statistics). Because of this specialist knowledge, they had been assigned the task of presenting to the others their evaluation of the research evidence concerned with the effects of erotica. The others were thus in the position of being dependent upon, and having to accept in 'good faith', the conclusions of these 'experts'. This applied especially since the technical volumes containing the research reports were not available until after the summary report had been published. Indeed, the technical volumes carry a prominent note to the effect that they had 'not been reviewed or approved by the full Commission'. The five members on the effects panel were in touch with the researchers and thus acquainted with the results before they were finally written up.

The eighteen committee members were all in employment elsewhere, and so, as with the violence commission, full-time staff were appointed to administer the research grants, collect material and prepare reports. Two of them, Weldon Johnson and Lenore Kupperstein, were employed for the very important job of reviewing the literature and preparing the report of the 'effects' panel. Perhaps unfortunately, both had been students of two very 'liberal' members of this panel – Otto Larsen and Marvin Wolfgang. These men became somewhat notorious in arguing for a repeal of all pornography laws, including those about the mailing of unsolicited pornography and those protecting children. While students are by no means always influenced by their professors, it does seem questionable to have appointed such an 'in-group' for these tasks that were so basic to the commission as a whole.

The committee met from time to time to discuss the findings of the four panels and to prepare the summary report. Unlike the outcome of the Surgeon General's enquiry, this committee could not reach a unanimous conclusion. As a compromise, they published a 'majority' report to which most of the members subscribed. This consisted of an overview of findings and a set of recommendations as well as the detailed reports from each of the four study groups. Following this was a 'minority' report consisting of statements by those members who wished to qualify items in the main body of the report. Some 'dissenters' wanted the recommendations to be more radical while others questioned the whole basis of the 'no harm' conclusion. It seems that by including members with very different attitudes to pornography a polarization of viewpoints resulted rather than the balanced conclusion that was intended.

The overview of findings in the 'majority' report summarized the results of studies concerned with the effects of erotica and noted major findings such as the following. First, 'that exposure to erotic stimuli produces sexual arousal in substantial portions of both males and females'. Second, 'that depictions of conventional sexual behavior are generally regarded as more stimulating than depictions of less conventional activity'. Third, 'that continued or repeated exposure to erotic stimuli over 15 days resulted in satiation (marked diminution) of sexual arousal and interest in such material'. Fourth, 'when people are exposed to erotic materials, some persons increase masturbatory or coital behavior, a smaller proportion decrease it, but the majority of persons report no change in these behaviors'. Fifth, 'statistical studies of the relationship between availability of erotic materials and the rates of sex crimes in Denmark indicate that the increased availability of explicit sexual materials has been accompanied by a decrease in the incidence of sexual crime'. Sixth, 'available research indicates that sex offenders have had less adolescent experience with erotica than other adults . . . The Commission cannot conclude that exposure to erotic materials is a factor in the causation of sex crime or sex delinquency'. These findings led to the 'no harm' conclusion which was expressed in various ways throughout the report, for example: 'Extensive empirical investigation, both by the Commission and by others, provides no evidence that exposure to or use of explicit sexual materials play a significant role in the causation of social or individual harms such as crime, delinquency, sexual or nonsexual deviancy or severe emotional disturbances.'

On the basis of the above conclusion and other considerations such as the entertainment value of pornography, the committee arrived at the following recommendation: 'In general outline, the Commission recommends that federal, state, and local legislation should not seek to interfere with the right of adults who wish to do so to read, obtain, or view explicit sexual materials.' Most of the committee agreed with this recommendation to repeal existing pornography laws. Their other main proposal was more conservative in saying 'we recommend legislative regulations upon the sale of sexual materials to young persons who do not have the consent of their parents, and we also recommend legislation to protect persons from having sexual materials thrust upon them without their consent through the mails or through open public display'.

In the 'minority' report there is a statement by Charles Keating, who was appointed in 1969 to represent President Nixon on the committee. Keating was so concerned by what he perceived to be personal biases that he dissociated himself from the others. He rarely attended meetings because he realized that his opinion would not be sufficient to reverse the tide of the majority opinion. Instead he issued occasional press releases denouncing the Commission as 'runaway' and oriented towards permissiveness. His qualifications were in law and so, unfortunately, he was not in a position to draw the attention of the others to the relevant research studies. He had apparently tried, since he relates how various research reports were denied to him, despite repeated requests. Perhaps as a result of his testimony, the Senate was later to reject by 76 votes to 3 the conclusions of the Commission, with Richard Nixon vowing 'so long as I am in the White House there will be no relaxation of the national effort to control and eliminate smut from our national life'.

The most important of the 'minority' reports is that by Morton Hill and Winfrey Link. It includes a section in which Victor Cline, acting as a consultant, claimed: 'A careful review and study of the Commission majority report, their conclusions and recommendations, and the empirical research studies on which they were based, reveal a great number of serious flaws, omissions and grave shortcomings which make parts of the report suspect and to some extent lacking in credibility.' He supported this claim by describing evidence indicative of adverse effects from pornography that had been omitted in the overview of findings. Such 'negative' evidence included research by Davis and Braucht (1971a) who found that exposure to pornography was related to promiscuity and sexual deviance. This research, which was contracted and financed by the Commission, was glossed over in the panel's report, not mentioned in the overview of findings, and apparently ignored in coming to the 'no harm' conclusion. Cline also noted how findings from inept research were presented as fact without mentioning their very serious limitations. For example, in a survey people were asked: 'Would you please tell me what you think are the two or three most serious problems facing the country today?' The 'effects' panel presented a figure showing that only 2 per cent mentioned pornography among their answers. The Commission took this as evidence for lack of public concern about pornography, despite a Gallup Poll result which indicated that 85 per cent of people favoured stricter laws on pornography. Later, Cline (1974) added to his critique by describing further research that was overlooked by the 'effects' panel, such as work carried out in our department indicating that a sexual deviation (a boot fetish) can be created in the laboratory using erotic pictures.

Many academics have challenged the validity of the Commission's conclusions. Typical of the criticisms offered was that by Eysenck (1972b) who wrote:

> It should be borne in mind that the Commissioners were concerned to 'make a case', and that in doing so they may not always have been entirely scrupulous about weighing the evidence impartially ... The writers of the majority report do not enter the necessary caveats in discussing these researches; they tend to generalize too freely, from one group to other groups dissimilar in age and character, and from short, often single exposures, to lengthy and multiple exposures. Such generalizations are not permissible, and though one may recognize the ethical difficulties involved in presenting such material to children, say, or of going beyond the limits of single or at most very limited presentations, nevertheless these limitations should be recognized and emphasized. Failure to do so implies a slide from scientific discussion to propaganda. Worse, the majority report suppresses information that goes against its recommendations.

The outcome of the commission may be interpreted in terms of the viewpoints held by the eighteen members before it started. Cline (1974) argues that the report seems to reflect their values, ideologies, suppositions and biases rather than the actual findings. Their general lack of expertise in interpreting scientific methodology and statistical data probably acted to allow greater scope for the intrusion of personal values. An extreme example of this is provided by two psychiatrists on the committee, Morris Lipton and Edward Greenwood, who wrote in their 'minority' statement and later in *Psychiatric News* that there was not even a 'significant correlation between exposure to erotica and immediate or delayed antisocial behavior among adults'. This statement hinges so much on the definition of 'antisocial' that it is difficult to understand how they came to make it without elaboration. It was clearly something they felt strongly about, since they continued by saying that 'to assert the contrary from the available evidence is not only to deny the facts, but also to delude the public by offering a spurious and simplistic answer to highly complex problems'. Cline cites this as a case of the social-political perceptions of the members leading to their omitting and distorting relevant evidence. He notes the irony that these men censored evidence even though they declared themselves to be anti-censorship.

The main effect of this commission has been to convince many people and authorities that pornography is not harmful. The majority conclusion is often quoted, for example in court cases, without mention of the dissenting reports or, indeed, of any of the arguments presented later such as that by Cline (1974). Moreover, the 'no harm' conclusion is often contrasted with that from the violence commission which claimed a 'modest link between viewing violence and subsequent aggression'. Dr Fox, consultant psychiatrist to the Samaritans, has been quoted as suggesting that TV could provide explicit sex instruction classes involving practical demonstrations of people making love. He considers that 'sexy' scenes of this nature could help lead to happier sex lives; in contrast he considers that violence shown on TV is only likely to 'breed violence'.

Not everyone has accepted the 'no harm' conclusion and acted upon it. It is, of course, possible to be opposed to the portrayal of explicit sex for reasons other than its supposed effects or lack thereof. The Commission presumably recognized such alternatives when it stated: 'If a case is to be made against "pornography" in 1970, it will have to be made on grounds other than demonstrated effects of a damaging or social nature.' Other grounds, such as viewers being offended, were probably involved when the ITV network announced in 1976 that it would not be screening *Straw Dogs* or *A Clockwork Orange* because of the rape scenes. Sex is also taboo in British TV advertising. In the IBA annual report for 1974, it was reported that over 100 commercials had been sent back to advertising agencies during the year for re-editing because 'we can't allow nudity to advertise something irrelevant, like chocolates'. Some parents, too, are likely to 'protect' their children from too much sex on TV. In a survey described in the above IBA report, it was found that parents who stopped their children watching a programme did this more often because it contained sex than because it contained violence. Anyway, even if TV sex is banned for reasons other than the findings of the pornography commission, it is still possible to challenge their 'no harm' conclusion.

In evaluating the usefulness of the 'commission' as a method of enquiry, it is clear that it is not easy for a group of men to impartially assess research evidence and to come to a balanced conclusion. Appointing members with 'permissive' attitudes along with members holding 'restrictive' views did not enable them to arrive at a joint conclusion. Perhaps it was expecting too much for men already committed to a particular point of view to modify this when confronted with a large array of research data. As it was, having both sides represented only led to failure to agree on any of the main points under consideration. This rather unsatisfactory state of affairs might have been predicted by reference to a classic study of religious beliefs. After finding that personal beliefs tend to be held, or rejected, with extreme rather than intermediate degrees of certainty, Thouless (1935) arrived at a law stated as follows: 'When, in a group of persons, there are influences acting both in the direction of acceptance and of rejection of a belief, the result is not to make the majority adopt a low degree of conviction but to make some hold the belief with a high degree of conviction while others reject it also with a high degree of conviction.' This is illustrated in Figure 3 which shows how a social attitude questionnaire prompted people to opt for extreme rather than intermediate degrees of agreement or disagreement. The Thouless law might well have operated in the pornography commission, with each member maintaining, and probably

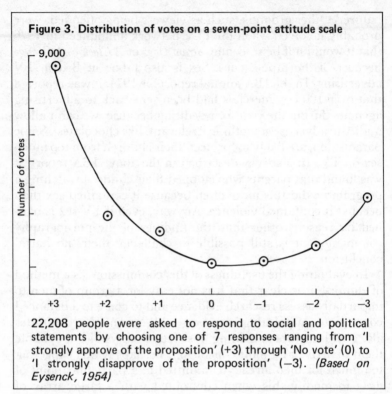

Figure 3. Distribution of votes on a seven-point attitude scale

22,208 people were asked to respond to social and political statements by choosing one of 7 responses ranging from 'I strongly approve of the proposition' (+3) through 'No vote' (0) to 'I strongly disapprove of the proposition' (−3). *(Based on Eysenck, 1954)*

increasing, his previously held feelings about the effects of pornography.

The above problem might also have been foreseen if attention had been paid to research on attitude change, which indicates just how difficult it is to change a person's attitude. Similarly, the history of science is replete with examples of the delay that occurs before new scientific findings come to be generally accepted. It seems that a better method of enquiry would have been to proceed along more conventional lines of scientific argument. Representatives of both sides of the controversy could have been encouraged to assemble the evidence and to say why it supported their particular point of view; they would also have been free to draw attention to the limitations of evidence running counter to their viewpoint. In this way separate reports could have been presented, and by giving an equal hearing to both sides a thorough debate might have ensued and critical research have been designed to settle the issue. Over a period of time, prevailing opinion might be expected to come down on the side of truth. The best way of speeding this process would appear to be that of funding more literature reviews and research rather than the appointment of committees.

SUMMARY

The US commissions on media violence and pornography are quoted, in both textbooks and courtrooms, as providing an 'official' viewpoint. The majority conclusions were that TV violence was probably harmful and should be substantially reduced, while pornography was not harmful and all restrictions, except those protecting children, should be lifted. This chapter describes some of the limitations in the organization of these commissions which involved lawyers, publishers and theologians rather than psychologists. As a result of the commissions' being unqualified to evaluate the research evidence, which was presented in the form of detailed technical accounts, many errors and omissions occurred in the final reports. The conclusions about TV violence were worded in such uncertain ways that many readers gained the impression that a 'no harm' conclusion had been arrived at. Many of the pornography committee members were known to hold liberal and anti-censorship views, and no one appeared to change his view as a result of looking at the research. Rather it seems that there was a polarization effect, with each member holding his personal viewpoint even more strongly as a result of serving on the committee. This outcome might have been predicted from research on political and religious beliefs, and it seems that a better way of evaluating the research would have been for both sides of the controversy to have assembled evidence to support their own particular point of view. By giving equal hearings to both sides, readers would then have been free to form their own conclusions. This would also have prevented such things as the 'blackballing' of well-qualified members of the committee on violence by interested parties.

5 Field Studies

In England in 1954, there were about 3 million TV sets in 15 million homes and less than half the population had been regularly exposed to TV. The BBC recognized this as an ideal opportunity to compare the habits of viewers and non-viewers, and suggested that the Nuffield Foundation sponsor a study into the effects that TV was having on young people. In order to arrive at an authoritative and independent enquiry, a team of social scientists from the London School of Economics was appointed. An advisory committee was also appointed being made up of academics and not, as with the later Surgeon General's committee, involving people with commercial interests. This enterprise was the first attempt to assess the effects of TV in a naturalistic setting, and was duly reported in a book by Himmelweit *et al.* (1958).

The research was concerned with the general effects of watching TV, such as whether it reduces the amount of time spent on homework, but a small part which has received most attention was concerned with the effects of violence. Two main studies were designed. The first involved a standard design in which viewers, who had been watching TV for at least three months, were compared with non-viewers. The children were matched individually on the four basic criteria of sex, age, intelligence and social background. A total of 1,854 matched viewers and controls in two age-groups, 10 to 11 and 13 to 14 years, were investigated in the four cities of London, Portsmouth, Sunderland and Bristol. A limitation of this design was that any differences discovered between the two groups might have existed before the viewers got their TV sets. That is, any differences in attitudes and behaviour could be due to factors that led to the purchase of a TV rather than to the effects of TV itself. The second study was designed to offset this limitation.

The second study approximated an experimental design by

seeing whether the behaviour of children changed over a one-year period during which they had become TV viewers. Although this method does not solve the problem that children who are about to become viewers are already different from those who are not, it is a more sensitive test than the usual comparison of viewers with non-viewers. This 'before and after' evaluation was made possible by a transmitter opening in the city of Norwich, which previously had been unable to receive TV properly. 370 matched viewers and controls were tested and a year later changes in those who had got a TV were compared with changes in those who had not. Because the children were first tested before the advent of TV in their lives, this approximation to a 'natural experiment' allowed baseline measurements for future viewers and future non-viewers. The advantage of this design may be illustrated by an example. It was found that viewers attended Sunday School less often than the non-viewers. It would be tempting to argue that this was due to the counter-attraction of TV, but this interpretation cannot be made since the baseline data indicated that the difference already existed between the two groups before TV came on the scene. It appears that the type of family susceptible to the attractions of TV tended to include children who were not very keen on Sunday School. Without the baseline data, there would have been a real danger of assuming that TV was responsible for reducing Sunday School attendances.

A limitation of the second study arose since all the children had been viewers for less than a year, and so only short-term effects could be assessed. The researchers realized that a more relevant question was the effects of long-term exposure. To cover this, a sub-group of viewers from the first study who had been watching for less than a year were compared with veteran viewers who had been watching for at least three years. In an attempt to throw light on the characteristics of the TV addict, another small study compared occasional with moderate and heavy viewers. Other studies were concerned with younger children, and with observing the behaviour of children before and immediately after viewing certain programmes.

In order to detect differences that might be attributable to TV, the children were given questionnaires concerned with personality, maladjustment, and what they did in their spare time. They were asked to keep a diary each day for a week in which to record everything they did between leaving school and going to bed, and to make a special note of the three things they had most enjoyed. The children were also assessed by their teachers on rating scales such as 'popular, many friends', 'moody', and 'wears glasses'; it was thought that any of these variables might reveal differences between TV viewers and non-viewers. Other forms of assessment included interviewing the children, their parents and teachers.

The outcome of this large-scale research project was disappointing in that very few differences emerged between viewers and non-viewers. Even such a seemingly obvious finding as viewers going to bed a bit later was offset by non-viewers being more likely to read in bed; time actually asleep was not thought to be different for the two groups. Viewers were more interested in ready-made entertainment such as comics and clubs, but this difference was also apparent along with an interest in radio prior to obtaining TV. With regard to personality, the viewers were no more aggressive or maladjusted than non-viewers. Some evidence of an effect of TV on aggression came from the mothers who related many examples of aggressive play after their child had been watching Westerns. Observation also indicated signs of tension and anxiety while a child was watching crime and violence. It was noted that the more personal and realistic the portrayal of violence, and the more that emotions were involved, the more disturbing was the programme. Children also claimed difficulty in falling asleep, and having nightmares, after watching frightening programmes.

That so few 'effects' from TV were revealed in this research is hardly surprising when we consider some of the limitations involved. First, the viewers may not have watched much in the way of violence, while the controls may have been exposed to just as much by going to the cinema or even by reading comics. There was not much violence shown on TV in those days. Moreover, the children were found to watch for just under two hours a day, this average being quite a bit less than the amount of viewing nowadays. Second, not many of the children had been exposed to regular TV for more than a few years. It was not possible to reliably assess the effects of long-term and repeated exposure. Third, the major focus of the research was on the displacement of other activities, such as finding whether schoolwork and general knowledge were affected by watching

TV. This meant that the effect of violent programmes on aggressiveness was not studied in detail. In fact, the only objective measure of aggressiveness appeared to be in the teacher ratings, which required a tick for each characteristic that applied to a child. An all-or-nothing judgement had to be made of whether each child was an 'aggressive type'. There was no provision for recording intermediate degrees of aggressiveness. This hardly constitutes a sensitive measure of this important variable.

The above research of Hilde Himmelweit and her colleagues is often quoted as finding that TV does not lead to aggression. In view of the limitations this is not a fair conclusion, nor is it quite what the results seem to indicate, and nor is it what the authors themselves concluded. To quote from one of their comments about violent programmes:

> We have not proved any causal relationship between seeing these programmes and behaving undesirably; but what relationship exists we have shown to be more likely to be harmful than desirable. We find little evidence that these programmes are desirable as a means of discharging tension (they often increase it), but do find evidence that they may retard children's awareness of the serious consequences of violence in real life and may teach a greater acceptance of aggression as the normal, manly solution of conflict.

They considered that the evidence was sufficient to warrant 'a reduction in the number of crime and violence programmes shown at times when children are likely to view' and 'more supervision of the vicious, though often short, episodes of violence and aggression in these programmes'.

The Himmelweit project was followed by a similar set of studies in North America (Schramm *et al.*, 1961). Two of the studies involved an assessment of aggression. In the first, children from a town in Canada where TV had been introduced were compared with children from another town judged to be similar except that it only had radio. The results indicated that younger children (11 to 12 years) from the TV town were less rather than more aggressive, while for older children (15 to 16 years) there was no difference. The reversal of the hypothesized result may merely reflect the usual problem encountered in studies of this type, namely that the two towns were not matched closely enough. The difference in aggressiveness might well be due to factors other than the presence of TV, such as differences in school discipline between the two towns.

In the second study, children in the Rocky Mountain area of the US were divided into 'high' and 'low' TV viewers. The results from this study indicated that the high viewers were slightly more aggressive than the low viewers, at least among the older children. A limitation of this study was that the children were not assessed for the amount of violence they actually saw. It is possible that the low viewers were more selective and chose to watch a lot of violence. If so, this would have acted to minimize the difference obtained. Another limitation, which applied to both studies, concerns the measure of aggression. The children were asked to agree or disagree with lengthy statements about aggression. It is known from social attitude research that lengthy questions often invite the tendency to acquiesce such that a personality characteristic is being assessed rather than the attitude intended (Wilson and Nias, 1973). Moreover, only four of the items in the scale were concerned with the relevant variable of anti-social aggression.

Because of the inherent problem of matching involved in the first study, the second probably carries more weight, and it is this study that gave a result in the hypothesized direction, albeit only just significant. Nevertheless, as with the Himmelweit research, this project is often quoted as finding no effects of TV on aggression, with attention being drawn only to the negative result from the first study.

An effort to overcome some of the limitations apparent in the above field studies was made by Eron (1963) who was specifically interested in aggression. In an attempt to obtain a more relevant measure of TV viewing, the parents of 875 children, aged eight to nine years, were interviewed about their children's actual viewing habits. They were asked 'What are Johnny's three favorite TV programs?', and their answers were then scored on a four-point scale according to the number of aggressive programmes that were given. To obtain a measure of aggressiveness more relevant to real life, the children were assessed by way of their classmates who were presented with ten 'guess who' items of the type 'Who pushes and shoves other children?'; the child named most often was judged to be the most aggressive.

The results indicated that boys who preferred violent TV

programmes, as reported by their mothers, tended to be more aggressive in school, as reported by their peers, the correlation being 0.21. The result for girls was not significant. The importance of assessing the nature of the child's favourite programmes was neatly illustrated by the finding of a negative relationship between time spent watching TV and aggressiveness. It seems on the basis of this study that aggressive children are less keen on the 'passive' pursuit of TV viewing, which means that had the children been divided simply into 'high' and 'low' viewers, as in the Schramm *et al.* second study, it might have appeared that high TV viewing leads to lowered aggression. It is apparently necessary to distinguish between watching a lot of TV and watching a lot of violent programmes.

The finding of a link between enjoying violent programmes and being aggressive can be criticized in terms of the two measures involved. Perhaps the parents, when not sure of their child's favourite TV programmes, tended to think of violent programmes if they perceived their child as aggressive. Similarly, most of the 'guess who' items were concerned with assertiveness rather than physical aggression, meaning that the demonstrated link is not necessarily with aggression. Apart from these limitations, there is the usual limitation involved in a correlational study. The correlation of 0.21 does not tell us whether there is a causal connection between watching violent programmes and aggressiveness, or whether it is just that boys who are already aggressive prefer violent programmes. This point was to be taken up by Eron and his colleagues in what was to become the most important of the field studies. Using the present study as a basis, the viewing habits and aggressiveness of the children concerned were followed up ten years later as part of the Surgeon General's enquiry.

A major advance over the usual type of field study was made by Eron and his team in an investigation of the long-term effects of violence-viewing (Eron *et al.*, 1972; Lefkowitz *et al.*, 1972). These researchers pointed out that only a longitudinal design could throw light on the cause and effect problem of correlational studies. They argued that if the relationship is causal, then childhood exposure to violent TV should be related to later rather than current aggression. Ten years after the previous study by Eron, they managed to locate and interview 427 of the original 875 children who were now aged eighteen to nineteen years. The subjects were asked to nominate their four favourite TV programmes, and their answers were scored as before in terms of the amount of violence represented. They were assessed for aggressiveness by their peers, using a slightly modified version of the 'guess who' technique used previously. The time elapsing since they had last seen one another varied, and so they were all asked to recall their classmates' behaviour when they were last at school together.

The results for boys are summarized in Figure 4, and the most relevant correlation is represented graphically in Figure 5. The latter is the correlation (r = 0.31) between early preference for violent programmes and later aggressiveness. This result together with the absence of a relationship between early aggression and a later preference for TV violence (r = 0.01), indicates that preferring to watch violence on TV is a cause rather than an effect of aggressiveness. The present study in combination with the previous one can be interpreted as suggesting that the more violent are the programmes preferred at age eight to nine, the more aggressive is their behaviour both at that time (r = 0.21) and ten years later (r = 0.31). Moreover, the indication that early TV preferences are more influential in causing aggression (r = 0.21) than are later viewing prefer-

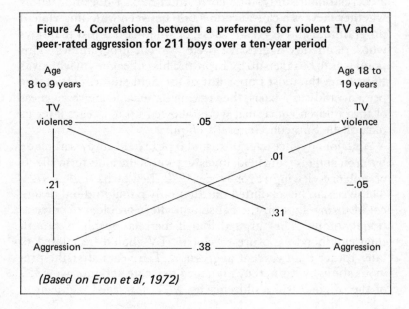

Figure 4. Correlations between a preference for violent TV and peer-rated aggression for 211 boys over a ten-year period

Age 8 to 9 years

Age 18 to 19 years

TV violence ———————— .05 ———————— TV violence

.01

.21   −.05

.31

Aggression ———————— .38 ———————— Aggression

(Based on Eron et al, 1972)

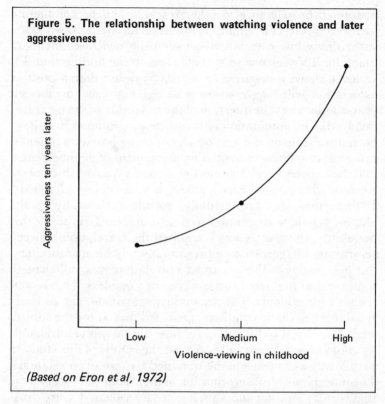

Figure 5. The relationship between watching violence and later aggressiveness

Aggressiveness ten years later

Low   Medium   High

Violence-viewing in childhood

(Based on Eron et al, 1972)

ences $(r = -0.05)$, is consistent with the theory that there is a critical learning period during which children are more susceptible to such influences as violent TV.

The above results were obtained for 211 boys; the results for a similar number of girls were not significant. Several reasons were advanced for this lack of an effect on girls. For example, girls might be influenced by female rather than male models on TV and it is relatively rare for female characters to be aggressive. Similarly, girls are less likely than boys to be reinforced by their peers for any display of aggression, so that socialization may be successful in counteracting any effect that TV might have on them.

The importance of this study has been reflected by the number of critical evaluations to which it has been subjected. It has been argued, on various grounds, that the conclusion of a causal relationship is not justified. Such criticisms have been countered by reference to other research and by conducting further analyses. For example, attention has been drawn to the surprisingly low correlation between the two assessments of liking for TV violence (r = 0.05), and to the finding that TV violence shows a negative (r = −0.05) rather than a positive association with aggressiveness at age eighteen to nineteen years. This raises the question of the reliability of the measures involved. The nomination of favourite programmes may have been unreliable on the first occasion, being based on parental rather than self assessment. The assessment of aggressiveness may have been unreliable on the second occasion since peers were asked to rate some individuals they had not seen for years. If these measures are virtually worthless, then any results obtained could be discounted as due to chance. To evaluate this possibility, the researchers computed the correlation between self-ratings of aggression, a presumably reliable measure, and the peer ratings. The obtained correlation was sufficient to indicate that the peer ratings were not worthless. This is consistent with evidence that personality assessment can be fairly reliable when made by others, provided they know the subject well. Anyway, it is difficult to see how limitations of unreliability could have differentially affected the results of this study in such a way as to provide the obtained pattern of correlations. The most plausible interpretation of the results does seem to be that regular viewing and a preference for violent TV are causally related to the formation of an aggressive life-style.

Partial support for the above result was provided by McLeod *et al.* (1972). In an approximation of the Eron *et al.* design, but involving a retrospective instead of a longitudinal approach, assessments were made of past and present violence-viewing and present aggressiveness. 473 adolescents in Maryland and 151 adolescents in Wisconsin were asked to indicate the frequency with which they watched 65 TV programmes, which had been independently rated for violence content. They were also given an aggression questionnaire with items such as 'If somebody hits me first, I let him have it'. The results gave a correlation of 0.24 between level of violence-viewing and overall aggressiveness. The Wisconsin children were also asked which of thirteen programmes, not currently being shown, they watched three or four years ago. Because of recall difficulties and because only thirteen programmes were used instead of sixty-five, this measure of past violence-viewing was not considered to be very reliable. Nevertheless, this measure correlated just as highly with current aggressiveness as did present violence-viewing. If the reliability of the past violence-viewing measure was indeed lower, then it follows that the correlation of a 'true' measure with aggression would probably have been higher. As with the Eron *et al.* analysis, this would have indicated that violence-viewing causes later aggressiveness.

Two other findings from the McLeod *et al.* study are worth mentioning. First, the amount of time spent watching TV was found to be positively related (r = 0.17) to aggressiveness, which contrasts with the negative relationship obtained by Eron (1963). It is difficult to think of reasons for these different findings, so perhaps they may just be taken as illustrating the need for studies to be repeated before much confidence can be placed in 'unexpected' results. Second, self-ratings of aggressiveness were more closely related to violence-viewing than were ratings provided by other people. Peer, teacher and mother reports of aggressiveness were collected for the Wisconsin sample. These gave an average correlation of 0.10 with violence-viewing, which compares with the figure of 0.24 from the self-ratings. The self-report figure may be an over-estimate since subjects who prefer violent programmes might perceive themselves as more aggressive than they really are. On the other hand, the figure from the ratings provided by other people is almost certainly an under-estimate because of the low reliability usually applying to ratings made by other people. The limited reliability of the ratings by the peers, teachers and mothers was demonstrated by calculating the correlations between them: the coefficients were only around 0.20.

A summary of the main results described so far, including those from the early studies, is presented in Table 1. The other field studies in the Surgeon General's enquiry were really just elaborations of the Eron study that compared heavy with light violence-viewers, but with various refinements in the measurement of aggression and TV viewing. Table 2 includes the most relevant findings from each of these subsequent studies. Because of their limited value, relative to those from the longitudinal study by Eron *et al.*, they need only be briefly discussed.

The remaining field studies were concerned with whether children who are keen viewers of TV violence are more aggress-

Table 1

Himmelweit *et al.* (1958)   No difference between TV viewers and non-viewers on a teacher rating of aggressiveness, but other evidence that children are adversely affected by violent programmes.

Schramm *et al.* (1961)   In one study, young TV viewers were less aggressive than children from a radio-only town. But in another study, children watching a lot of TV were found to be more aggressive than light viewers.

Eron (1963)   Liking for violent TV correlated 0.21 with aggressiveness for boys, but the result for girls was not significant. Amount of general TV viewing was negatively related to aggressiveness.

Eron *et al.* (1972)   Ten years later 211 of the boys from the above study were reassessed for aggressiveness. Early preference for violent TV was correlated 0.31 with later aggressiveness. Again the result for girls was not significant.

McLeod *et al.* (1972)   Past and present watching of violent TV had similar correlations with present aggressiveness. The correlations were higher when aggression was rated by the self rather than by others. Amount of general TV viewing was correlated 0.17 with aggressiveness.

ive than light viewers. Dominick and Greenberg (1972) gave children a questionnaire covering approval of violence, willingness to use it, perceived effectiveness of it, and suggested solutions to conflict situations. The results indicated that children who are heavy viewers of TV violence, and whose parents have not pointed out that violence is noxious, have a more positive view of aggression as a mode of conduct. Robinson and Bachman (1972), working with boys who had left school, administered a self-report check list with items such as 'Gotten into a serious fight at school or work' and 'Used a knife or gun or some other thing (like a club) to get something from a person'. Admitting acts that involved aggression rather than general delinquency was more often found among boys who nominated violent TV programmes as among their favourites. This result was also obtained by McIntyre and Teevan (1972) with a larger sample that included girls. These results are consistent with expectation in that viewing violence was specifically related to aggressive delinquency.

The above studies are important because the amount of violence viewed on TV was assessed rather than just viewing *per se*, which may be why each has detected an association between the two variables. But in spite of popular opinion and the funding of such studies by the Surgeon General's Commission, field studies are not the best way of investigating the effects of TV. Demonstrating that children who watch a lot of violence are more aggressive does not tell us which causes which or whether each is a reflection of a third variable such as basic personality. For this reason these studies do not throw much light on the issue. A notable exception, however, is provided by the ten-year follow-up study of Eron *et al.* Finding that an early preference for TV violence is related to later aggressiveness provides evidence that the obtained connection between the two variables is causal, with the viewing of TV violence occurring first. Similarly, the finding that early aggression is not related to a later preference for violent programmes is evidence counter to the possibility that boys who are predisposed to aggression will prefer violent programmes.

Table 2

Dominick and Greenberg (1972)   434 boys and 404 girls aged 10 to 12 years were assessed for the number of violent programmes watched, together with their parents' and their own attitudes to the use of violence. Children believing in aggression, and having parents approving of it, had higher exposure to TV violence.

Robinson and Bachman (1972)   1,500 males, one year out of school, were assessed for liking violent programmes and for aggression and delinquency. Preference for violent TV was related to being aggressive in interpersonal situations rather than to general delinquency.

McIntyre and Teevan (1972)   2,229 children listed their favourite programmes and were assessed for anti-social acts. Liking violent programmes was related to aggressive and serious rather than petty deviance. Children perceiving the use of violence as effective were also more likely to be aggressively deviant.

The conclusions reached by the Surgeon General's Commission, and reviews of field studies in general, often give the impression that the findings have been inconclusive. This is not the conclusion we have gained from our review, nor is it the conclusion that Chaffee (1972) reached in his technical report to the Commission. He pointed out:

> A significant positive correlation has been found much more often than not, and there is no negative correlational evidence. That correlation stands up consistently in varying samples of different sexes, age levels, and locales, and with a variety of measures of aggressiveness. It persists in the face of attempts to partial out many other variables that might have explained it away.

The only major field study since the work of the Commission has been carried out in London by Belson (1978). At the time of writing this study is unpublished, but previews allow us to briefly describe the project. In an effort to obtain a random sample, 21,600 homes were called at until 1,650 boys aged 13 to 16 years were located. Of these, 82 per cent (1,565 boys) were persuaded by attractive female researchers to attend for interview. The first stage of the interview was concerned with assessing the boys for violent acts committed over the previous six months. To help ensure truthfulness, the boys sorted cards describing violent acts into 'yes' and 'no' categories anonymously, and were later questioned in detail about their answers. The second stage of the interview was concerned with how much violence on TV they had been exposed to over the previous twelve years; they were asked to estimate how often they had watched sixty-eight programmes which were independently rated for degree and type of violence.

The basic analysis involved comparing the boys with above-average exposure to TV violence with the other half of the sample. This indicated that boys in the 'high exposure' group were more likely than those in the 'low exposure' group to have been involved in violent acts. The next step was to see if this result still held when the two groups were 'matched'. In contrast to previous research, this task was taken seriously and no less than 227 possibly relevant variables, or correlates. of violence, were considered. Matching was systematically performed in terms of each variable where a difference existed between the two groups. After this matching, the difference in violent acts between the high and low TV exposure groups was reduced but was still significant. More detailed analyses were conducted in terms of types of violent act and types of TV violence. One of the more interesting findings was that while exposure to most types of TV violence was related to violent acts, cartoons were an exception along with violence in comedy, science fiction and sport.

In spite of the impressive nature of this research, three limitations may be noted. First, while various strategies were adopted to obtain truthful answers, there is still the possibility that boys who watched a lot of TV violence were more likely than the others to exaggerate their participation in violent acts. Differential truthfulness of this type could be sufficient to explain the results obtained. Similarly, boys who were violent may have been less inclined than the others to admit to watching cartoons. If only for this reason, the claim that cartoons are 'harmless' should be regarded as tentative until supported by laboratory evidence. Second, even though 227 variables were considered in matching the groups there is still the possibility that other relevant variables, such as subtle aspects of personality, were overlooked. Third, because the sample was split into only two groups, any effects of TV violence, such as in cartoons, within either one of these groups may have gone undetected. For example, it is possible that cartoons increased the aggressiveness of non-violent boys but decreased that of violent boys, thus having little or no effect overall. That such limitations can still apply to a study that is by far the most elaborate yet conducted, clearly illustrates the inherent problems and complexities involved in the field study method. This same point is also apparent in the research on the effects of pornography to which we shall now turn.

The first field studies on the effects of pornography consisted of interviewing sex offenders and seeking the opinions of psychiatrists who dealt with them. While many of the offenders felt that they had been influenced by pornography, and some of the psychiatrists were inclined to agree with them, this information is of very limited value, being based on merely subjective judgement. Prior to the Pornography Commission there had been only one major study conducted with any degree of scientific sophistication. This was a monumental enquiry carried out by a team from Kinsey's Institute for Sex

Research and reported in a 923-page book (Gebhard *et al.*, 1965).

Gebhard and his colleagues set out to discover ways in which the sexual histories and social backgrounds of sex offenders differed from those of non-offenders. Personal interviews were carried out among 1,356 convicted sex offenders, who were sub-divided into fourteen categories such as incest and peeping. The answers from these groups were compared with those from 888 other prisoners and with 477 men from the general population. The two control groups were roughly matched with the sex offenders in terms of age, social class, amount of education, and urban or rural residence. In order to find whether the sex offenders were characterized by greater exposure or sexual responsiveness to pornography, the interviews included questions about experience with such material.

The results indicated that the sex offenders were not differentiated from the others by possession of pornography, or by their reactions to it. It was found that almost all the men had seen pornography at some stage in their lives. In response to the question, 'Does it arouse you sexually to see photographs or drawings of people engaged in sexual activity?', 31 per cent of the 'normal' and 36 per cent of the prisoner control group reported being 'strongly aroused'. The corresponding figure for the sex offenders tended to be slightly lower, although there was much variation among the fourteen sub-groups. For example, among offenders against adults, 43 per cent of the homosexuals reported strong arousal compared with only 18 per cent of the heterosexuals. The failure to find enhanced interest in pornography for the average sex offender is often stressed as the main outcome of this study. But such a failure is hardly surprising when it is considered that the sex offender tends to be a man of action rather than imagination and fantasy, which after all is why he gets into trouble!

Apart from the general limitations of studies of this kind, this particular one can be faulted in several ways. The matching of the three groups was far from perfect. For example, the sex offenders tended to include more rural dwellers and men with less education than either of the control groups. Both these differences meant that the sex offenders had less opportunity for obtaining pornography, which goes some way towards explaining the results obtained. But more importantly, no systematic attempt was made to link specialized types of pornography with specific offences. A clue that such a connection exists came from a question about sado-masochism, which asked 'Do stories of rape, torture, or violence arouse you sexually?' Although most of the men denied being aroused by such themes, the highest responders were predictably 'heterosexual aggressors' with 16 per cent admitting at least a moderate degree of sexual arousal as compared with only 8 per cent of the controls. But, of course, even this tenuous link does not tell us which came first, the pornography or the sadistic interests.

In spite of the limitations of field studies highlighted by the Gebhard *et al.* enquiry, the Pornography Commission still attached much importance to them by funding six studies of this type. The studies yielded various results indicative of both a positive and a negative relationship between experience with pornography and sexual deviance. Four studies that found either a negative or no relationship overall are listed, together with the Gebhard *et al.* study, in Table 3, while two studies that found evidence of a positive relationship overall are listed in Table 4.

A retrospective study based on interviews by Goldstein *et al.* (1971) provides an example of a negative relationship. Because sex offenders were found to have been exposed to less pornography than controls, this study is often cited as supporting the view that pornography does not lead to sexual offences and indeed that pornography may even 'immunize' people against such deviance. A 267-item interview concerning experience with erotica, attitudes to sex, and a sexual case history was administered to sex offenders, sexual deviants, and controls. The sex offenders, consisting of 19 rapists, 20 boy molesters and 20 girl molesters, were at Atascadero State Hospital, an institution for the 'criminally insane' in California. The 'deviant' group were 37 homosexuals from a local club, 13 transsexuals who had applied for a sex change, and 52 users of pornography responding to advertisements placed in 'porno' bookshops and cinemas. The controls were 53 men from the general population matched with the patients on age and education. Various other groups were also interviewed including 22 unemployed blacks, 16 'drop-outs' and a few deviant females.

The sex offenders tended to report less exposure to erotica compared with the controls, especially in adolescence. Even the users of pornography and the homosexuals reported less exposure to erotica during their adolescence. The rapists in particular had less often received a sex education course at school, and had less early as well as less recent experience with erotica. This applied even when the analysis was in terms of exposure to sado-masochism. For example, only 6 per cent of the rapists had been to live shows of sado-masochism compared with 8 per cent of the controls and 19 per cent of the homosexuals. Moreover, no connection was found between recalling 'peak experiences', in which activities portrayed in pornography had an impact at the time by standing out vividly in their minds, and subsequently committing sexual offences.

Can the above results be taken at face value? Unfortunately, the limitations of the study make any conclusions very uncertain. The study, while more specific to the effects of pornography than that by Gebhard *et al.*, was even less useful because the numbers involved were much smaller. Moreover, the matching of the control groups with the sex offenders was far from satisfactory. The authors admitted this when they wrote: 'Time was an ever-present burden in this study and its extreme brevity – necessitated by the Commission's schedule – accounted for many methodological variances [*sic*]'. One 'methodological variance' was that people were not always asked exactly the same questions. The failure to make the groups comparable, in respects other than that of being sex offenders, is important, since other surveys have found that exposure to pornography is related to being young, of higher social class, and better educated. The control groups in this study differed from the sex offenders in all three of these directions, meaning that the finding of a negative relationship between pornography and deviance could well be just an artifact of sampling.

Another source of error which could have led to the negative relationship is apparent in the way the groups were selected. The sex offenders, for genuine or other reasons, had already convinced the authorities that they should be sent to hospital rather than prison. It is possible that those having, or claiming, less experience with pornography would have stood more chance of being classified as psychiatrically disturbed and receptive to rehabilitation, the criteria for hospitalization. Similarly, it is possible that the controls who volunteered had more experience with pornography than those who refused. The controls were essentially volunteers since seventy of those approached had refused to be interviewed, compared with only two from the group of offenders. The possibility that inclusion of the seventy 'refusers' would have given different results, illustrates the difficulty that arises when the experimental method of randomization cannot be applied.

The above limitations, taken together, suggest that no weight can be attached to the results of this study. As if this were not enough, Cline (1974) has pointed out inconsistencies that appear in a later report of this study (Goldstein and Kant, 1973). For example, in spite of a claim that only rarely did the offenders act out their pornographic desires, the results show that the majority of people claimed to have 'tried out' sexual activities depicted in pornography. If true, this could have

---

Table 3

Gebhard *et al.* (1965) Compared with controls, sex offenders reported similar exposure and reactions to pornography. But rapists were more likely than controls to report being aroused by sadistic themes.

Goldstein *et al.* (1971) Compared with poorly-matched controls, sex offenders were found to have less experience with pornography, especially in adolescence. But many people claimed to have 'tried out' sexual activities depicted in pornography.

Walker (1971) Sex offenders in prison were compared with other prisoners and those in hospital with other patients. There was a non-significant trend for the sex offenders to report less exposure to pornography than the controls. But the sex offenders claimed a greater increase in sexual activity after viewing pornography.

Cook and Fosen (1971) Sex offenders were compared with other prisoners. While the two groups were similar in their reactions to erotic slides, the sex offenders reported less frequent and milder exposure to pornography.

Johnson *et al.* (1971) Interviews with sex offenders and a random sample from the general population revealed very similar experience with pornography.

serious consequences if the activities concerned are of an
aggressive nature.

A study attempting to provide more suitable control groups
was carried out by Walker (1971). Sex offenders in hospital
were compared with other patients, while those in prison were
compared with other prisoners. There was a slight, but not
significant, trend for 30 sex offenders, mostly rapists, to have
less experience with pornography than 30 controls. On the
other hand, the sex offenders claimed more often than the
controls to increase their sexual activity after seeing pornography. If their sexual activity was deviant, then this could
be a serious consequence of viewing pornography.

A study by Cook and Fosen (1971) was different in that
subjects rated their degree of sexual arousal to erotic slides as
well as being interviewed about previous exposure to pornography. While 63 sex offenders and 66 controls at Wisconsin
State Prison were similar in their arousal ratings, the sex offenders reported less frequent and milder exposure to pornography. This finding occurred in spite of the claim that
criminals have a low interest in sex generally, because if they
did value an active sex life they would be less likely to risk being
sent to prison! This illustrates the impossibility of ever finding a
perfectly matched control group with which to compare the sex
offenders. The final study in Table 3 simply compared sex
offenders who were receiving psychiatric treatment with age-
matched controls drawn at random from the general population. Although no statistical tests were carried out, the sex
offenders reported very similar experience with erotic materials
to that of the controls.

Table 4

Davis and Braucht (1971a)   Among prisoners and students,
exposure to pornography was related to sexual deviance and to
low moral character. Exposure to pornography was not related
to having deviant friends.

Propper (1972)   Prisoners with high exposure to pornography
were found to have had earlier experience with sex, and to have
engaged more often in group and oral sex. Contrary to the above
study, they were also more likely to have friends involved in
sexual deviance and anti-social behaviour.

The two studies in Table 4 were something of an exception in that a positive relationship was found between exposure to pornography and sexual deviance. In the Davis and Braucht (1971a) study, 365 male prisoners and students were assessed for experience with pornography and for signs of deviant sexuality and for lack of moral character. The latter was defined in terms of moral blindness, defective moral reasoning, and defective interpersonal character. While these variables were positively related, exposure to pornography was not related to having deviant friends, a result which helps rule out the possibility that the positive relationship is due to peer influence.

The other study that found a positive relationship between exposure to pornography and sexual deviance was by Propper (1972). 464 incarcerated males were classified as having high or low exposure to pornography, and were compared in terms of their sexuality. Those with high exposure to pornography tended to have started sexual intercourse at an earlier age, to have been more promiscuous, and to have indulged more often in oral and group sex. Unlike the above study, the high exposure group also tended to have more friends involved in unusual sexual practices and in anti-social behaviour. This means we are left with three alternative interpretations of the positive relationship. Pornography may have played a role in the development of deviance, men who were already deviant may have sought out pornography, or deviant friends may have influenced them both in becoming deviant and in developing an interest in pornography.

A criticism applying to both the above studies is that deviance was defined more in terms of sexual variety than in terms of seriously anti-social sexual practices. A criticism common to all the field studies is that type of pornography has not been systematically related to type of sex crime. The sex offenders have been assessed for their interest in pornography concerned with nudity, sex play and intercourse rather than with rape scenes and sex with children. The latter type of pornography has not, until recently, been readily available, and so it has not really been possible to assess its effect in a field study. Perhaps this may be added to the various reasons offered to account for the overall failure of field studies to find a clear link between pornography and sex crime.

The field study approach has been used to compare the

incidence of sex crimes in countries over a period in which pornography has become freely available. The press often report that sex crimes declined in Denmark with the repeal of pornography laws. Although the Pornography Commission interpreted this as a beneficial effect of pornography, it is possible to challenge the validity of such a conclusion. Two statistical surveys in Copenhagen and one in the US were sponsored by the Commission, and police records from several other countries have since been investigated.

Pornographic material first became readily available in Denmark about 1965 and over the next few years it grew rapidly in popularity, with legal restrictions finally being lifted in 1969. The Commission took advantage of this change by asking Ben-Veniste (1971) to conduct a survey of police statistics on reported sex crimes in Copenhagen for a twelve-year period. The results indicated a decline in various sex offences since 1965, although this did not apply to rape which remained constant at around twenty cases a year over the whole period. This survey is often quoted as showing that pornography has led to a decrease in sexual deviance, or at least that it has not led to a sudden increase as was feared in some quarters. As such the survey is seen to indicate that pornography is harmless or even therapeutic. Two objections can be made to this interpretation. First, most of the data are only up until 1969 and it is possible that an increase in sex crimes will become apparent later. This is not unlikely when it is realized that the more 'abnormal' types of pornography, such as sadistic and rape scenes, have recently become increasingly popular. Second, it is possible that both the police and the victims have become more tolerant of sex crimes, and so the apparent decline may merely reflect increasing permissiveness and less reporting. Such an increase in permissiveness may have gone hand in hand with the increase in the availability of pornography. The other survey in Copenhagen was concerned with this very question.

Kutschinsky (1971a) designed a survey to find whether the decline in reported sex crimes was due to changes in public attitudes. A random sample of people in Copenhagen were asked various questions. For example, they were asked whether they would report sex crimes, and whether they would have been more or less likely to report such an act to the police ten years ago. They were also asked whether they considered various sex acts to be crimes, and whether they had changed their mind recently over the seriousness of various sex crimes. The possibility that the decline in sex crimes was due to changes in the law or to changes in police attitudes was also investigated. The results indicated that while the law and law enforcement practices had not changed, people had certainly become more permissive, especially for less serious offences such as peeping, exhibitionism and indecent interference. Changes in public attitudes could thus at least partly explain the drop in reported sexual offences. While arguing that the decrease in serious offences, such as child-molesting, was probably genuine, Kutschinsky concluded that 'the decrease in exhibitionism registered by the police during the last ten years may be fully explained by a change in people's attitudes towards this crime and towards reporting it to the police'. The Pornography Commission, however, considered that 'the decrease in reported sexual offenses cannot be attributed to concurrent changes in . . . public attitudes toward reporting such crimes to the police'.

The results from the two Copenhagen surveys are difficult to evaluate. In particular, the results for the important crime of rape are unreliable for two reasons. First, only a small proportion of cases actually come to the notice of the police, which allows added scope for a change in the incidence of rape to occur without being accurately reflected in the police records. Second, the number of reported rape cases is low. For example, in a table in the Commission's report 'Intercourse on threat of violence or by fraud, etc.' is shown to have declined by 37.5 per cent, but the actual numbers involved were eleven and eight which hardly warrants conversion to a percentage; statistically the change is not significant. It would have been better to have presented figures for the whole of Denmark. Cline (1974) by referring to the *Danish Statistical Yearbook* for 1970 noted that violent sex crimes have remained at around 220 a year since 1960. Thus the conclusion from this country seems to be that the less serious sexual offences have undergone a dramatic reduction with the increasing availability of pornography, while the frequency of violent crimes such as rape has not changed. An increase in permissive attitudes may be sufficient to explain the reduction in the reporting of less serious sex crimes.

Table 5   Reports to the police of rape and attempted rape

Rate per 100,000 population

	1960	1965	1970	1973
USA	10	12	19	24
Copenhagen		3.5	9.2	8.6
New Zealand		5.1	6.0	8.6
South Australia	2.4	2.3	2.7	8.4
Australia		2.2	3.3	5.1
Singapore	1.9	2.2	2.3	2.4
England and Wales	1.1	1.3	1.8	2.0
London	0.8	1.0	1.8	2.0

(Based on Court, 1977)

The other Commission survey was carried out in the US by Kupperstein and Wilson (1971). They found that between 1960 and 1969, when pornography was becoming freely available, arrests for sexual offences increased by 18 per cent with rape showing the greatest increase at about 50 per cent. However, the rape figure appears less ominous when put in the context of a general increase in crime. Cline (1974) has extended this survey by two years and found that the increase in rape has recently accelerated. He also found a similar trend for divorce rates, a more general index of sexual morality, with increases of 50 and 68 per cent for the two periods respectively.

A recent survey of sex crimes and availability of pornography in several countries, including personal visits to each in order to check for flaws in the statistical records, was made by Court (1977). The results indicated that reports to the police of rape and attempted rape have recently increased, and that this increase has usually coincided with an increase in the availability of pornography. Table 5 presents a summary of the figures available. In Singapore, pornography is still largely controlled, and the stable incidence of rape thus provides an interesting comparison with the increase apparent elsewhere. Nevertheless, when interpreting these results many problems are apparent. Three examples will suffice. First, the recent influence of the Women's Liberation movement may have increased the chances of a girl reporting rape, and so be responsible for the increase rather than pornography. Second, public attitudes to the reporting of rape can be changed by all manner of 'unknown' influences. For example, following a TV film called *Cry Rape* there was a sharp decrease in reported rape. The theme of this film, in which the rapist argued that he had been seduced by the woman, was that a victim undergoes in court an ordeal that may be worse than rape itself. Third, if young people are tending to move out of a city, as is happening in London, then this will act to reduce the incidence of sex crimes for that city. Ideally rates should be based on the population at risk, but instead they are usually reported in terms of absolute numbers and sometimes as a proportion of the total population. Because of the many reservations that are attached to rape statistics as well as to the field study method, it is difficult to draw any conclusions. The conclusion drawn by the Pornography Commission, namely that availability of pornography has been associated with a reduction in sex crime, is, to say the least, misleading.

SUMMARY

The field study method of observing naturally occurring behaviour is popular and is often taken seriously. But it involves the inherent problem that because subjects are not randomly assigned to different conditions, a causal relationship cannot be established. Because it is never possible to equate groups on all relevant variables, any differences emerging between them may be due to unknown factors. Early comparisons of TV viewers and non-viewers found little difference between the groups, but with improved methods of detecting effects there are now indications that people who view a lot of violence tend to become more aggressive. Sex offenders have rarely been found to differ from other prisoners with respect to exposure to pornography, but researchers have not looked for a *specific* link between the type of pornography that is read and the type of sex crime committed. To find that rapists are not particularly interested in looking at pin-ups is hardly surprising when it is considered that their problem is one of acting out a harmful desire in a specific situation. Statistics on sex crimes are unreliable since many factors can influence whether such crimes are reported. For what it is worth, they tend to reveal an increase in violent sex crimes, along with an increase in crimes of violence generally, and a decrease in minor sexual offences in the period after the repeal of restrictions.

6 Experimental Field Studies

The first application of the experimental method in a naturalistic setting to the effects of TV violence was by Feshbach and Singer (1971). The dormitories of three private schools and four boys' homes were restricted to a diet of either violent or neutral TV. The boys were required to watch for at least six hours a week for six weeks, being allowed to choose from a list of violent programmes such as *The Untouchables* or from neutral programmes such as *Lassie*. Naturally occurring aggressive behaviour during this period was recorded each weekday by houseparents and teachers who were familiar with the daily activities of the boys. Rating scales were used with items of the type 'Was in a fist fight, hit or kicked somebody'. The results obtained were claimed to support the catharsis theory. There was a cumulative trend over the period of the study for the violent TV group to become less aggressive than the neutral group. This result, however, was significant only for the boys' homes; for the private schools there was virtually no difference between the two groups. The difference between the two groups was greater for aggression directed towards peers rather than authority. The average scores for aggression are presented in Table 6. Why violent TV should have led to less aggression than neutral TV only in the boys' homes is not clear. Explana-

---

Table 6 Aggression scores towards peers and teachers for boys restricted to six weeks of either violent or neutral TV

| | Boys' homes | | Private schools | |
	Peers	Authority	Peers	Authority
Violent TV	2.47	1.36	0.93	0.74
Neutral TV	4.98	1.98	1.00	0.74

(Based on Feshbach and Singer, 1971)

tions have been sought in terms of this group's working-class origins, and in particular their tendency to be more aggressive to begin with. The difference between the two types of TV was greater for boys who were already high on aggression. According to the catharsis theory, it is such boys who have most to gain by watching TV violence since they have more aggression than the others to get rid of.

The finding of less aggression in boys who watched violent rather than neutral TV has become one of the best-known instances of support for catharsis. Unfortunately for the theory, however, there is a simpler explanation of the results. The boys in the neutral TV group were not very keen on their programmes and often made protests about being so restricted in their choice. This resentment may have been expressed in the form of aggression, thus accounting for their scores relative to the violent group. Similarly, the incidence of aggression, especially towards each other, may have been higher in the neutral group simply because they were in poor humour and bored, having nothing better to do. There are thus two ways in which failure to match the two sets of TV for degree of interest could have resulted in the neutral group becoming more aggressive than the violent group. There is also an explanation for the high level of aggression among the working-class boys in the neutral group. They may have just been less able than the middle-class boys to tolerate such a restriction of their freedom, and to have expressed their frustration by fighting. The researchers were aware of the problem of resentment and tried to reduce it by promising a payment of ten dollars for those boys who completed the study. In spite of this, however, some of the boys in the neutral group insisted on *Batman*, a violent programme, being included among their choices. By yielding to this pressure, the researchers may have actually encouraged aggression in this group. Indeed, one of the principles of learning theory is that reward, in this case being able to watch Batman, leads to an increase in the behaviour that preceded it, which in this case was the expression of annoyance.

While annoyance and boredom among the boys in the neutral group is probably sufficient to discount the results of this experiment, a few other limitations may be noted. Some of the boys inevitably guessed the purpose of the study and this may have affected their behaviour; those in the violent group may have been particularly keen not to give the impression that their favourite programmes led to fighting. Similarly, the teachers and houseparents who made the ratings of aggression were aware of the purpose of the study, and they knew the group to which each boy belonged. The possibility that this knowledge may have affected their ratings is very real, especially since they were untrained and no check was made on the reliability of their ratings. Similarly, no check was made to see how well the groups were initially matched for aggression; had the neutral group included some very aggressive boys, then this could be sufficient to account for the results obtained.

A small-scale, but well-controlled, study with pre-school children was conducted by Steuer *et al.* (1971). To provide baseline scores, the children were rated for signs of physical interpersonal aggression, such as hitting or pushing another child, during ten daily sessions in a play room. On the basis of these scores, and how much TV they normally watched, ten children were matched into pairs. For the next eleven sessions, half the children were shown ten minutes of violent TV, mostly cartoons, while the other member of each pair was shown a neutral programme. They were again rated for aggression, through a one-way mirror, immediately after each of these sessions. Although the results were of only borderline significance, the trend was in the opposite direction to that of the previous study. The children in the violent TV group tended to become progressively more aggressive as the study continued. This increase was most apparent for those already above average on aggression; two pairs of children who showed little or no increase in aggression had baseline scores of near zero aggression.

One limitation of this study was that the children were observed for signs of aggression for only two minutes each session; in view of this it is hardly surprising that a clear result was not obtained. Another limitation concerns the fact that the children were placed together in the same play room for observation. If only one of them had become aggressive, whether or not because of the influence of TV, then some of the others may have obtained high aggression scores simply because they were retaliating. This probably acted to obscure any real differences in aggression between the violent and the neutral TV groups.

In spite of the relatively large number of ordinary field

studies, only one experimental field study was included in the Surgeon General's enquiry. Stein and Friedrich (1972) assessed the naturally occurring aggression of children who had been specially enrolled in a nursery for nine weeks. After baseline scores for aggression had been recorded for three weeks, the children were randomly assigned to one of three groups; slight adjustments were made to ensure that the groups were equated for age and social class. The children then watched either violent programmes, such as *Batman*, neutral TV represented by various children's films, or episodes from the pro-social *Misterogers Neighborhood*. Three programmes were shown each week for four weeks, and the free play of the children was assessed during this period, and for two weeks afterwards, by observers who did not know to which group each child belonged. Three five-minute assessments were made each day for physical and verbal aggression and for pro-social behaviour such as rule obedience and tolerance of delay. Among the children who were initially above average in aggression, there was a tendency for those watching violent TV to be more aggressive than those in either the neutral or the pro-social group. The value of including observations of pro-social behaviour was revealed in that self-controlling behaviour, such as tolerating minor frustrations, was significantly lower in the group who had watched violent TV than in either of the other two groups. The children below average in aggression during the baseline assessment did not respond differentially to the three conditions, and little effect was apparent for any of the children during the two-week follow-up period. Nevertheless, the trend of the results for the aggressive children was, it may be noted, in the reverse direction to that predicted by catharsis theory.

The two previous studies, because they involved nursery-school children rather than adolescents, are not really replications of the original Feshbach and Singer study. Catharsis from watching violence on TV may be achieved only by children above a certain level of maturity, and fortunately there are several other studies involving older children. In one of these, boys in ten residential schools were restricted to either violent or neutral TV for seven weeks (Wells, 1973). Precautions were taken to ensure that the two groups were matched for initial aggression by including a baseline assessment. In addition, outside observers were recruited for making the ratings of aggression, which were sub-divided into physical and verbal. Among the boys who were above average on the baseline measure of aggression, the violent group were significantly more physically aggressive than the neutral group. With respect to verbal aggression, however, it was the neutral group who obtained the higher scores. This latter result may be taken as evidence of catharsis, but it seems more likely to reflect this group's complaints about having to watch 'lousy' shows. Anyway, the different results obtained for the two types of aggression neatly illustrates the value of making such a distinction in order to appreciate the subtle effects from deliberately changing people's viewing patterns. Wells also took the trouble to ask whether any of the raters had inadvertently become aware of the group to which a boy belonged. Some of them had done and this knowledge was found to be related to the results, with a boy being more likely to be perceived as aggressive if he was discovered to be in the violent group. This demonstration of observer bias, while possibly sufficient to discount the results of the study, may also be taken to suggest that Feshbach and Singer obtained the results they did merely because their observers, who were fully aware of the group to which each boy belonged, happened to be sympathetic to the basic tenets of catharsis theory.

The catharsis theory was supported in the original study only for subjects in the boys' homes, who tended to be aggressive and to come from working-class backgrounds. A replication of this study should, therefore, involve a similar group. Parke *et al.* (1977) approximated such a requirement by studying juvenile delinquents known to have a prior history of aggression. After three weeks of baseline assessment, the boys watched full-length films for a week instead of their customary TV, and were then assessed for a further three weeks. Slightly more aggression was observed in the group who watched violent as opposed to neutral films, and this was apparent for boys both above and below average on initial aggression. The study was then repeated with two improvements. Observations were made for five instead of three days a week, and an extra effort was made to find neutral films that were just as interesting and exciting as the violent ones. Ratings for degree of interest in the two sets of films by the boys, helped confirm that this important matching had been achieved. Again there was a tendency for more aggression to occur in the violent group. Similar results have also been reported from a replication of this study in Belgium (Leyens *et al.*, 1975). It is not just in the US that people respond to filmed violence!

One of the main limitations of an experimental field study concerns the reaction of subjects when they become aware that an experiment is being conducted. Inevitably there will be rumours as to what it is all about, and even if the subjects do not guess the true nature of the enquiry their behaviour may not be as natural as one would hope. In particular, subjects are likely to react to having their choice of programmes restricted. As Stein and Friedrich (1975) point out: 'When one intervenes arbitrarily in people's lives by governing what they watch on TV, one is not assessing the effects as they might occur when programs are selected by the subjects themselves. If children are not interested in the programs, their reactions might reflect irritation and frustration at being required to watch rather than imitation of program content.' As we have seen, the results obtained for verbal aggression by Wells are consistent with this interpretation, and a similar argument can be used to repudiate Feshbach and Singer's claim for catharsis.

A unique experimental field study, which largely circumvents the problem of restriction of choice, was carried out by Milgram and Shotland (1973). They were concerned with theft rather than aggression but because of the methodology it is worth describing this study; it is included with the others in the summary provided by Table 7. Through the co-operation of a local TV network, the researchers had control over the content of a TV programme itself. Subjects attended a preview in which they saw one of three parallel versions of the popular *Medical Center*. In one episode, a situation was portrayed in which money was stolen from charity collection boxes with the thief escaping; in another episode the thief was caught and punished, while in a third he made a donation instead of helping himself. There was also a control group who saw a neutral episode not involving theft or donation. Attendance at the preview entitled the subjects to a transistor radio, but some of them were frustrated when they arrived to collect this gift at a box office by finding it closed. Nearby a collection box was clearly visible with a dollar bill sticking out, and the measure of

Table 7

Feshbach and Singer (1971)   For six weeks, boys were restricted to choosing from either 72 violent or 152 neutral programmes. For those resident in working-class boys' homes, there was a tendency for the violent TV group to be less aggressive than the neutral group. Full data were collected from 395 of a total of 625 boys aged 9 to 15 years.

Steuer *et al.* (1971)   10 pre-school children were paired in terms of aggressiveness and previous TV exposure. Over the course of eleven sessions one member of each pair was shown 110 minutes of cartoons and the other neutral programmes. In a free play situation, it was the child who had watched the violent cartoons who tended to become the more aggressive.

Stein and Friedrich (1972)   Among 92 pre-school children, those who were above average on aggression tended to become more aggressive and less pro-social if they had been assigned to four weeks of violent TV rather than neutral or pro-social programmes.

Wells (1973)   Boys above average in aggression were rated as becoming more physically but less verbally aggressive after watching violent rather than neutral TV for seven weeks, especially if the rater inadvertently discovered to which group a boy belonged.

Parke *et al.* (1977)   Delinquent boys aged 14 to 18 years tended to become more aggressive during the week in which they watched violent rather than neutral films. The study was repeated with more frequent assessments of aggression and with neutral films rated just as exciting as the violent ones; similar results were obtained.

Leyens *et al.* (1975)   Similar results were also obtained in a replication in Belgium with delinquent boys aged 12 to 19 years. Ratings for aggression were made twice a day for one week before, during and after five days of films.

Milgram and Shotland (1973)   In a series of eight experiments, men aged 16 to 40 years did not respond differentially to experimental and control TV programmes about stealing from medical charity collection boxes or making abusive telephone calls.

the differential effect of the films was whether a subject took this money, ignored it, or pushed it into the box. While boys who had been frustrated were more likely than the others to take the money, the film groups did not differ significantly from one another. This evidence has been quoted as showing that TV crime is unlikely to influence real-life behaviour, but perhaps it is overly optimistic to expect the effects of viewing one film to become apparent against the background of years of previous viewing. Stealing from a charity is a rare occurrence, and one may hope that it would need more than exposure to a single film to induce such an act!

A problem with all experimental field studies is the effect of previous viewing experience. Because most subjects will have watched a great deal of TV, it is unreasonable to expect experimental manipulation of what they watch for a day, or at most a few weeks, to have much lasting effect. Even conducting experiments with pre-school children does not appear to get round the problem. Stein and Friedrich (1972) estimated, from interviews with mothers, that the children in their study watched TV at home for an average of more than thirty hours a week, which represented about 37 per cent of their waking hours. One compromise, which is adopted in most laboratory-type experiments, is to limit the investigation of effects to those that can be detected immediately after exposure to a particular film. Even then, as we shall see in the next chapter, to obtain differential film effects it is usually necessary to assess anti-social behaviour in a relatively mild form or in the context of a 'permissive' atmosphere.

With many of the above studies it was noted that the effects were more apparent for children who were initially high rather than low on aggression. Does this mean that such children are more susceptible to the influence of TV violence? Not necessarily, since there must be more opportunity for differential film effects to become apparent for boys who are already aggressive and, indeed, for those who are frequently provoked by their peers. An increase in aggression for a peaceful individual may go undetected if it does not result in an overt act, while an equal increase for an aggressive person may result in a fight that becomes very serious. The question of who is most at risk is difficult to investigate and will be considered again later. It will suffice to say at this point that an increase in aggression for an already aggressive person is of particular concern, if only because of the more serious consequences that it may have for his victims.

What do we learn from the studies discussed so far in this chapter? The balance of the evidence indicates that any effect from TV violence is as predicted by imitation and disinhibition rather than catharsis theory; this conclusion is amply confirmed by other methods of enquiry. Whatever effect TV violence has is almost certainly in the direction of increasing rather than decreasing aggression. If the direction of effect is not in much doubt, then what about its degree? The evidence described suggests that it is slight, but there are obvious reasons for this. If one week in an experimental field study has a detectable effect, then what effect does a lifetime of viewing have in a lifetime of opportunities to express aggression? This question, like that of who is most at risk, is difficult to investigate. Perhaps the most convincing conclusion from the experimental field studies is that it is not the method of choice for evaluating the effect of TV. There are just too many practical difficulties to overcome, such as the need to control all relevant variables. With researchers who adopt a 'head in the sand' attitude and try to forget the influence of uncontrolled factors, there is always the danger that their results are due to these very factors. When researchers assess the effect of these factors, such as Wells's check on observer bias, then the possibility of an alternative interpretation becomes a reality. It is necessary that each of these difficulties is specified and if necessary studied in isolation under laboratory conditions. Just as an aircraft design is tested on stress machines and in wind tunnels before being tested in the air, so too with social psychology it is the laboratory experiments which should come first. With a better understanding of the factors involved, perhaps then we would be in a position to mount an experiment in a naturalistic setting and obtain a result not surrounded by ambiguity.

Researchers have not yet explicitly designed experimental field studies on the effects of pornography. A number of studies have involved deliberately exposing people to erotica in order to observe their reactions in the laboratory, and have then gone on to record how their sexual behaviour at home is affected. These studies, however, have not involved true-to-life exposure sessions as would be required in a proper experimental field study; the erotic materials have been presented in a laboratory-type setting rather than in a more natural setting such as a cinema or, better still, given to the subjects to take home. Nevertheless, because these studies included collections of data on subsequent behaviour in the natural environment, this aspect of the work will be considered in this chapter. We shall deal first with studies that assessed the delayed effects of a single session of exposure to erotica, and then move on to the more important studies that involved several sessions of such exposure.

The final report of the Pornography Commission summarized the results of experiments on the delayed effects of erotica as follows:

> When people are exposed to erotic materials, some persons increase masturbatory or coital behavior, a smaller proportion decrease it, but the majority of persons report no change in these behaviors. Increases in either of these behaviors are short lived and generally disappear within 48 hours. . . . In general, established patterns of sexual behavior were found to be very stable and not altered substantially by exposure to erotica. When sexual activity occurred following the viewing or reading of these materials, it constituted a temporary activation of individuals' preexisting patterns of sexual behavior.

This statement is a reasonable summary of the results taken at face value, except that no study found a decrease in masturbatory or coital behaviour. The committee was probably referring to the obvious fact that in any given experiment some individuals will show a decrease, but what they fail to make clear is that such a finding does not necessarily constitute evidence that these individuals will characteristically respond to erotica in this manner. It is possible that the sexual activity of some people will be inhibited by exposure to erotica, but no study has yet obtained such a result. All that can be concluded from the evidence so far is that the subjects as a group tended to react to erotica with a slight and temporary increase in their usual sexual activities. This conclusion is specific to the type of study that has been conducted, and, as we shall see, the studies have not really been designed to show anything more than this.

The first study to look for effects beyond the laboratory was carried out in Germany prior to the Commission's work. Schmidt *et al.* (1969) found that orgasms, usually through masturbation, were more frequent among male students in the twenty-four hours following exposure to erotic slides than they were for the preceding day. Intercourse, spontaneous erections, and petting also increased, but not significantly. There was a tendency for the increase in sexual activity to apply more to radical than to conservative students. None of the students admitted to practising a new or perverse type of sexual activity; this led the researchers to point out that there was no evidence of 'sexual disinhibition as is often postulated by advocates of censorship'. In other words, any rise in sexual appetite or reduction of inhibitions was not sufficient to lead to new or uncontrolled activities.

This study was repeated several times with the addition of female subjects and erotic films and stories. The results were similar each time, and as an example those from the third study are presented in Table 8. In this study, for what it's worth, three subjects reported adopting a new coitus position or fore-play technique. A more important finding was that of those who subsequently masturbated, a sizeable proportion of both the men and the women thought about scenes from the erotica while doing so. According to the conditioning theory of how sexual preferences are developed, erotic scenes imagined immediately before orgasm are reinforced and thus become a

Table 8 Effects of erotica on sexuality

Behaviour increased	Males	Females
Masturbation	19	10
Total orgasms	26	17
Fantasies	31	33
Talk about sex	16	33
Sexual tension	13	17
Wish for sex	27	35

Students tended to report an increase rather than a decrease in sexual activity in the twenty-four hours after viewing erotica. The figures shown represent the net percentage change, which in each case was significant.

(Based on Schmidt and Sigusch, 1970)

more potent source of stimulation. Another finding from this series of studies was that the increase in sexual activity applied to both sexes, and in the case of the erotic stories it was the women who were more affected than the men (Schmidt *et al.*, 1973).

The basic design of the German studies was to become a prototype for several of the Commission studies, which was unfortunate since it has a number of limitations. It is just conceivable that it was attendance at the sessions, irrespective of their nature, that led to the increase in sexual activity, and to check for this possibility a control group of subjects shown non-erotic material should have been included. But more importantly, if the aim was really to find evidence of 'sexual disinhibition' from viewing pornography, then it would have helped if the subjects had been exposed to material of a novel or 'abnormal' nature and then provided with opportunities to indulge in these new activities. As it was, there was nothing in the materials that was illegal and very little that would have given the students 'new ideas'. Apart from 'normal' sexual activities such as petting, oral sex and intercourse, the slides portrayed 'pin-up' type poses that could hardly be copied. Had the erotica been concerned with, say, fairly novel forms of petting, then it is possible that a few of the students may have been prompted to imitate this behaviour. The few scenes of oral sex may have been sufficient to lead to imitation had an opportunity arisen in the twenty-four hours, but, since nearly all the students were single, few of them may have had this opportunity. While it was noted that most of the students volunteering for the experiments had previous experience of coitus, no attempt was made to find out how many of them had a current sexual partner. These studies, which were carried out among students at the University of Hamburg, are summarized in Table 9.

One way of increasing the chances of indulging in new sexual activities is to allow more time for such activities to occur. In one of the Pornography Commission studies, male students at the University of Waterloo were assessed for the week before and after exposure to erotic slides (Amoroso *et al.*, 1971). Although there was a large increase in masturbation on the day of viewing, reported sexual activity over the rest of the week was similar to that of the previous week. As the researchers concluded, 'sexual behaviour was affected little by the viewing of

---

Table 9

Schmidt *et al.* (1969)   The sexual activity of 99 male students was greater in the twenty-four hours after being shown 72 erotic slides than in the twenty-four hours before. The increase was for their usual sexual practices, mainly masturbation, and not for new activities, and was greater for liberal than conservative subjects.

Sigusch *et al.* (1970)   In a replication of the previous study, 50 male and 50 female students were shown 72 erotic slides. The results were similar to before, with an increase in sexual desire, masturbation and coitus being reported by both sexes over the next twenty-four hours.

Schmidt and Sigusch (1970)   In another replication, 128 male and 128 female students were shown a ten-minute erotic film or 24 slides. The results were again similar, and this time it was noted that of those who did masturbate in the following twenty-four hours, 68 per cent of the men and 43 per cent of the women imagined the erotic scenes while doing so.

Schmidt *et al.* (1973)   120 male and 120 female students read an erotic story about foreplay and intercourse. Sexual drive and activity again increased over the next twenty-four hours, and this time significantly more so for females than males.

---

the slides, and . . . the behaviors affected were those the subjects tended to engage in most initially . . . Moreover, these activities were all autoerotic; there was almost no change in heterosexual activity.'

A more obvious way of helping to ensure that subjects have an opportunity to indulge in new sexual activities is to employ married couples. It 'takes two to tango' and the availability of a willing partner reduces the moral and legal restrictions that might otherwise prevent sexual intimacies. For this reason, Byrne and Lamberth (1971) assessed the effects of erotica on married couples, one or both members of each pair being a student at the University of Purdue. The erotica consisted of nineteen themes in which the subjects were shown slides, or short passages from erotic books, or were asked to imagine the erotic scenes. One week later the couples were assessed for any changes in their usual pattern of sexual activity for that week.

Very few subjects reported any changes, and overall it appeared that sexual behaviour was 'about the same as usual'. Even the few changes that were reported were interpreted as positive in nature, namely 'increased love, increased willingness to experiment, and increased feelings of closeness'.

The original German work included an assessment of various forms of sexual behaviour which might have been affected by exposure to erotica. Davis and Braucht (1971b) conducted one of the more detailed of the Commission studies. College-educated men were shown films portraying couples undressing each other, petting and then engaging in oral sex and coitus. Questionnaires were designed to assess the thoughts and actions of the subjects in the twenty-four hours before and after the film session. The results revealed an increase in daydreams and talking about sex, interpreted as substitute behaviour. There was also evidence of an increase in tension, desire for sex, masturbation, and thinking about the films to provide a source of added stimulation while engaging in sex.

In a similar study with students, sexual fantasies and discussions increased but no increase in masturbation was detected (Mosher, 1971). There was also a significant increase in sexual tension, internal unrest and, for males, aggression. A further finding was that attitudes toward premarital sex became more liberal for the sexually experienced, and slightly more conservative for the less experienced; this may be another example of the phenomenon discussed in Chapter 4 of how attitudes tend to 'polarize' when existing beliefs are 'put to the test'. Although not significant, it was noted at follow-up after two weeks that a few of the subjects reported adopting new techniques of lovemaking, some of which were apparently modelled directly from the films. For the male students a measure of 'sex calloused' attitudes to women was included; this measure is concerned with treating women as sex objects for the pleasure of men and approving of sexual exploitation generally. It was thought that the erotic films would strengthen any such attitudes, but, contrary to prediction, 'sex calloused' attitudes were found to decrease. After viewing the erotica the male students were less inclined than before to approve of the use of force or tactics, such as plying a girl with alcohol and falsely professing love, for the purposes of seduction. This is evidence contrary to the popular view that erotica tends to degrade or humiliate women.

The studies discussed so far have involved material that might be classified as soft-core pornography or more simply as just erotica; the scenes depicted were of a relatively 'non-kinky' nature being concerned with normal rather than abnormal sex. In another of the Commission studies, which are listed in Table 10, Kutschinsky (1971b) decided to investigate the effects of exposure to material that was closer to being 'hard-core'. Graduate students, who were mostly married, were shown films of sexual practices including troilism (triangular group-sex) and lesbianism, coloured pornographic magazines, and a fifteen-minute recording of pornographic literature by a poet.

Table 10

Amoroso *et al.* (1971)   The sexual behaviour of 116 male students was similar in the week before and after viewing 27 erotic slides, there being a slight increase only for masturbation.

Byrne and Lamberth (1971)   42 young married couples who were presented with 19 themes of erotica rated their sexual activity for the following week as being 'about the same as usual'.

Davis and Braucht (1971b)   The sexual thoughts and activities of 121 male adults changed in the twenty-four hours after being shown three ten-minute erotic films. There was an increase in masturbation, pornography-aided sex, and sexual fantasies and discussions.

Mosher (1971)   Sexual fantasies and conversations increased for 377 students in the twenty-four hours after being shown an erotic film in a group setting. There was no increase in masturbation, and 'sex calloused' attitudes to women decreased. Changes in attitudes to pre-marital sex were apparent at follow-up after two weeks.

Kutschinsky (1971b)   Coitus rather than masturbation increased in the twenty-four hours after exposure to one hour of pornography for 72, mostly married, graduate students. This increase applied mainly to those who were most aroused when viewing the pornography. Longer follow-ups did not reveal any changes in sexual activity.

Although fairly 'tame' by present-day standards, the material was considered the 'best' available at the time in Copenhagen. Assessment the next day revealed an increase in coitus rather than masturbation, which may be explained in terms of nearly all the students being married or 'going steady'. This increase in coitus was particularly likely to occur where both members of a pair had viewed the pornography. It was also noted that the students who had been most aroused during the one-hour session were the ones most likely to increase their sexual activity. Later assessments, over the following two weeks, failed to detect any clear changes in behaviour. There was no indication that the subjects had developed an interest in pornography as a result of the session; indeed many of them spontaneously mentioned that they had lost interest in it. Moreover, there was evidence contrary to the notion that 'pornography breeds prurient interest' since there was a decline in interest for trying out 'deviant' practices of the type depicted during the session. These observations of diminished interest in pornography may be an example of 'anticipation being better than reality'. It could also be a reflection of the materials selected or, more likely, the fact that they were presented to all the subjects at the same time in a large hall. It is possible that this group-exposure condition acted to inhibit full appreciation of the materials.

A limitation of all the studies discussed so far is that the subjects were exposed to erotica on only one occasion, with the length of the sessions ranging from only an hour down to a mere few minutes. If the subjects were already familiar with erotica, then it could hardly be expected that this new exposure would have much impact. Unfortunately, the investigators did not attempt to recruit subjects with little or no previous experience of erotica. It is reasonable to suppose that the subjects had already been well exposed to erotica since surveys indicate that it is the young college male, of the sort used in most of the studies, who is most likely to have had such exposure (e.g. Abelson *et al.*, 1971). If pornography does have a 'corrupting' effect then this is likely to have already started and any extra exposure, especially if it is of a relatively brief nature, is unlikely to have much additional effect. The following studies are, surprisingly, the only ones to have involved exposing subjects to more than one session of erotica.

An investigation of the effect of four sessions of erotic films

was carried out in Palo Alto by Mann *et al.* (1971). The film
sessions were held once a week for a month, and portrayed male
and female homosexuals engaging in various acts, troilism, a
Japanese couple whipping each other, and more standard
activities. For the first time, control groups of couples who saw
only neutral films or no films were included in a study of this
type. The subjects were middle-class couples who had been
married for at least ten years; it was noted that they had little
prior experience of erotic films. They made daily reports of
their sexual activity for the month before, during and after the
film sessions. On the night after the films there was an increase
in sexual activity, but it was only their usual sexual habits that
were activated. A greater frequency of sexual activity on film
rather than other nights was reported by 77 per cent of the men
and 63 per cent of the women; the corresponding figures for the
control group seeing neutral films were 41 and 35 per cent
respectively. Remembering that the subjects were married
couples, the higher sexual activity reported by the men might
be seen as evidence of extra-marital affairs, but in the event it
seems to have merely represented fuller reporting and a higher
incidence of masturbation in the men compared with the
women.

There was no evidence of imitation in that there was no
tendency for the subjects to copy the unconventional sex acts
they saw on the screen. Nor was there evidence of disinhibition
in that there was no tendency to engage in sex with other than
their partners after seeing the erotic films. Apart from the
temporary increase in their usual frequency of sex, the only
change detected was for the females to become more permissive
towards the legalization of pornography. There was also a
tendency for the couples to become more open in discussing sex
and less inhibited in their sex play, but this applied equally to
the control group who watched neutral films. It appears that
the daily completion of the questionnaire was responsible for
producing this change, which nicely illustrates the importance
of having a control group in studies of this kind.

A later analysis of the same data indicated a satiation effect
with repeated exposure to the erotic films (Mann *et al.*, 1974).
The increase in sexual activity on the film-viewing nights
tended to decline over the four sessions. Figure 6 gives the
average incidence of intercourse reported by males for each of

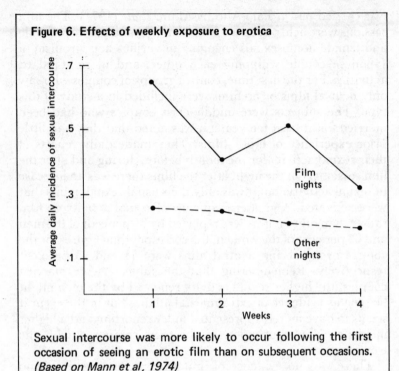

Figure 6. Effects of weekly exposure to erotica

Sexual intercourse was more likely to occur following the first occasion of seeing an erotic film than on subsequent occasions. *(Based on Mann et al, 1974)*

the four film nights compared with the average for the other nights in each week. A similar pattern was also apparent for sexual activities other than intercourse. With an interval of a week, the erotic films thus tended to become less effective as elicitors of sexual activity. Had there been a longer interval between each of the sessions, it is possible that this satiation effect would not have occurred. The importance of a control group was again apparent since the incidence of intercourse, although lower than after seeing erotic films, was slightly higher for the control group who saw neutral films rather than nothing. Going to see non-erotic films may be enough to cause a temporary increase in the lovemaking of couples.

Only one study has investigated the effects of prolonged exposure to erotica; this is summarized along with the other studies involving repeated exposure in Table 11. Male students at the University of North Carolina were provided with a range of erotic materials for ninety minutes a day for fifteen days

---

Table 11

Mann *et al.* (1971)   85 married couples were assessed for the month before, during and after being shown twenty-minute erotic films once a week for four weeks. Relative to 66 control subjects, there was no change in sexual behaviour, except for an increase on the four film nights, and no change in attitudes, except that the females became more permissive about pornography.

Mann *et al.* (1974)   In the above study, the average incidence of intercourse after seeing the erotic films was 46 per cent while the corresponding figures for the neutral and no-film control groups were 31 per cent and 20 per cent respectively. While the incidence of intercourse remained stable for the two control groups, and for the experimental group on non-film nights, at 23 per cent, it tended to decline over the four sessions of erotic films.

Howard *et al.* (1971)   23 male students were exposed to erotica for ninety minutes each day for fifteen days. Their interest in the materials declined over this period, but their sex life did not change. There was also an increase in self-esteem and attitudes to pornography became more permissive. Relative to a control group of 9 students, response to a 22½-minute erotic film declined during the study. Responsiveness appeared to be partially re-awakened at follow-up after eight weeks.

(Howard *et al.*, 1971; Reifler *et al.*, 1971). They had access to erotic films, photographs, magazines and novels as well as to non-erotic materials. During the first session, the students spent nearly all the time looking at the erotic materials, but for subsequent sessions the amount of time spent looking at them gradually declined. Satiation was specific to the erotica and not to their sex life; the frequency of sexual intercourse and other activities remained stable over the course of the study. Sexual responsiveness to erotica was assessed at the beginning by showing a 'stag' film; all the subjects had at least a partial erection during this screening. Another film was shown at the end of the daily exposure sessions, and this time fewer subjects had erections. This diminished responsiveness was significant relative to a control group of nine subjects who were not exposed to the erotica but who were assessed for responsiveness. Further evidence of satiation was provided by the subjects who all expressed an initial interest in seeing the erotica but who, by the end of the study, all reported being bored by the thought of it. Perhaps this sentiment is what a judge had in mind when saying: 'Hard-core pornographers should be made to watch their films for four hours a day for six months'. Since it was not in his power to order such a punishment, the judge had to be content with giving suspended prison sentences.

Presumably because of the prolonged exposure and their reduced interest, the students no longer saw pornography as having any importance as a social issue requiring legislation. All twenty-three subjects, except the two most conservative, moved towards a more permissive attitude to pornography with most of them ending up by favouring the abolition of all controls over the sale of pornography to adults. Another attitude change was the realization that unconventional sex, specifically group sex and homosexuality, was not for them. Their experience, however, had led to a significant increase in the desire to be promiscuous as assessed by a questionnaire, but there was no indication that this change had been translated into action. The study ended with a follow-up assessment after two months when a partial re-awakening of interest was indicated by most of the subjects having erections during the screening of another 'stag' film.

Among the people assumed to be most at risk from pornography are those who are inclined to deal with stress by action rather than thought. Accordingly the subjects had been assessed for what was thought to be a relevant personality dimension, namely 'psychopathic deviance'. But even for the students with high scores on this scale, there was no indication of a change in their sexual activities as a result of the prolonged exposure. There was, however, a tendency for them not to tire of the erotica as much as did those with low scores. The scale of 'psychopathic deviance' may thus indicate the type of person who is most susceptible to becoming a pornography 'addict'. It is a pity that more researchers have not included an assessment of relevant individual differences in response to erotica. Concern over the pornography issue is centred on unstable and deprived individuals thought to constitute those most likely to rape or torture someone. In spite of this, the investigations described in this chapter have nearly all been on students, with the only exceptions being on married couples who were college-educated and on middle-class men. While the investigation of groups at risk of becoming sex offenders may present practical difficulties, there is no reason why a student sample should not be sub-divided in terms of relevant personality dimensions, as was done in the present study.

The observed decline in interest is often quoted to support the view that people will soon tire of pornography if it is made freely available. This claim is made in spite of observations that permanent satiation does not occur in real life. According to surveys, the majority of sex-movie attenders and book-shop customers admit to being regulars (Winick, 1971). Even if he does get bored, the typical pornography addict does not give it up but instead continually searches for new materials. Most people do not quickly tire of having the same sex partner; over-activity may lead to satiation, but this is only temporary and the appetite soon returns. Similarly, there is no evidence that too much violence on TV leads to permanent satiation. Perhaps temporary satiation occurred in this study because the exposure was too heavy and the conditions of viewing were not true to life. Because the students were encouraged by money and by a sense of responsibility to the experiments to over-indulge it seems hardly surprising that satiation occurred. Another factor contributing to boredom was the amount of variety offered. Although a wide range of erotica was provided, new material was not introduced until the eleventh day and even this, being of the same type as before, was not novel. Moreover, the subjects probably selected the 'best' material on the first day, and this too would have contributed to a decline in interest on the subsequent days. Even though by the end there were reports of feeling bored by the thought of pornography, this does not mean that the students would not have been keen to view materials of a different kind. A more appropriate study would be to provide subjects with new materials, preferably of a more exciting nature on each occasion, and to have an interval of at least a week between each viewing. Under such conditions it is an open question as to whether or not satiation would occur.

On the evidence provided by the above studies, the behavioural effects of viewing erotica are 'transitory, there being an increase in sexual activity, but only on the night following exposure. Although changes in the subjects' attitudes to their sex life and to pornography were detected in several of the studies, the 'triggering' of new, let alone perverse, activities has not been demonstrated. But were the studies really designed to have such an effect? Several design limitations have already been mentioned, such as exposure being too mild and too brief, and the use of students or middle-class volunteers rather than potential sex offenders. Another limitation concerns the issue of whether subjects would readily admit to having engaged in anti-social sex acts. Surprisingly, none of the studies included a discussion of this point with the subjects; it is quite possible that a few subjects would have been unwilling to reveal such information even in the interests of science! Similarly, subjects who know they are going to be asked questions about their sex life will surely think twice before indulging in deviant practices. Under such conditions, it was optimistic of the researchers to expect to uncover dramatic changes in behaviour.

The most basic limitation, and one that applies to all the studies, is that they were not designed on the basis of appropriate theoretical considerations. The only theory implicit in their design was that subjects on seeing erotica would be sufficiently excited or 'turned on' to lose their normal inhibitions and to commit some sort of deviant act. This is the 'triggering' theory described in Chapter 2, which has little scientific value since it does not specify the particular acts that will be indulged in or why. A more promising theory is the one by Clark Hull who argued that performance at any task is a multiplicative function of both drive and habit strength; these variables being multiplicative rather than additive means that both are necessary in order for performance to result. Applying this theory to the present case, it can be seen that even if exposure to erotica does result in the losing of inhibitions, this would not result in deviant acts unless they were already habits. Rather any increase in drive strength, which results from viewing erotica, would lead to the stronger expression of existing habits. And this is precisely what happened since all the studies were designed, in effect, to alter drive strength and not to replace such existing habits as masturbation and coitus with new ones. In the study involving daily exposure to erotica, drive may have been reduced, but in all the others it was probably increased by the erotica. Consistent with Hull's theory, this increase in drive was expressed in the increased performance of existing repertoires of sexual habits.

According to Hull's theory, a new sexual performance would result only with the development of a new habit. Imitation is one learning mechanism by which such a habit might be created. To maximize the chances of imitation occurring, it would have been better for the erotica to have portrayed a particular activity rather than the range that was presented in all the studies. If a subject were to copy what he saw, then he would probably choose one of the activities that was already a favourite.

Another learning mechanism is conditioning. It was noted in some of the studies that subjects would imagine scenes from the erotica while engaging in sex. This could lead to new ideas being sufficiently rewarded by sexual excitement and orgasm to become regular fantasies and perhaps also part of an individual's repertoire. But this would take time and it would help if the subjects were informed of the theory of 'orgasmic reconditioning', as is the case when this method is used in sex therapy. If the imagined activity happens to be, say, SM (sadomasochism) or TV (which stands for transvestism on this occasion) then the possibility of serious consequences becomes apparent. An obvious ethical problem arises when the sexual preferences of subjects are deliberately manipulated for research purposes. David Holbrook and Mary Miles expressed such a sentiment in the Lord Longford report when responding to a review of research by Maurice Yaffé (1972). After questioning the value of research in assessing the effects of pornographic materials, they commented: 'Nor do we feel that to use students in such tests is justifiable, and we cannot therefore endorse the suggestions for future research.' Nevertheless, the important point to emerge from the studies that have been conducted is that because they were not designed with the explicit aim of producing immediate changes in sexual attitudes or preferences, let alone behaviour, it is unfair to conclude that pornography has little effect.

SUMMARY

The experimental field study method represents a compromise in that subjects are randomly assigned to groups and their behaviour is observed in a naturalistic setting. This is often seen as the ideal method since it involves controlled manipulation and a situation that is less artificial than the laboratory. But the very fact that subjects know they are in an experiment can have all manner of unknown effects and it is harder to control these extraneous influences in the field than it is in the laboratory. The resentment of subjects restricted in their choice of TV viewing has usually been greater for those in the non-violent than in the violent condition, and this has acted to obscure any differential effects. Where efforts have been made to reduce this problem, there has usually been a tendency for more aggression to occur in subjects assigned to a diet of violent rather than neutral TV. No true-to-life exposure sessions have yet been arranged for assessing the effects of pornography, but follow-ups of laboratory experiments have been conducted to see if any effects are apparent in the natural environment of the home. Studies with single students have not found any changes, except an increased incidence of masturbation on the night following exposure, but no checks have been carried out to discover whether these students would have practised new sexual activities had they had the chance. Studies with married couples have usually indicated a temporary increase in their usual sexual practices and no tendency to indulge in new activities. This type of result could have been predicted from learning theory; it will need more than a few sessions of looking at erotica and the usual one-week follow-up before any changes in behaviour would be predicted.

7   Laboratory Experiments

According to the catharsis or 'safety-valve' theory, watching a violent film should act to reduce any tendency to be aggressive. Siegel (1956) put this prediction to the test by showing pairs of nursery-school children a Woody Woodpecker cartoon, regarded as violent, and a non-violent cartoon. After each film the children, who were friends, were observed for fourteen minutes while in a playroom, and special note was taken of any signs of aggression directed towards each other. Although not statistically fully significant, a comparison of the two conditions revealed more rather than less aggression after the violent cartoon. This result, while contradicting the catharsis theory, tends to support instead the theory of disinhibition. This theory predicts that a violent film will act to remove the inhibitions that normally prevent a person from expressing aggression.

True to the scientific tradition, various safeguards were incorporated in the design of the experiment. Steps were taken to ensure that the observers were 'blind' in that they did not know which of the two films had just been shown; such a precaution was necessary in case their ratings of aggression were influenced by this knowledge. Other safeguards included checking that degree of interest in the two films was roughly the same, and the use of a one-way mirror so that the children would not become aware that they were being observed. Since this first laboratory experiment on the effects of film violence became very well known, it might be thought that the safeguards would have been incorporated in subsequent studies, and fortunately this has indeed been the case in laboratory work with only a few exceptions.

Siegel's result might have reached significance if the children had been given more opportunity to become aggressive. This possibility was taken up by Hapkiewicz and Roden (1971). After pairs of children had been shown either a violent cartoon, a neutral cartoon or nothing, they were invited to watch a 'peep show' through a toy box with a small hole. Because only one of them could view at a time, they had the chance to argue and fight over who it should be. Boys who had just seen the violent cartoon were less inclined to be polite and co-operative in sharing the peep show, but were not significantly more aggressive than the two control groups. It seems that any 'disinhibiting' effect from the violent cartoon was not sufficient to override the normal habits of children who are taught to stand in line, to wait and to take turns. Before considering ways round this difficulty, let us look at some tests of imitation theory.

Tests of imitation theory have been conducted by showing children a film of a child or adult model threatening and attacking an adult dressed up as a clown. In contrast to tests of disinhibition, a film for testing imitation is very specific in suggesting ways of expressing aggression in a situation that the child is about to face. The effects of the film are usually assessed by placing each child in a room with a female dressed as a clown. In two such studies, mere exposure to the film was sufficient to produce imitation of physical aggression in most of the children (Hanratty *et al.*, 1969; Savitsky *et al.*, 1971). None of the children in the control group, who did not see the film, attacked the human clown. In an effort to encourage aggression, some of the children were frustrated by withdrawing the promise of a toy they had earlier chosen, telling them that they had lost it because their partner in a game had performed badly. Contrary to prediction, this frustrating experience did not enhance the effect of the violent film. Frustration was found to be necessary, however, in another study when the film alone was not sufficient to produce imitation of aggression against the human target (Hanratty *et al.*, 1972). Why there was a different outcome in this study is not clear, but it does serve to illustrate that some children will have developed sufficiently strong inhibitions against hitting or kicking another person; such children may need extra encouragement, in the form of both film and frustration, in order to do so.

For ethical reasons, only a few studies on the effects of viewing violence have involved direct attacks on a human victim. But it may be noted that all three of the studies on the imitation of interpersonal aggression, which are outlined in Table 12 along with the two on disinhibition, produced evidence of film effects; the volunteers who acted as the clowns had

---

Table 12

Siegel (1956)   Twelve pairs of nursery-school children, aged 4 to 5 years, watched a ten-minute violent cartoon and an instructional cartoon. For fourteen minutes after each film, aggression in a playroom was recorded by observers. There was a non-significant tendency for the children to be more aggressive after the violent than after the neutral film.

Hapkiewicz and Roden (1971)   Ten pairs of children, aged 6 to 8 years, were shown a twelve-minute violent cartoon and then observed for signs of aggression. Compared with 40 other children who had seen either a neutral film or nothing, they were less co-operative but not significantly different in terms of aggression.

Hanratty *et al.* (1969)   Nursery-school children shown a 2½-minute film of a child model threatening and attacking a human clown tended to copy this behaviour when in a playroom. Imitation occurred whether or not the children were frustrated.

Savitsky *et al.* (1971)   In a replication of the above study using the same film, very similar results were obtained with 48 boys aged 6 to 8 years.

Hanratty *et al.* (1972)   In another replication, 30 boys aged 6 to 7 years imitated an adult model hitting a female clown only when they were frustrated.

---

the bruises to prove it. Since children probably feel inhibited about attacking an adult, greater effects would probably have been achieved with a child acting the role of the clown. But for ethical reasons, the experimenters felt constrained about having a child as the target for aggression.

A way round the ethical problem of encouraging subjects to attack another person is to trick them into thinking that they are punishing someone. With the Arnold Buss 'aggression machine' method, a subject is led to believe that he is assisting in a separate experiment which happens to be concerned with the effects of punishment on learning. He is asked to administer electric shocks to another subject whenever a mistake is made on a learning task. Aggressiveness is assessed in terms of the intensity and duration of the shocks applied. The victim is in fact a confederate of the experimenter and just pretends that he is receiving the shocks; it is assumed that the aggressor will be so absorbed in his task that he will not see through the deception.

In the first study with the aggression machine for testing the effects of violence-viewing, male hospital attendants were shown the exciting knife fight scene from the James Dean film *Rebel Without a Cause*. Aggression was assessed before and after, and compared with that from a control group who had seen an innocuous educational film. The results, presented in Table 13,

Table 13 Effects of films on aggressive expression				
	Violent film		Neutral film	
	Before	After	Before	After
Shock intensity	4.3	4.9	5.0	4.9
Intensity × Duration	42.8	47.2	41.1	35.3

Men shown a violent film tend to administer higher and longer shocks to another person.
(Based on Walters et al., *1962)*

show that the group who saw the violent film punished errors more severely than did the controls. Here, then, is the first laboratory study with positive evidence for the disinhibition theory. In a replication of this study, similar results were obtained for younger males and for females from a hostel for working girls (Walters and Thomas, 1963). Some of these subjects went so far as to administer the highest level of shock; they had earlier experienced the lower levels and so must have realized how painful the highest shocks would be. Further illustration of the 'disinhibiting' effects of the violent film came from remarks, such as 'I bet I made that fellow jump', made by some of the subjects who appeared to actually enjoy administering the shocks.

The studies discussed so far have involved children or working-class adults who, it might be argued, have relatively weak inhibitions about hurting other people. Exposure to a single violent film may not be sufficient to 'disinhibit' other groups who have been more strongly 'socialized' in this regard. One such group could be university students for whom it may be necessary to provide frustration or provocation in order to produce the effect. This is in fact what happened in a study with students at the University of Wisconsin (Berkowitz and Geen, 1966). Those who were shown a boxing scene from the Kirk Douglas film *The Champion* were no more aggressive than those in a control group who were shown the Bannister–Landy track duel from the Commonwealth Games. The effects of the violent film became apparent only for students who had been angered. They were angered by an accomplice of the experimenters who, in judging their ability at a 'creativity' type task, decided to give them a large number of shocks for a poor performance. Their chance for revenge came later, after seeing one of the two films, when the roles were reversed and they were asked to judge the performance of the accomplice. It was the subjects who had been shocked many times who now gave more shocks to the accomplice, especially if they had seen the violent rather than the sports film.

A modification of the 'aggression machine' was designed for children in one of the Surgeon General's studies (Liebert and Baron, 1972). It consisted of a box with a 'hurt' and a 'help' button. The subject was told that a child in another room was playing a game involving the turning of a handle. A light would come on every time the handle was turned, and each time the subject was required to press one of the buttons. It was explained that if he pressed the 'help' button this would make the handle easier to turn and so help the child win the game, but if he pressed the 'hurt' button the handle would become hot so forcing the child to let go. The subject was also told that the longer he held down the button the more it would help or hinder the other child. Children were given twenty trials on this machine after seeing either a fight scene from *The Untouchables* or an exciting sports sequence. As predicted, it was the violent film group who were more likely to press the 'hurt' button and to press it for longer.

In an interesting replication of this study, the facial expressions of children were also recorded (Ekman *et al.*, 1972). Boys who expressed happiness or pleasure during the scenes of violence were more likely to press the 'hurt' button than boys whose facial expressions revealed pain, surprise or lack of interest. It was only emotional reactions to violence that were related to subsequent aggression and not reactions to the sports sequence. Thus we have evidence that a viewer who responds to screen violence with pleasant emotions is especially likely to be aggressive when given the chance.

Another technique for assessing aggression involves the use of insults or verbal aggression (West *et al.*, 1975). Female delinquents were given a puzzle to solve while another subject, who was in fact a confederate of the experimenters, made insulting remarks such as 'You stupid idiot!' After watching either violent or neutral films, the roles were reversed and the subject was asked to comment on the performance of the confederate. Judges rated the degree of aggression expressed and, in line with prediction, it was the girls who had seen the violent films who were the more verbally aggressive. Since many of their comments were identical to those made earlier, this study probably demonstrates the effects of imitation as much as those of disinhibition.

The results from this group of studies, outlined in Table 14, are consistent in providing evidence that film violence increases our willingness to hurt or insult another person. This finding applies to both children and adults, and was obtained by providing a 'permissive' situation in which aggressive urges could be freely expressed. A reservation concerns the extent to which the subjects were convinced that they were hurting another person. A subject who sees through the deception might be more aggressive simply to please the experimenter by giving the result he wants. The usual practice is to explain the deception to the subjects after the experiment, and to ask if any of them had guessed what was happening. This check usually indicates that subjects really believe that they are hurting someone. Another important check is to see whether the scores obtained are related to real-life aggression. This was done by Shemberg *et al.* (1968) in an effort to establish the validity of the 'aggression machine' method. Children were rated for general aggressiveness by two counsellors who knew them well, and in this way two groups were obtained regarded by both raters as either high or low on aggressiveness. When tested on the aggression machine, the group regarded as generally aggressive administered significantly higher shocks than did the unaggressive group. Consistent with this result, other researchers have noted that subjects with a previous history of aggression are usually more prepared to hurt another subject.

Table 14

Walters *et al.* (1962)   28 men were assessed, in terms of their willingness to administer shocks to another person, before and after seeing either a violent or an educational film. The violent film group gave significantly higher and longer shocks.

Walters and Thomas (1963)   Results similar to the above were obtained with 24 boys aged 14 to 16 years and 32 females aged around 20 years.

Berkowitz and Geen (1966)   88 male students were given either one or seven shocks by an accomplice of the experimenters. Among the subjects who received seven shocks, those who saw a seven-minute violent film later administered more shocks to the accomplice than did those who saw a sports film.

Liebert and Baron (1972)   68 children, aged 5 to 9 years, who were shown a 3½-minute violent film were more willing to hurt rather than help another child in comparison with a control group who were shown a sports film. Mild frustration did not significantly enhance the effect of the violent film.

Ekman *et al.* (1972)   In a replication of this experiment, involving 30 boys and 35 girls aged 5 to 6 years, facial expressions were also recorded. Boys who responded to the violent film with positive rather than negative expressions were later more likely to hurt another child. The results for girls were not significant.

West *et al.* (1975)   63 delinquent girls were verbally harassed by a confederate while attempting to solve a puzzle. Later the roles were reversed and girls who had seen violent films were more verbally aggressive than those who had seen neutral films.

Another way of detecting increases in aggression is to look for changes in attitude. This approach is particularly useful where an increase is insufficient to result in an overt act of aggression. Mussen and Rutherford (1961) used the technique of simply asking children whether they wanted to 'pop' or just play with a balloon. Some of the children had previously seen an animated cartoon about a weed attempting to choke a flower with a panda bear struggling in turn to destroy the weed; others had seen a film of a frog and duck playing co-operatively, and the remainder nothing. Table 15 shows that the group who saw the violent cartoon were more likely to express a desire to burst the

Table 15 Effects of films on aggressive intentions		
	Frustrated	*Not frustrated*
Violent cartoon	17	20
Neutral cartoon	7	8
No cartoon	5	7

Whether or not they had been frustrated, children were more likely to express an aggressive desire if they had just seen a violent cartoon.

(Based on Mussen and Rutherford, 1961)

balloon than were the other groups. The violent cartoon appeared to stimulate aggressive impulses, which were expressed verbally in terms of intent. Frustration was induced in half the children by giving them the tedious task of copying numbers while their teacher criticized them, but this did not make them more aggressive.

Leifer and Roberts (1972) used the method of presenting children with descriptions of day-to-day conflict situations, to which physical or verbal aggression would be a possible response. The children were asked to say which of several alternatives they would actually choose when in such a situation. An example of an item was 'You're walking down the street. Some kid is mad at you and comes up and hits you. What do you do?', and the alternative responses were 'Hit them', 'Call them "Stupid" ', 'Leave them', or 'Tell a grown-up'. For ease of understanding, these four alternatives were illustrated by 'stick figure' drawings. As expected, children who had just been watching a violent rather than a neutral film were more likely to select aggressive responses. This result was obtained in spite of asking the children what they would normally do – a clearer result might have been obtained by asking them what they would choose to do at that moment.

The above studies are listed in Table 16 along with an interesting variation. The effect of film violence on dreams was investigated in a sleep laboratory by Foulkes *et al.* (1972). After spending a night adapting to the conditions, boys watched a violent and a non-violent episode from a Western on the next two nights before going to bed. During the night they were

---

Table 16

Mussen and Rutherford (1961)   36 children, aged 6 to 7 years, watched either an eight-minute violent cartoon, a neutral cartoon, or nothing. The violent cartoon group were the most likely to express an impulse to burst a balloon.

Leifer and Roberts (1972)   In a series of experiments, children aged 3 to 18 years were more likely to claim aggressive responses to six interpersonal conflict situations in real life if they had just see a violent rather than a neutral film.

Foulkes *et al.* (1972)   40 boys, aged 10 to 12 years, were shown a fifty-minute violent or neutral episode from a Western. Dreams were recalled 73 per cent of the time when the boys were woken during the night, but the content of their dreams was unrelated to the type of film watched.

---

woken while dreaming, as indicated by rapid eye movements, and asked to describe their dreams. These descriptions were later analysed for emotional content but, contrary to prediction, the films were not related to the amount of aggressive imagery. The violent film did not increase hostility, anxiety, guilt or unpleasantness, nor did it disturb sleep. This finding applied even to boys who had been selected as having little previous exposure to TV violence. Nevertheless, even these boys were probably used to some degree of violence, especially that in Westerns, which could explain why the film did not appear to influence their dreams. Another limitation of the study became apparent when a third of the boys claimed to have previously seen the film; it would have been better to have used an extremely violent film that had not been seen before. On the basis of the evidence so far, we cannot conclude that dreams are unaffected by what is seen before going to bed.

Apart from the effect of violence on dreams, studies have been concerned with its effect on fantasies or daydreaming. The Thematic Apperception Test involves the writing of 'imaginative' stories under pressure of time, and these are assumed to reveal clues as to the writer's fantasies. Barclay and Haber (1965) used this method with students and found that those who were angered and humiliated expressed more aggression in their stories. This was not surprising, but it was also found that they expressed more sexual themes as well. Perhaps this helps explain the historical observation that after witnessing tortures, people often became so infected with blood-lust that they engaged in spontaneous sex orgies (Hurwood, 1969).

Several replications of the Barclay and Haber experiment have since been carried out and similar results obtained; these are summarized in Table 17. Of particular interest is the objective measure of sexual arousal used by Barclay (1969); he detected a higher level of acid phosphatase in 'angered' males. This enzyme is secreted by the prostate gland and has often been found to increase under conditions of sexual arousal (Zuckerman, 1971). Although Barclay's set of studies has been concerned with the effects of anger arousal by insults rather than the showing of violent films, it nevertheless suggests that one of the effects of witnessing violence may be an increase in the desire for sex. It is unfortunate that this interesting possibility has not yet been followed up.

An approach to studying the effects of witnessing violence that has been thoroughly investigated concerns the use of toy dolls. An inflated Bobo doll is weighted so that it returns to an upright position when struck, and for many children it 'invites'

Table 17

Barclay and Haber (1965)   64 students were made angry by insulting and humiliating comments. Compared with a control group of 60 students, they produced not only more aggressive themes in TAT stories but also more themes of a sexual nature. This result was obtained with both males and females.

Barclay (1969)   In a replication of this study involving additional measures, similar results were obtained. Urinary acid phosphatase, which is believed to be a physiological indicator of sexual arousal in males, was enhanced in the 'angered' group. Themes of ambition and affiliation were not increased by the anger-arousing procedure.

Barclay (1970)   In another replication, in which the students were angered by a female rather than a male experimenter, similar results were again obtained. The 'anger provoking' female was particularly effective in eliciting sexy stories from the male students.

attack. This toy doll has been used in many studies to assess aggression, the usual procedure being for an adult model armed with a mallet to assault Bobo with accompanying cries such as 'Kick him!' and 'Pow!'. The first study of this type was by Bandura *et al.* (1961). Nursery-school children, matched for previous aggression, were assigned to one of three groups in which they watched either a violent model, a subdued model, or nothing. A frustrating experience, in which the children started playing with very attractive toys but were then stopped, was introduced at this point to increase the chances of aggression occurring. Each child was then placed in a room with an assortment of ordinary toys including a mallet and a Bobo doll. As expected, those who had seen the violent model tended to imitate the various forms of physical and verbal aggression. There were also signs of disinhibition since these children would also punch Bobo, even though this particular action had not been modelled.

Many other studies have been conducted along similar lines, but usually with the primary aim of investigating some other issue, such as the relative effectiveness of an adult versus a child model. For this reason we shall refer to these studies later when dealing with the particular issue concerned. Suffice it to say at this point that the studies have invariably found that children do tend to imitate an aggressive model when given the chance. In fact, it is generally easier to demonstrate imitation than disinhibition.

Another method involving toys was designed by Lövaas (1961). Before watching either a violent or a neutral cartoon, children were shown two toys, each operated by a lever. In one a doll hits another over the head with a stick, and in the other a ball runs through obstacles in a cage. The children were then given the chance to play with the toys, and encouraged to play most with the one they preferred. Whereas the neutral group spent most of their time operating the ball game, the violent group tended to play with the aggressive doll as much as the ball game. The violent cartoon appeared to have a 'disinhibiting' effect in making them prefer to operate an aggressive toy. This study along with some Bobo doll examples is listed in Table 18.

Throughout this book we have been painting a rather negative picture of the effects of TV by repeatedly giving examples of how screened violence can lead to aggressive behaviour. There is, however, a positive side and this is well illustrated by research on the so-called 'pro-social' effects of TV (Comstock and Lindsey, 1975). Children and adults too, as we shall see in the next chapter, have a tendency to be influenced by 'good' as well as 'bad' models. One example will perhaps suffice to show that the many studies concerned with aggression have been paralleled by a few concerned with 'pro-social' effects.

Sprafkin *et al.* (1975) assessed the effects of a *Lassie* TV episode, in which a boy helps the dog recover a trapped puppy, relative to another *Lassie* episode and a *Brady Bunch* comedy. Thirty children, aged six to seven years, watched one of these three half-hour programmes. They were then given a game in which they were competing for a prize, but at the same time they were given earphones and asked to summon help by pressing a button if they heard any barking from puppies that the experimenter was meant to be looking after. The results indicated that the children who had seen the 'pro-social' *Lassie* episode were much more likely to sacrifice their chances of winning a prize by persistently pressing the 'help' button than were either of the other two groups. Future research might with advantage seek to further identify the types of programme that are most likely to lead to an increase in altruistic behaviour.

The laboratory experiments which we have described in this chapter have consistently indicated that violence-viewing increases aggression. This has been detected in a variety of ways and, even though each study may have certain limitations, the overall result seems impressive. A few studies did not obtain an effect, but in each case an obvious reason was apparent. In the dreaming study we noted that a Western may not be violent or frightening enough to influence a child's dreams. Similarly, in the study by Siegel it may be a bit much to expect children, who were friends, to start hitting each other on account of having just seen a short cartoon. To obtain direct aggression against another person requires a good deal of provocation. It is easier to elicit an indirect form of aggression, such as getting a subject to administer electric shocks to someone else as part of a scientific experiment. Only for university students was this form of aggression not elicited by a violent film, although it was for students who had been made angry. The conclusion from all this work must be that viewing violence increases the chances of aggression occurring, and this aggression is most likely to be detected if a permissive atmosphere for the expression of aggression prevails.

Critics of this work point out its artificial nature and the tendency for only the immediate effects of a film to be assessed. Artificiality is the price we have to pay for gaining close control over the variables involved, such as making sure that control group subjects watch only a neutral film, and for arranging a situation in which it is possible to detect the small increases in

---

Table 18

Bandura *et al.* (1961)   72 nursery-school children, aged around 4 years, watched an adult model either attacking or just playing with a Bobo doll, or nothing. After a frustrating experience, the violent group were markedly more aggressive than the other two groups when they found themselves in the presence of a Bobo doll. This reaction was observed for twenty minutes through a one-way mirror.

Lövaas (1961)   20 nursery-school children, aged 4 to 6 years, watched either a five-minute violent or a neutral cartoon. Those who had seen the violent cartoon were more likely to choose an aggressive toy, when later given the chance to operate a couple of 'action' toys.

Kniveton and Stephenson (1970)   20 middle-class boys, aged 4 years, who were exposed to a 3½ minute filmed model displayed more imitative aggression against an inflated doll than did 10 control subjects. Imitation was significantly reduced, however, by giving the boys fifteen minutes' prior experience of playing with the doll.

Hicks (1965)   30 boys and 30 girls, aged around 5 years, watched an eight-minute film of a model hitting a plastic doll. Relative to a neutral film, imitation was found to occur whether the model was an adult or a peer, male or female. Imitation was also apparent when the children were tested for retention six months later.

Kniveton (1973a)   32 working-class boys, aged around 6 years, were shown a film of modelled aggression. Relative to a neutral film, imitation occurred whether they were tested immediately or one week later. Retention of the modelled aggression was also apparent four to five months later.

aggression that are predicted to occur in response to a short film. If these small increases are also short-lived, then of course it is necessary to assess them immediately after the film. But for imitation, at least, it seems that the effects are far from being short-lived. Hicks (1965) noted that retention of modelled aggression was good even after six months in nursery-school children. Kniveton (1973a) took this a step further by testing some children immediately after exposure to a film and others after a day or a week. Imitation occurred whatever the delay, and the children could still recall most of the aggressive acts when retested four to five months later. Both these researchers had taken the trouble to replicate their findings (Hicks, 1968; Kniveton and Stephenson, 1972), but in spite of their results we still hear the criticism that laboratory-demonstrated imitation is only short-lived.

Ideally, the laboratory method should include having continuous and long-term control over the behaviour of subjects. But this involves the practical problem of expecting subjects willingly to give up part of their lives in order to take part in such a study. It would not be easy to gain control over the viewing habits of subjects by keeping them in the laboratory for weeks at a time. Apart from accepting the less rigorous method of the experimental field study, there is another alternative and that is to consider theories relevant to the long-term effects of violence-viewing and then to investigate these theories in the laboratory. Desensitization is one such theory and to this we shall turn in the next chapter, but first we must look at the laboratory studies on the effects of exposure to pornography.

Unlike the laboratory studies of violence-viewing, those on pornography have not been designed with a particular theory in mind. Researchers have instead adopted the approach of simply presenting subjects with a variety of erotic materials and then searching for any effects. Nowhere do we find studies directly aimed at inducing imitation; this is probably because imitation is considered relevant only to children who in turn, for ethical reasons, have not been involved in laboratory experiments on the effects of pornography. But modelled sexual behaviour is a technique used in sex therapy, and it appears to work. Implicit in the design of the studies is the theory of disinhibition. It appears to be thought that as a result of seeing erotic materials, subjects will be sufficiently disinhibited to express all manner of perversions. But again, in contrast to the violence studies, only for one set of studies – those concerned with the sex–violence link – do we find an explicit attempt to provide a situation where an 'abnormal' effect can be readily expressed. Bearing these points in mind, it might be predicted that little will be detected from experiments on the effects of erotica. Most of the laboratory studies have included a follow-up over the next day or week, and these results were described in the previous chapter. Here we shall report on the immediate effects from viewing erotic materials, but first a brief consideration of imitation.

In Western society there is little in the way of direct training on how to make love, and so young people have to rely largely on what they see and hear in the media. Films probably fulfil an important role in depicting techniques of lovemaking, which the viewer can later imitate. The need for this form of instruction is stressed by sex therapists who frequently encounter patients who literally do not know what they are meant to do when making love. Although learning by imitation is an important technique in sex therapy, it has not been directly investigated by research. There is, however, evidence that a person's approach to looking at erotic pictures can be influenced by a social model (Walters *et al.*, 1964).

Male students were led to believe that they were taking part in advertising research concerned with the 'eyecatching' qualities of different pictures. To demonstrate the procedure they were shown a film of another subject being tested; this subject was in fact a confederate of the experimenters and served as the social model. The pictures consisted of females who were fully clothed or in various states of undress, and the model acted in either an 'uninhibited' manner by dwelling over the erotic poses or in an 'inhibited' manner by quickly passing them by. After observing the model, the students were tested by a female experimenter and, true to prediction, the amount of time spent looking at the erotic pictures depended on the model's behaviour. Students who witnessed the 'uninhibited' model spent twice as much time examining the erotica as did the students who witnessed the 'inhibited' model. Because of the presence of the female experimenter, it seems that the students were uncertain as to how to conduct themselves in this potentially awkward situation and so fell back on the example provided by the model. Consistent with this interpretation, the students were not influenced by the model's approach to the neutral pictures; with these pictures there was no problem as to how to behave.

Imitation almost certainly plays a role in the development of sex-appropriate play in children (Kobasigawa, 1966 and 1967). Boys were more likely to play with female toys, such as a dolls' house, if they had just witnessed another boy doing so. Similarly, boys were inhibited from playing with female toys by an adult model who played with neutral toys but avoided female toys with comments such as: 'These are nice toys, but I'm not going to play with them. They are for girls. Boys won't play with this kind of toy.' These demonstrations of how sex-appropriate behaviour can be vicariously modified by modelling suggest that other forms of sexual behaviour can also be modified. If true, this means that pornography can only act to increase the chances of people modelling their own behaviour on what they see portrayed. Details of the three studies relevant to this issue are given in Table 19.

Table 19

Walters *et al.* (1964)   24 male students who witnessed an 'uninhibited' model looking closely at sixteen erotic pictures spent more time looking at these pictures themselves than did 22 students who had witnessed an 'inhibited' model. Imitation occurred only for the erotica; for sixteen neutral pictures the model's looking behaviour did not have a significant influence on the subject.

Kobasigawa (1966)   45 boys aged around 6 years tended to copy another boy, but not a girl, who chose to play with female rather than neutral toys. 45 girls who observed models playing with male toys were not significantly influenced.

Kobasigawa (1967)   Children observed an adult model playing for two minutes with neutral or sex-inappropriate toys. In seven minutes of subsequent play, children tended to avoid sex-inappropriate toys if they had witnessed the model doing likewise.

Many studies have assessed the immediate effects of exposure to erotica, including each of those listed in Tables 9 and 10.

Dealing first with the Hamburg series, most of the students reported some degree of sexual arousal when questioned afterwards. Table 20 presents the results from one of these experiments, which may be taken as fairly typical. The females were

Table 20 Students reporting sexual arousal during the viewing of erotica			
Males (%)		*Females(%)*	
Full erection	31	Genital sensations	65
Partial erection	55	Breast sensations	9
Pre-ejaculatory emission	25	Vaginal lubrication	28
Any genital reaction	87	Any physiological reaction	72
(Based on Schmidt and Sigusch, 1970)			

almost as likely as the males to report signs of physical arousal, although the figures are not directly comparable because of certain well-known anatomical differences between the sexes. Taken at face value, the results appear to show that a majority of the students were 'turned on' by the erotica, but the actual figures have little absolute meaning. In the case of pre-ejaculatory emission and vaginal lubrication, the figures may be regarded as underestimates since around 20 per cent of the remaining students were unsure as to whether or not such a reaction had occurred. On the other hand, all the figures may be regarded as overestimates since 20 per cent of both sexes reported stimulating themselves during the viewing session – with 4 per cent of the males actually ejaculating through masturbation. Moreover, many of the students probably used their imagination to elaborate on the scenes shown and so increased the chances of being 'turned on'. Perhaps a more valid indication of the impact made by the erotica is provided by subjective feelings, which were rated on a nine-point scale ranging from low through moderate to high sexual arousal. The students reported being only 'moderately' stimulated by the erotica with average ratings of 5.2 and 4.7 by males and females respectively.

The main purpose of the above study was not to investigate the 'arousal' value of erotica as such, but rather to investigate sex differences in responsiveness. Although the males were more aroused than the females, the differences were very slight and applied only to the more intensive themes involving oral sex. Another finding was that males were more likely than females to report a favourable rather than an unfavourable reaction, although both groups tended to report 'neutral' or indifferent reactions. Other emotions were assessed before and after seeing the erotica, and numerous changes were detected. For males, these changes included a decrease in the tendency to feel composed, innerly calm, interested and friendly. For females, the changes included a decrease in the tendency to feel composed, unconcerned, lazy and interested. Relative to males, the females were more likely to report changes in the direction of feeling shocked, irritated and disgusted. The issue of sex differences will be taken up again in Chapter 9.

The main findings from the German studies are summarized in Table 21. Apart from reports of sexual arousal from most of the students, the main point to note is that both favourable and unfavourable feelings were evoked by the erotica. The more explicit scenes evoked feelings of shock and disgust for the more conservative students; both sexes were 'put off' by unaesthetic poses taken out of context and males were put off by the presence of the male character in explicit intercourse scenes.

The Commission studies were designed to confirm and extend the findings from the Hamburg series. A wealth of information was collected in these studies but it is very difficult to interpret. The problem concerns the degree to which the subjects' reactions were a result of their own fantasies rather than the erotica. As before, around 80 per cent of subjects reported signs of sexual arousal but, again, the erotica were subjectively rated as only moderately stimulating (e.g. Mosher, 1971). Indications that the subject's own fantasies were responsible for this discrepancy between objective and subjective measures of arousal emerged from two of the studies. First, in the study by Amoroso and his colleagues, 60 per cent of the subjects were later reported as having elaborated on the erotica by the use of fantasy (Brown *et al.*, 1976). Second, sexual arousal was found to be greater in response to imagining specified sexual themes than it was in response to the same themes presented in pictures or stories (Byrne and Lamberth,

Table 21

Schmidt *et al.* (1969)   When viewing erotic slides, 79 per cent of male students reported at least a partial erection. The more stimulating pictures tended to give rise to unfavourable feelings, there being a correlation of −0.38 between rated degree of sexual arousal and favourableness of feelings.

Sigusch *et al.* (1970)   In a replication of the above study involving both sexes, 80 per cent of males reported an erection and 70 per cent of females reported sensations (warmth, pulsations, itching) in the genital area. Except for slides with romantic content, females rated most of the pictures as less arousing and more unfavourable than did males.

Schmidt and Sigusch (1970)   Male and female students reported on signs of sexual arousal and changes in mood in response to seeing ten minutes of slides or erotic film. Most reported genital reactions, but they considered the erotica had only 'moderately stimulated' them.

Schmidt *et al.* (1973)   Erections or genital sensations were reported by nearly all the male and female students who read one of two erotic stories, but they rated them only 'moderately sexually arousing'. For a story without any affection or tenderness, there was an increase in aggressive feelings.

1971). It does seem, therefore, that the results from all these studies were partly due to 'unknown' fantasies of the subjects.

Evidence relevant to this problem was available at about the time that the Commission studies were getting under way. After establishing that four of seven men responded to an erotic film with erections, Laws and Rubin (1969) instructed them to develop an erection in the absence of a film and found that all seven were able to do so. The men had done this simply by relaxing and fantasizing. They were also able to inhibit erections while watching a film by 'thinking of other things'. An important aspect of this experiment was the recording of erections by a mercury strain gauge; in all the above studies reliance had to be placed on the subjects' testimony and memory. Mechanical recording of erections allowed an important discovery: erections to the film were more sudden and smoother in their development than were erections produced by fantasy.

Had this information been available to the Commission researchers, then it is possible that they could have designed their studies so as to distinguish between 'genuine' and 'fantasy induced' erections. As it is, we have no way of telling the extent to which their results are distorted by the fantasies of their subjects. To find that 80 per cent of male subjects report erections when viewing erotica means little if some of them are trying to enhance and others to inhibit this reaction. Similarly, to find that conservative subjects are less likely than others to have erections may simply mean that they happen to be motivated not to display such a reaction.

The experiment of Laws and Rubin involved only seven subjects and so might be dismissed as being of little value. But to do so would be to miss the point that it highlights a variable that was uncontrolled in all the studies that assessed erections in response to erotica; the researchers should have considered controlling for the effect of fantasy unless they could be certain that it would not influence their results. This is the type of consideration stressed in cognitive psychology, which is an area explicitly concerned with the role played by the subject's own thoughts. If it is not possible to control for the 'fantasy' variable, then the alternative is to estimate its importance, for example by questioning the subjects afterwards. Only Brown *et al.* (1976) appreciated the necessity to do this and, with the exception of Byrne and Lamberth (1971), the other researchers do not fully discuss the issue and, amazingly, none refer to Laws and Rubin's work. Their studies are thus open to the criticism that they involved 'demand' characteristics, with the results being distorted because the subjects felt that they were expected to behave in a certain manner. In the case of viewing erotica, subjects may well feel that they are expected to become aroused and try to do so in order to accommodate the desires of the experimenter; they may also respond in this way simply because they want to give an impression of themselves as sexually responsive.

The report of the US Commission (1970) states: 'Experimental and survey studies show that exposure to erotic stimuli produces sexual arousal in substantial portions of both males and females.' Had the committee been acquainted with Laws and Rubin's work, they might have added that exposure to one's own imagination produces sexual arousal in even more substantial portions of both males and females! To claim an important effect from erotica, it really is necessary to demonstrate something over and above that which could be produced by mere fantasy. Apart from the basic requirement of a control group of subjects who just fantasize, this might be done by monitoring the development of erections, which as we have seen may be different for erotica as opposed to fantasy. Another way might be to present forms of sex that are unlikely to be part of a subject's fantasy life; even with the fairly standard varieties of sex play presented in the Amoroso *et al.* study, it was found that 29 per cent of the subjects indicated that they would like to try some of the new techniques they saw depicted in the slides (Brown *et al.*, 1976). Even if this expressed intention is not translated into action, and it would need longer than a one-week follow-up before such an answer could be suggested, it still provides evidence of a psychological effect from erotica.

Because of the doubt over the part played by erotica in producing arousal, the most useful aspect of the research concerns the subjective reports of the subjects. Some of the more interesting results are summarized in Tables 22 and 23. Consistent with the German research, the impact of erotica is indicated by the mood changes which took place, and the diversity of individual reactions by the reports of negative emotions as well as arousal. Of particular interest were the subjects' judgements made while watching the films in the research by Davis and Braucht (1971b). Compared with their initial expectations, the men were less likely to label themselves as 'deviant' for watching the films; there was also a tendency for them to be less afraid of such detrimental effects as the films making them 'sexually abnormal or queer'. But in contrast, they were more likely to consider that such films should not be freely available to the general public. This increased belief in censorship applied especially to those who had rejected oral sex practices in their own personal life. Presumably the films were less exciting and impressive than they expected, which might explain the decrease in feeling deviant about watching them. The increase in pro-censorship views might be explained in terms of the nature of the films where the emphasis was on oral sex, which many of the men did not favour. As we shall see in Chapter 9, views on censorship seem to depend, very much, on the personal preferences of the person making the judgement.

Table 22

Davis and Braucht (1971b)   While viewing three ten-minute erotic films, 75 per cent of men reported erections and 72 per cent felt the desire to masturbate. As a result of the experience, they reported being less likely to feel deviant about watching pornography but, paradoxically, more likely to recommend its restriction.

Mosher (1971)   In response to watching one of two erotic films, 79 per cent of male students reported at least a partial erection while 85 per cent of the females reported strong genital sensations. But the films were rated as having induced only a 'moderate' level of sexual arousal. The films were more likely to be seen as disgusting and offensive by females, and by those who were sexually inexperienced.

Laws and Rubin (1969)   Seven men were shown eleven-minute erotic films. Four responded with full erections, but when instructed to inhibit this reaction, there was at least a 50 per cent reduction in each case. When instructed to develop an erection in the absence of a film, all seven subjects were able to do so within 30 per cent of their maximum.

It was noted in Table 9 that after seeing an erotic film or slides, 68 per cent of males and 43 per cent of females who masturbated during the next twenty-four hours thought about the erotic scenes whilst doing so (Schmidt and Sigusch, 1970). Similarly, Brown *et al.* (1976) noted that 67 per cent of their subjects reported thinking about the erotica later with 23 per cent reporting the onset of spontaneous sex arousal accompanied by thoughts of the erotica. In the Kutschinsky (1971b) study, 20 per cent of the men and 5 per cent of the women declared they would sometimes use pornography when masturbating. All these observations point to the likelihood of the material acting to modify existing sexual preferences in accordance with conditioning theory. Unfortunately, no information is given in these studies on the types of sexual activity that people are most inclined to incorporate into their fantasies. On the other hand, although the final report erroneously states that 'The Commission has limited its concern to sexual obscenity, including sadomasochistic material', it is perhaps fortunate that the researchers instead tended to employ only 'soft-core' material.

The Commission overlooked two areas relevant to the conditioning of new preferences, namely research on the development of a sexual attraction to boots and research on the effectiveness with which erotica are used by therapists to change sexual orientation; both of these areas were being researched before the Commission started and will be discussed in the next chapter. The Commission also overlooked evidence pertaining to a link between sex and violence when summarizing its findings on anti-social behaviour. This was particularly surprising in view of therapists often citing cases where pornography is believed to be an instigator or contributor to sex crimes or other anti-social acts, and also in view of the original German studies finding changes in mood in the direction of increased aggressiveness and decreased friendli-

---

Table 23

Amoroso *et al.* (1971)   Male students spent more time looking at erotic slides when alone than when observed by graduate students. Although none of the slides were considered 'hard-core', the more pornographic were rated as both stimulating and unpleasant and were looked at for longer – provided there was not an audience.

Brown *et al.* (1976)   In a later analysis of the above study, 77 per cent of the students rated the session as enjoyable while 21 per cent reported feelings of disgust. Significantly, 60 per cent admitted 'using their imagination to add to the slides', while 21 per cent tried to control their sexual arousal.

Byrne and Lamberth (1971)   Married couples who rated their feelings before and after a session of erotica revealed an increase in arousal, disgust and boredom, and a decrease in anxiety, fear and curiosity. Imagining each of nineteen erotic themes led to much greater arousal than did exposure to either pictorial or prose presentation, especially for females.

Kutschinsky (1971b)   During exposure to one hour of pornography, married students reported an increase in boredom and a decrease in mirth. For males, there was also an increase in disappointment and a decrease in tension. Sexual arousal was felt from the beginning of the session by 42 per cent of males and 9 per cent of females while at the end it was felt by 24 per cent of both sexes.

ness after viewing erotica (Schmidt and Sigusch, 1970; Schmidt *et al.*, 1973). Moreover, one of the Commission's own studies revealed an increase in feeling angry for men relative to women after reading erotic stories (Byrne and Lamberth, 1971), and another two of the studies dealt specifically with the link between sexual arousal and aggression (Mosher and Katz, 1971; Tannenbaum, 1971). Because of the potential importance of this issue – there were 60,000 cases of marital violence reported last year in Britain – and because the Commission overlooked even its own evidence, we shall describe the two most relevant studies and then briefly outline the research that has since been conducted.

Mosher and Katz (1971) provided evidence that the desire for sexual stimulation can override conscience and guilt by allowing verbal aggression to be expressed against a female. What they did was to show male students examples of aggressive and derogatory comments and accusations (e.g. 'You really are a dumb ——!') and then asked them to be as verbally aggressive as possible against a female assistant. After being shown a film, the students were asked to repeat their attack against the female, being told that they had to achieve an increase in their level of aggression if they wanted to see an exciting sex film. Needless to say, aggression did increase when made instrumental to seeing this sex film. Although this result was fairly obvious, it may generalize to a real-life situation in which obtaining sex with a female can depend on the forcefulness with which the man 'encourages' her. A more interesting finding was that even males with a severe conscience and guilt about aggression increased the severity of their attack. It appeared that the female assistant was perceived to have a 'spoiled' or 'bad girl' image which made her a suitable target; after all, the morals of a girl who willingly takes part in such an experiment must be suspect! Although not specifically investigated, an even more interesting finding was that different females elicited different degrees of aggression. More detailed work along these lines will help identify the type of girl who is most vulnerable as a potential victim of sexual assault.

Tannenbaum (1971) provided evidence that censorship of an erotic scene in a film can increase aggression. A romantic setting, involving ocean waves crashing onto rocks and dappled sunlight streaming through leaves, was artistically portrayed with two lovers engaged in sex play and intercourse complete with a symbolic representation of its aftermath. Male students were shown one of three versions: the original with or without the intercourse scene, or a 'scenario' version in which the intercourse was replaced by a written description of it. The students had earlier been angered by a confederate of the experimenter, and now they had the chance for revenge, being asked to administer electric shocks to him as part of another study. A significantly higher level of shock was applied by those students who had seen the scenario version of the film. It appeared that their feelings of aggression had been intensified by the frustration of having their sexual appetite whetted and then having their attention drawn to the nature of the censored scene.

A similar study involved a direct test of the hypothesis that sexual arousal can facilitate aggression. Students were shown excerpts from an erotic film (*The Couch*), a violent film (*Body and Soul*) or a neutral film (*Marco Polo*). Table 24 shows that higher

Table 24	Effects of films on aggression	
Type of film	*Mean shock intensity*	*Mean blood pressure index*
Erotic	5.1	17.8
Violent	3.9	4.7
Neutral	3.1	2.6

Higher shocks were administered in revenge by students who had seen an arousing erotic film rather than a violent film.

(Based on Tannenbaum, 1971)

shocks were administered to the confederate after the erotic film than after the violent film. This must not be taken as evidence of catharsis, since the neutral film resulted in less aggression than either. A possible explanation for this result was suggested by blood pressure measures being highest for the erotic group, which points to a general heightening of arousal as a result of the erotic film. Blood pressure change is an index of drive which, in accordance with Clark Hull's theory, will tend to be expressed in terms of predominant habits, which in this case are concerned with the taking of revenge. In the light of subsequent research, however, this appears at best only a partial explanation.

Many studies have been designed along similar lines, and three examples are included in Table 25. Consistent with the above results, Zillmann (1971) found that an erotic film had significantly more effect on a subject's aggressiveness than did a neutral or even a violent film. Several other researchers, however, have found evidence of the very reverse. For example, relative to neutral pictures, pin-ups were found to actually inhibit aggression (Donnerstein *et al.*, 1975). This result is difficult to explain. Since the erotica were almost certainly more arousing than the neutral material, a reduction of aggression below that of the neutral group cannot be explained in terms of lowered drive levels. Nor can it be explained in terms of sexual desires being frustrated in the experimental situation.

How, then, can the contradictory results be explained? Clues can be sought in terms of differences between the two sets of research, but a definite answer is unlikely because they involved different procedures as well as different types of erotica. Unfortunately, work in this field has not proceeded along the conventional scientific lines of first replicating and then extending by changing only one variable at a time. It is not even possible to compare the intensity of the different erotica employed, since measures of physiological arousal were taken in some studies and subjective ratings in others. Nevertheless, it appears that mild forms of erotica have tended to inhibit aggression while more explicit or 'hard-core' material has acted to facilitate it. This makes sense in terms of the different mood states generated by the two types of material. Mild erotica involving aesthetically pleasing poses, or tender and affectionate lovemaking, might be expected to give rise to pleasurable feelings which would appear incompatible with the expression of aggression. Explicit or 'hard-core' material, on the other hand, might be expected to induce unpleasant feelings along with arousal which would be compatible with aggression. Consistent with this interpretation, it may be noted that Schmidt *et al.* (1973) found evidence of increased feelings of aggression only after reading erotic stories devoid of love and affection. Baron and Bell (1977) made a direct attempt to reconcile the divergent outcomes from previous research by comparing the

Table 25

Mosher and Katz (1971)   120 male students were asked to verbally assault one of four female assistants for two minutes, while she was completing an IQ type task, before and after viewing a ten-minute erotic or neutral film. A significant increase in aggression did not result from seeing the erotic film, but it did when made conditional upon seeing a more exciting erotic film.

Tannenbaum (1971)   In a series of studies, male students were shown excerpts from one of several films. Aggression towards someone who had earlier shocked them was higher after seeing erotic than either violent or neutral films. It was particularly high for an erotic film where attention was drawn to a censored scene.

Zillmann (1971)   In previously angered subjects, an erotic film induced higher shocks on the 'aggression machine' than did a boxing or neutral film. Strong physiological arousal was indicated only for the erotica.

Donnerstein *et al.* (1975)   Relative to neutral pictures, mild erotica reduced aggression while scenes of lovemaking had no effect in previously angered subjects. For subjects angered after exposure, however, aggression was facilitated by the erotic pictures.

Baron and Bell (1977)   85 male students were shown pictures ranging from neutral to explicitly erotic. Relative to the amount of aggression expressed by the subjects who had seen the neutral pictures, slightly less resulted from scenes of lovemaking and least of all from pin-ups.

effects of different levels of erotica. The intensity of shocks administered via the 'aggression machine' was lowest for pin-ups, intermediate for scenes of lovemaking, and highest for neutral material. Unfortunately, no 'hard-core' material was included and so the chance was missed of completing the picture by seeing if this resulted in more aggression than the neutral material.

Future research will need to take into account the reactions of individual subjects as well as the type of material. What is pleasantly erotic to one person may be unpleasantly por- nographic to another, and to combine results from such diverse groups can only act to obscure the issue. Apart from subjective ratings of the emotions aroused by the material, it is necessary to include objective measures, such as blood pressure, in order to determine the effect of general arousal on aggression. The complexity of this issue will be referred to again in Chapter 10 in connection with individual differences; at this point we may just note the advantages of the laboratory approach over less refined methods in the isolation and investigation of relevant variables.

SUMMARY

The laboratory method has scientific rigour and it is usually possible to arrange for optimal conditions for maximizing the chances of detecting effects. Even though criticized as artificial, it is the method of choice since the problems involved are at least known and steps can be taken to control them. Modelled aggression for children has invariably led to imitation, and usually disinhibition as well, especially if the subject is frustrated and encouraged by the provision of a permissive atmosphere. Similarly, violent films have a disinhibiting effect on people if they are presented with an acceptable opportunity to express their aggression. Moreover, boys who expressed pleasure while watching violence were particularly likely to hurt another child when given the chance. In studies that have not obtained these effects, it is usually apparent that conditions were acting to prevent the expression of all but the most extreme feelings of aggression.

In the only study of its kind, imitation of an uninhibited model has been demonstrated for male students in looking at erotic, but not neutral, pictures in the presence of a female experimenter; this suggests that imitation is particularly likely under conditions of emotional arousal and uncertainty, as in many sexual situations. The immediate effects of erotica are reported to include physiological arousal, such as erections, but it appears that subjects facilitate this reaction by adding their own imagination to the erotica. Mood changes tend to accompany exposure to erotica, and for explicit materials these changes tend to involve negative emotions together with arousal, especially among sexually inexperienced subjects. Other experiments have demonstrated that the viewing of mild erotica acts to inhibit the expression of aggression, while more explicit material acts to facilitate aggression; it appears that emotional arousal combined with the negative hedonic tone that usually accompanies 'hard-core' pornography is responsible for the facilitating effect.

8 Investigation of Basic Issues

When the second moon walk was televised, there was a marked reduction in the number of viewers. A similar problem confronts the producers of films and TV programmes that depend for their appeal mainly on the portrayal of violence. Audience figures are not going to be maintained if each time only one man gets killed by shooting; producers are for ever on the look-out for new, and more extreme, forms of violence. This is why we have been treated in *Marathon Man* to the sight of Laurence Olivier torturing Dustin Hoffman with a dentist's drill! To quote the head of the film company that made *Death Race 2000*: 'Violence is going to escalate because the public always demands more than they saw last time out.' Among the issues dealt with in this chapter, we shall be concerned with the question of whether people really do develop a 'thick skin' and get used to violence. The relevant theory here is that people, by constant exposure to violence, will eventually become 'desensitized' and no longer be upset or aroused by witnessing violence.

When feeling emotional we tend to sweat, and very slight increases in moisture can be detected electrically by what is known as a 'galvanic skin response' or 'skin conductance' measure. This highly sensitive indicator of emotional arousal, which is used in 'lie detector' tests, was being used in a study in which students were shown a film of an aboriginal ceremony that vividly depicted a sequence of crude operations performed with a piece of flint on several adolescent boys (Lazarus *et al.*, 1962). Skin conductance tended to 'peak' every time there was a particularly gory scene, but these peaks were not as high towards the end of the film as they were at the beginning. This is evidence of desensitization, but, because this demonstration was not the main point of the study, no attempt was made to control for alternative interpretations such as the later scenes being less horrific and so accounting for the decline in emotional responsiveness.

Fortunately this necessary control was incorporated in the design of an experiment by Berger (1962). Galvanic skin responses were monitored in fifteen subjects who either watched a man being given a series of electric shocks in order 'to see what level he could take' or the same man merely having his galvanic skin responses recorded. The 'victim' was in fact a confederate of the experimenter, and the subjects were reassured that it would not be necessary to give them shocks. Skin responses were evident in the experimental subjects each time the victim jerked his arm at the shock, but their emotional response became less with each repetition of the procedure.

Heart rate and self-reported distress were monitored as well as skin conductance in a study of habituation to an industrial accident film (Averill *et al.*, 1972). Male students were shown twenty repetitions of either a gruesome accident or a benign scene, and then the complete film involving three accidents. This procedure was repeated on three occasions, and each time prior exposure to the accident scene was found to reduce emotional arousal when that same scene was viewed in the context of the whole film. There was, however, little evidence of generalization since emotional responses to the other two accidents were similar for the control and experimental subjects. This lack of desensitization to the new accidents helps explain why the interest of existing TV audiences is maintained if producers provide them with new forms of violence. Nevertheless, generalization is known to occur in other situations and it may not have become apparent in this study simply because it may need more than three days of brief exposure to one type of violence in order to manifest itself. Evidence from a field study does in fact suggest that generalization to TV violence occurs in real life; this study is listed together with the above in Table 26.

Boys were shown a sequence, including a brutal boxing scene, from a Kirk Douglas film (Cline *et al.*, 1973). Galvanic skin response and blood volume pulse amplitude were recorded before and during this film for two groups of boys. One group had been selected on the basis of having watched TV for twenty-five hours or more a week over the previous two years, and the other for four hours or less a week. Emotional arousal during the violent scene was less for the 'hardened' viewers than it was for the 'low exposure' controls, whereas before this scene the physiological measures were similar for the two

Table 26

Lazarus *et al.* (1962)   A progressive drop in skin conductance was noted for 70 students while watching a seventeen-minute film of primitive mutilation.

Berger (1962)   Compared with a control group, galvanic skin responses occurred more frequently for subjects who were witnessing a man being shocked, but these responses steadily declined over thirteen trials.

Averill *et al.* (1972)   For three days, 45 students watched a twenty-five second accident scene twenty times at half-minute intervals before seeing a twelve-minute film in which this was one of three accidents. Compared with 23 control subjects, emotional arousal was significantly reduced only for the accident to which they had been desensitized.

Cline *et al.* (1973)   Boys aged 5 to 14 years were selected on the basis of high or low exposure to TV. While watching an eight-minute violent scene in a fourteen-minute film, emotional responses were lower for 17 'high exposure' than for 15 'low exposure' boys.

groups. Because this was a field study, the results suffer from a weakness inherent in the method, namely that alternative interpretations are always apparent. For example, if boys who are particularly sensitive to violence are less inclined to watch TV, then this alone could be sufficient to account for the results obtained. Because of this limitation we shall return to laboratory studies, which also provide important evidence of desensitization to violence generalizing to another situation.

In one of the few studies in the Surgeon General's Commission to be concerned with desensitization, children were shown either a violent *Peter Gunn* or a neutral *Green Acres* TV episode, and then compared in a test for awareness of violence (Rabinovitch *et al.*, 1972). The test involved a stereoscopic projector by which two slides can be presented simultaneously to each eye so quickly that only one is seen. Nine pairs of slides were used in which one portrayed a violent and the other a neutral scene. For example, a man hitting another over the head with a gun was paired with a picture of a man helping another hit a pole into the ground with a gun butt. The children were asked to write down descriptions of what they saw, and it was the group who had just seen *Peter Gunn* who identified fewer of the violent pictures. This constitutes evidence that the violent programme, by making them temporarily less sensitive to violence, blunted their awareness of the violent pictures. It is difficult to think of an alternative interpretation of this result unless it was catharsis making the violent group think of peaceful rather than violent scenes.

Evidence that attitudes in real life can be influenced by a violent film is provided in an ingenious experiment by Drabman and Thomas (1974). Children who had watched a violent scene from *Hopalong Cassidy* were compared with a control group, who had not seen a film, for tolerance of violent acts. This was done by asking each subject to keep an eye on a couple of children who were playing in another room, and to summon the experimenter if there was any trouble. They were able to watch the children by way of a videotape monitor; by this technique it was possible to arrange for both groups of subjects to see exactly the same sequence of events. After playing peacefully the two children started to abuse each other verbally and then to fight during the course of which the TV camera was knocked over and contact was eventually lost. The measure of attitude to aggression was the time taken before the subject sought help from the experimenter, and these results are presented in Table 27.

Table 27	Effects of films on toleration of aggression	
	Violent film	*No film*
Boys	104 seconds	63 seconds
Girls	119 seconds	75 seconds

Time taken before notifying the experimenter of an altercation between two younger children for whom the subject had taken responsibility.

(Based on Drabman and Thomas, 1974)

Just over half the control subjects notified the experimenter of the argument before physical fighting began, whereas only 17 per cent of the film group did so. Whether these results were obtained because of a temporary reduction in emotional responsivity in the film group, or simply because the argument and fighting appeared trivial in comparison with the filmed violence, they constitute strong evidence that a violent film can lead to increased tolerance of aggression. One criticism, however, is apparent and this concerns the possibility that the film group took less notice of their responsibility because they were still thinking of the exciting film. It would have been better if the control subjects had been shown an exciting but non-violent film instead of nothing. This was duly done in a replication by Thomas and Drabman (1975) and the result still held; children who had watched an excerpt from *Mannix* took an average of 145 seconds before summoning help, whereas those who had watched an exciting baseball film took only 88 seconds.

Thomas *et al.* (1977) attempted to produce temporary desensitization by showing children a violent TV police drama, and then assessed the effect in terms of their response to a videotape of two pre-school children fighting. Compared with a control group who were shown an exciting volleyball game, the 'desensitized' children responded with fewer galvanic skin responses when shown the videotape of 'real' aggression. This again provides evidence that the viewing of TV violence can make children inured to real-life violence, only this time there is the additional information that after watching TV they feel less emotional when witnessing scenes of real fighting. The study was repeated with students, except that news films of riots were used instead of the fighting scenes, and similar results were obtained at least for males.

The above studies, which are summarized in Table 28, have all provided evidence of desensitization to violence. That desensitization occurs is not really in doubt, although we have noted that generalization to other forms of violence is a very gradual process. It probably requires years of ardent viewing before people become immune to whatever type of violence is next to appear on the screens. According to the reports of cinema managers, some members of the audience fainted or were sick during the screening of *Soldier Blue* and *A Clockwork Orange*. Presumably these viewers had not been sufficiently 'desensitized' for films of such a violent nature. Carruthers and Taggart (1973) took electrocardiogram recordings and other physiological measures from adult men and women watching these two films. Reactions to the violent scenes were assessed

Table 28

Rabinovitch *et al.* (1972)   57 children, aged 11 to 12 years, watched either a violent or a neutral TV programme, and were then shown pictures of violent and neutral scenes flashed momentarily before them. The violent group were less likely than the controls to notice the violent pictures.

Drabman and Thomas (1974)   44 children, aged 8 to 10 years, watched either an eight-minute violent film or nothing, and were then asked to keep an eye on two younger children. The violent group were less likely than the controls to call the experimenter when the children started to fight.

Thomas and Drabman (1975)   In a replication of the above study, 20 children who had just seen a fifteen-minute violent detective film on TV were slower to summon help than were 20 controls who saw an exciting non-violent film. This result was not apparent, however, for younger children aged 6 to 7 years.

Thomas *et al.* (1977)   28 boys and 16 girls, aged 8 to 10 years, were shown either a violent police drama or an equally emotion-arousing sports film. Subsequently, a videotape of real-life aggression (children fighting) produced less emotional response (skin resistance) in the violent group. Similar results were obtained for 29 male students, but not 30 females, in a replication. In both studies, amount of TV violence normally viewed was negatively related to responsivity while viewing aggression.

relative to baseline measures taken during pre-film commercials. The interesting observation was made that although there was increased adrenaline excretion, indicating excitement or arousal, there was also a slowing of the heart, indicating horror or revulsion, during the most violent scenes. In some people the heart rate slowed even below forty beats per minute; this provides an explanation for the fainting attacks since with a drastically slowed heart beat insufficient blood may be reaching the brain to retain consciousness. A very interesting extension to this research would be to observe changes in these physiological measures during a process of desensitization. If the aversive reaction habituates more rapidly than the excitement reaction, then we would have the ominous prospect of the 'hardened' viewer responding to such films only with excitement.

In an earlier review of the desensitization evidence, Howitt and Cumberbatch (1975) commented that 'it is very likely that this process of habituation does occur for mass media violence . . . but the social consequences of this are unclear'. One such consequence is that desensitization, by reducing anxiety, may make people more likely to carry out acts of aggression in the future. In other words, in order to commit an act of aggression it may be necessary to overcome certain inhibitions, and this is where prior exposure, even if only to acts of a similar nature on the screen, probably helps. The experiment by Drabman and Thomas indicates another social consequence. As people become more and more used to violence, there is the danger that they will come to accept and tolerate it. If witnessed continually, violence may eventually come to be regarded as normal behaviour.

The effects of desensitization to violence have been generally overlooked by theorists in favour of the imitation and disinhibition effects that were discussed in the previous chapter. But it seems to us that the consequences of a nation 'desensitized' to violence are just as serious, if not more so, than one which is merely exposed to examples of how to be violent. To complete this section of the present chapter we need to consider the evidence for two other theories, starting with the one proposed by Gerbner and Gross.

Children and, to a lesser extent, adults often see TV fiction as true to life, and sometimes even look upon fictional characters as real people. During the first five years of *Marcus Welby, M.D.*, viewers sent him 250,000 letters, mostly with requests for medical advice. In an early study, children with high and low exposure to TV were referred to such programmes as *The FBI* and asked 'Do things like this happen in real life?' Those who watched a lot of TV were more likely than the others to give an affirmative answer, especially if they also admitted to having many problems (Bailyn, 1959). This does not necessarily mean that heavy viewing contributes to the belief that TV represents reality; the connection could equally well be due to such other factors as low intelligence being related to both frequent viewing and the tendency to confuse fiction and reality. Frequent viewing is part of a syndrome that includes low education, low geographical mobility, low aspirations and high anxiety, and any of these could be associated with seeing TV as portraying everyday events. Bearing this in mind, it makes sense to compare heavy with light viewers only if they are matched in terms of all relevant characteristics, but since the nature of many of these may not be known, the task becomes impossible. Nevertheless, as an academic exercise we shall describe a widely quoted large-scale study where at least some effort was made to match the two groups of viewers.

Gerbner and Gross (1976) compared adults in the US who watched TV for at least four hours a day with those who watched for two hours or less a day. They were asked questions such as 'About what percent of the world's population live in the United States?' Because most of the leading characters on TV are American, it was predicted that heavy viewers would tend to over-estimate. Given the choice of 3 or 9 per cent, the true answer being somewhere in between, heavy viewers were 19 per cent more likely than light viewers to choose the higher figure. For each question, people were asked to select from two answers, one of which was slanted in the direction of how the world is presented on TV. For example, for the question 'During any given week, what are your chances of being involved in some type of violence?', they were given the choice of 1 in 10 (the 'TV answer') or 1 in 100. Table 29 gives the proportion of people who chose the 'TV answer' in response to this and two other questions. In each case, heavy viewers were more likely to select the 'TV answer', which was interpreted as indicating a heightened sense of fear and mistrust of other people.

The next step was to see if differences still existed between

Table 29   Beliefs of TV viewers

	Heavy viewers	*Light viewers*
Number of men involved in law enforcement	59	50
Most people cannot be trusted	65	48
Chances of being personally involved in violence	52	39

Scores refer to the percentages of people giving answers slanted in the direction of the 'TV world'.

(Based on Gerbner and Gross, 1976)

the groups when they were matched for certain characteristics. After dividing the sample into people with and without a college education, there was still a tendency within each of these sub-groups for the 'TV answer' to be given by heavy rather than light viewers. The same applied when the sample was divided in terms of sex, age, and whether or not they were regular readers of a newspaper. Rather than equating the groups on each of these variables in turn, it would have been preferable to have matched them on all the variables at the same time in the first place. If this had been done, it is possible that the results obtained for heavy and light viewers would no longer have differed. This is in fact what happened when the study was repeated in London with two groups equated from the beginning for sex, age and social class (Wober and Dannheisser, 1977).

The Gerbner and Gross theory is, firstly, that constant exposure to TV will give people the impression that the world is a more violent place than it really is and, secondly, that this impression will cause them anxiety and encourage paranoid feelings about their fellow citizens. Evidence for the first part of this theory has not been established, with the best controlled study finding no difference in the beliefs of heavy and light viewers. Moreover, the second part of the theory conflicts with the 'desensitization' evidence that exposure to TV violence leads to a decrease rather than an increase in anxiety. On this evidence, it should be people with low rather than high exposure who react to scenes of violence with heightened anxiety. Some people are undoubtedly prone to interpret TV as depicting what life is like on the outside, and they may also react to this with feelings of anxiety and depression. But it seems more likely that people respond in this way because of personality characteristics than because they watch a lot of TV.

Another theory that conflicts with predictions from 'desensitization' theory is catharsis. Although very few studies have provided support for catharsis while many have indicated the exact opposite, the theory is widely accepted. A doctor advised a distraught client, whose wife had just left him for another man, to take up football and pretend that the ball was the other man's head. The advice was taken, but giving his rival a make-believe booting did not relieve his stress and anger, and he ended up in court charged with smashing the other man over the head with a metal cosh. Had the doctor been aware of the extremely tenuous nature of the evidence for catharsis, he might have been inclined to offer a more effective form of advice. We noted earlier that an experimental field study which was claimed to support the catharsis theory could be readily interpreted in another way. Alternative explanations are also apparent for the few other studies which run counter to the general weight of evidence that viewing violence leads to aggression rather than contentment.

Feshbach (1955) angered students by making derogatory comments about them and requesting that for the purposes of an experiment they act like adults rather than adolescents. They were then given the chance to discharge the aggression they felt as a result of being insulted by writing dramatic stories in a measure of fantasy known as the Thematic Apperception Test. Predictably, they expressed significantly more aggression in their stories than did control subjects who had not been insulted. The effect of the 'substitute' activity on their level of aggression was then assessed by means of a questionnaire concerned with attitudes to the experimenter and the experiment, and by a Sentence Completion Test in which the number of aggressive responses was taken as an index of aggression. Compared with subjects who had been involved in aptitude tests rather than the writing of aggressive stories, they obtained significantly lower scores on these two measures of aggression. This was presented as evidence that aggression can be partly discharged by a substitute activity, in this case the mere writing of aggressive stories.

In another experiment, Feshbach (1961) used a ten-minute film clip of a fight, instead of story writing, as the substitute means of discharging aggression. Using a similar procedure to the above, students who had been insulted by unwarranted and extremely critical remarks appeared to successfully discharge part of their resulting anger by watching the violent film rather than a neutral film about a factory. It is important to note that this result is the very opposite to that obtained in most other studies; the viewing of a violent film usually leads to more aggression than does a neutral film. Feshbach argued that his study differed from previous ones in that his subjects were angry at the time of viewing, and so they were able to use vicarious participation in the film to satisfy and thereby reduce their hostility. This argument, however, no longer applies since in subsequent studies the subjects have been angered before as well as after seeing a film, and in either case a violent film tends to increase rather than decrease aggression. Viewed in the context of these other results, it appears likely that the present results were due to some accident of chance. Nevertheless, even taken at face value, do they really provide evidence of catharsis? An alternative interpretation of the results in that guilt, revulsion or anxiety, aroused by the watching of a violent film or the writing of aggressive stories, was responsible for the apparent lowering of aggression merely by inhibiting its expression.

Berkowitz and Rawlings (1963) provide an interesting example of a study that attempted to control for the possibility that a violent film arouses inhibitions by introducing the film clip in such a way that the violence could be justified, and so be less likely to arouse inhibitions. According to the catharsis theory, the angered subjects could enter vicariously into the scene and work off their aggression by identifying with the winning fighter. But, consistent with the 'inhibition' interpretation, these subjects instead expressed more aggression than did others who had seen the same film but with an introduction that did not serve to justify the violence. A control condition of a neutral film was not included and so the chance was missed of checking whether Feshbach's original result could be replicated; but, as we have noted, this has since been done – the relevant experiments being described in other chapters.

In two recent and very comprehensive reviews it was concluded that violence, whether actually indulged in or just viewed vicariously, tends to facilitate aggression (Geen, 1978; Geen and Quanty, 1977). What little evidence there is for catharsis can be re-interpreted in terms of inhibitions against the expression of aggression because of the procedures used; when such inhibitions are minimized the opposite of catharsis occurs. Not only is it untenable to argue that 'the battle of Waterloo was won on the playing fields of Eton', it is also untenable to argue that wars can be prevented there.

Theories that appear particularly relevant to predicting the effects of pornography include imitation, conditioning and desensitization. The absence of experimental studies designed to evoke imitation of modelled sexual activity was noted in the previous chapter. Similarly, there are no studies directly aimed at increasing sexual activity by 'desensitizing' inhibitions that may be preventing it. Nevertheless, techniques in therapy are based on these theories; some examples will be given presently. But first we shall turn to a consideration of conditioning theory.

Conditioning appears directly relevant to the development of sexual deviations, and yet only two studies have been conducted. Rachman (1966) was interested in the possibility that a boot fetish could be created by 'classical conditioning'. Three male students were selected who responded with some degree of erection when shown slides of sexually provocative women. A picture of a pair of black knee-length female boots, which did not evoke such a response, was then shown to each subject immediately before one of the pin-ups. This procedure was repeated eighteen times during each of several sessions. According to the theory of conditioning, the neutral stimulus of the boots should in time become associated with the reward provided by the pin-ups. This is what happened, since after thirty or so pairings each of the subjects began to respond with erections to the boots. They were then tested by showing them pictures of other boots and shoes, and consistent with the principle of 'generalization' there was a slight tendency for erections to occur with these objects. For ethical reasons it was decided not to leave the subjects with their new-found interest in female footwear, and so a procedure of 'extinction' was instituted. The boots were shown continuously without the reward of an accompanying female until any sign of an erection had vanished. The subjects were re-tested one week later, and consistent with the principle of 'spontaneous recovery', erections were again apparent when the boots were presented. Extinction trials were again carried out and the subjects were eventually declared officially 'cured'.

Because of the potential importance of this demonstration, the study was repeated and a similar result was obtained with another five subjects (Rachman and Hodgson, 1968). To help rule out the possibility that the results were due to faking or pseudo-conditioning, a control condition was instituted. In this control condition, the subjects were shown the scantily-clad females immediately before rather than after the presentation of the boots. This is the procedure for 'backward-conditioning', which is known from other work to be very hard to establish, and so it proved in the present case with none of the subjects responding with erections to the boots under these 'reversed' conditions.

These studies provide evidence that sexual arousal can be conditioned to a previously neutral stimulus, and may explain why some men prefer a naked woman, others a woman in clothes, and yet others clothes without a woman in them! To demonstrate a 'true' fetish it would of course be necessary to demonstrate that the boots had become the only sexual interest, or at least that the boots had acquired more arousal value than the pin-ups. It is only when a fetish reaches such a stage that the preference seems likely to be transformed into real-life behaviour. In the case of the experimentally conditioned interest in boots, the pin-ups were still preferred and so the subjects would have been unlikely to need to include boots in their sexual adventures.

The theory of conditioning, combined with the evidence from the above studies, indicates that it might be possible to create a rapist or sadist in the laboratory by presenting scenes of rape or sadism immediately prior to normally arousing scenes. Had this been done then perhaps the Pornography Commission would not have overlooked this line of research! An interesting extension would have been to see whether erections could be conditioned just as easily to 'truly' neutral stimuli; it seems likely that such conditioning is easier for stimuli that already have 'symbolic' sexual significance, which may well be the case for knee-length female boots. Relevant research has in fact been conducted, and it appears that it is indeed difficult to condition men to respond with erections to pictures that have no sexual association. Although evidence of slight arousal to coloured circles and triangles was obtained by McConaghy (1967), virtually no response to pictures of polygons was apparent in research by Langevin and Martin (1975) even when they used the potentially stronger reward of erotic films rather than pin-ups. The significance of this research will be considered in a moment in connection with the theory of 'preparedness'.

In the original McGuire et al. (1965) study, it was considered to be early real-life experiences that led to the development of sexual deviations. Could pornography, by providing an early sexual experience, have a similar effect? Many claims have been made that exposure to pornography can lead to sexual

deviancy. It has been reported to increase the desire to masturbate, with some men preferring to look at pornography rather
than interacting with a real wife (Cline, 1974). The story has
also been related of how some men got the idea from pornographic films and magazines of persuading their wives to
have sex with other women while they watched. The men
thought that this might provide a source of excitement for
themselves, but in the event it was the wives who 'benefited'
with 65 per cent of them coming to prefer the lesbian acts to
heterosexual group sex (Bartell, 1970). Similarly, Cline points
out the possible dangers involved in the homosexual practice of
showing erotica to boys in order to get them aroused before
attempting a seduction; it is suggested that the boys' arousal
could through conditioning become linked with the homosexual act.

It is unlikely that exposure to pornography on its own is
sufficient to lead to sexual deviations. But there are several
ways in which it might be supplemented. According to the
McGuire *et al.* theory, it is sexual fantasy reinforced by orgasm
that leads to the development of sexual preferences. Among the
deviates they studied, a common fantasy was their first real
sexual experience; in their case it happened to be of a deviant
nature. Apart from providing this first sexual experience,
pornography could possibly influence sexual development by
suggesting new fantasies. It could also have an influence by
providing additional stimulation during masturbation; some
men do in fact use it for this purpose (Athanasiou and Shauer,
1971). Through the positive feedback provided by sexual
excitement and orgasm, images from pornography or fantasy
would tend to acquire an increasing degree of significance.

In addition to fantasy reinforcement, it is also possible that
some degree of predisposition or 'preparedness' is necessary in
order for a full-scale fetish or sexual deviation to develop. In
connection with phobias, Seligman (1971) has pointed out that
they are selective or 'non-arbitrary', being usually concerned
with objects or situations of natural importance to the survival
of the species. This suggests that phobias may represent 'prepared' learning, an idea reinforced by the observation that they
can be acquired in a single trial and by their tendency to be
peculiarly resistant to extinction. In contrast, conditioned fears
to 'neutral' objects in the laboratory require many trials and

soon extinguish. It is possible that a combination of biological preparedness and learning applies in the case of sexual deviations, although here there does not seem to be any evolutionary significance involved. Consistent with this extension of the theory of 'preparedness' to sexual deviations is the evidence that it is easier to develop a 'conditioned' attraction to boots than it is to geometrical shapes. Predisposition to acquire a sexual deviation would probably be transmitted genetically, although there is little evidence for this.

The possibility of a genetic influence was raised by Gorman (1964) who, after noting reports of homosexuality and transvestism in identical twins, described a case of rubber fetishism. A pair of identical twins developed an attraction to rubber independently and unknown to each other, and under similar circumstances and at a similar age (five and six years). In both cases, it was based on an initial sexual experience; in one case being wrapped after a bath in a rubber cape which was found to be highly pleasurable and in the other finding erotic stimulation from a rubber cot sheet. Following these discoveries, the boys often used the cape and sheet and also rubber garments for obtaining erotic sensations. It was not until they were aged ten years that they disclosed to each other that they had this interest. While this case history is consistent with heredity playing a part in the development of sexual preferences, it hardly constitutes scientific evidence, nor does it rule out the possible role of conditioning. In the absence of more information, all we can say is that both mechanisms may be involved in the formation of sexual preferences.

Consistent with the notion of preparedness is the early age at which awareness of having a fetish or sexual deviation first occurs. According to 100 members of the 'Mackintosh Society', their attraction to rubber was first experienced at an average age of ten years (Gosselin, 1978). Although most of the 'rubberites' claimed that their particular interest was an adjunct to 'normal' sex and not a substitute, preparedness may also be indicated by an early awareness of a lack of interest in normal sex. McGuire *et al.* (1965) reported that many of their deviates held the belief that a normal sex life was not possible for them, and that this belief usually predated awareness of their particular deviation – which again tended to occur before puberty.

When fetishes are held in addition to conventional sexual

desires, they may be regarded as a harmless extra interest. It is only if they interfere with a normal sex life that treatment may be requested. Similarly, in the case of the potentially more serious deviations such as sadism, treatment is likely to be indicated only if other people are suffering. Before turning to a consideration of the part that pornography plays in modern treatment, we must again mention the absence of experimental demonstrations on the effects of 'desensitization'. Although several such studies have been carried out for violence, none have yet been reported for pornography. Partial evidence for desensitization is available from those studies that assessed changes in attitude to sex as a result of a single exposure to pornography. As we saw in the last chapter, the finding was that most subjects tended to become more liberal in their attitudes; the exceptions tended to include the more religious, conservative and sexually inexperienced subjects who reacted by adopting a more restrictive outlook. Even for these latter subjects it would presumably be possible, by repeated exposure under relaxing conditions, to demonstrate a reduction of anxiety, guilt and other negative feelings about sex. For ethical reasons this has not been done; it is pertinent to note that desensitization to the expression of aggression is considered more acceptable than a similar procedure for the expression of sexual desires.

Erotica are used in treatment for a variety of reasons. Explicit films are used to illustrate techniques of lovemaking in sex education. If it is important that this information is conveyed in the context of a loving relationship, this can be done much more effectively on film than as a lecture. The films used for sex education classes have had to be made specially since commercial films are considered generally unsuitable; the typical pornographic film does not portray positive sexual experiences, nor does it involve a gradual build-up of sexual arousal. Because of the assumed critical experience of a child's introduction to sex, whether in theory or practice, it is a source of some amazement that it is still left to chance factors such as seeing pornography or receiving a 'cold' biologically-oriented lecture.

Films are also useful for 'attitude restructuring' in sex therapy. Watching other people indulging in activities which the viewer considers unacceptable tends to result in a relaxation of existing taboos. Again, this has to be done in the right way, for example, by showing the people in the film really enjoying themselves. This approach is adopted for patients with a very restrictive view of sex, and is carried out in a gradual fashion, starting off with mild scenes of kissing and undressing and eventually ending up with advanced forms of petting, such as oral sex, and various techniques of intercourse. The idea is to give the patient the idea that 'anything goes' in sex, and it is claimed that this method tends to work even if the patient adopts only the milder techniques portrayed in the films.

Erotica are also used for dealing with specific difficulties such as anxiety preventing the occurrence of orgasm. An example will serve to illustrate the sort of thing that is done. Reisinger (1974) was treating a 23-year-old college girl who enjoyed sex but had never experienced orgasm. To maximize the chances of success it was decided to reduce anxiety by training the girl in relaxation, and to begin with a technique most likely to produce an orgasm. Many women claim that their most intense orgasms occur when masturbating, rather than during intercourse (Masters and Johnson, 1966), and so the girl was instructed to locate her most sensitive areas and to masturbate while concentrating on pleasant sexual scenes in fantasy. This procedure was followed for eight sessions during which she often became excited but never reached orgasm. Erotic films portraying 'fore-play' and other practices, which she did not find anxiety-provoking, were then provided to accompany her masturbation for the next eight sessions. Orgasm now began to happen, as indicated by her subjective report and by signs of a greatly increased heart rate. The next step was to revert to masturbation accompanied only by her own fantasies, but which now incorporated memories from the films, and this was sufficient to produce orgasm on each of eight occasions. Following this treatment, and at follow-up six months later, the girl reported experiencing orgasm nearly every time during sexual intercourse.

The 'standard' form of treatment for sexual deviancy or unwanted sexual preference is aversion therapy. A typical procedure involves a male patient being shown pictures of acceptable sexual stimuli, such as provocative women, as well as unacceptable stimuli such as children or men. The patient will have been diagnosed as deviant if erections occur only to the unacceptable pictures. Size of penis is continually monitored, and when erections begin to occur in the presence of an unacceptable picture electric shocks sufficient to cause the erection to subside are given. The acceptable pictures are shown at a time when the patient is feeling relief that the shocks have stopped. The success of this treatment is considered to be rather limited, and 'cultured' variations have been developed which appear to be more effective as well as less painful.

One of these is 'covert sensitization' in which the patient is instructed to imagine unpleasant consequences of his deviation or to otherwise associate it with painful thoughts. Another is 'orgasmic reconditioning' therapy, which was developed by McGuire *et al.* (1965). The idea is to treat deviations by changing the fantasies assumed to be responsible for maintaining the deviant behaviour. Patients are instructed to start masturbating while concentrating on their deviant fantasies, but when sexually aroused to switch to a normal fantasy. To start with they make this switch immediately before orgasm, but are then told to do it earlier and earlier on each subsequent occasion. It is hoped that eventually the deviant fantasy will no longer be necessary for inducing sexual arousal, and that the normal fantasy will take its place, having been repeatedly reinforced by sexual excitement and orgasm. Patients usually improve with this treatment, and in one study eleven out of twelve men were reported to have been successfully treated (Marshall, 1973). Although both these methods are based on fantasy, they could presumably be carried out using erotica.

Another method that does involve erotica has been developed by Feldman and MacCulloch (1971). The 'anticipatory avoidance' method is based on active avoidance rather than passive punishment, and has been applied to the treatment of homosexuals who want to change their sexual orientation. The patient is instructed to look at a male picture that is presented to him for as long as he finds it sexually attractive. If after eight seconds he has not rejected it by pressing the switch provided, he receives an electric shock. He can avoid this shock by rejecting the slide, but is told to do so only when he genuinely finds the slide no longer attractive. A female picture is also presented but is not associated with shock, and the patient can press a switch whenever he wants to see this slide. Changing the orientation of a homosexual has long been regarded as very difficult, but following a slightly more complex form of this procedure, 58 per cent of homosexual men were reported to have achieved some degree of success when followed up at least one year after treatment.

It would be nice if we could furnish scientific evidence that treatment involving exposure to erotica, and based on established psychological theory, was more effective than treatment not so based. This would provide evidence that the theories we have used to account for the effects of exposure to erotica really do have factual support from a variety of sources. Unfortunately, very few properly controlled studies have been carried out in which different treatments have been compared. Most of the evidence comes from individual case reports and group studies without the necessary control groups. For what it is worth, this evidence does support the validity of the theories, such as desensitization and modelling, when applied to the use of erotica in treatment. Moreover, evidence of a more convincing nature is now beginning to appear of which the following are examples.

McMullen (1978) compared the progress of 40 frigid women given sex therapy with another 20 who were on the 'waiting list'. The treatment group were instructed in relaxation and masturbation techniques, and also in the development of sexual fantasies. They were instructed to imagine making love while they were masturbating, this being aimed at generalizing any sexual excitement from masturbation to intercourse. The instructions were provided in the form of detailed illustrations given on film or in a booklet. Twenty-four of the 40 women experienced their first orgasm during the course of this treatment, while this did not happen with any of the women in the control group. Of the 24 experiencing orgasm, 13 were able to transfer this response to sexual intercourse. There was a slight, but not significant, tendency for the group given the booklet to improve more than the film group. Compared with the lack of response in the control group, this study indicates that erotica can have beneficial effects when used in treatment.

Gillan (1978a) was interested in the question of whether erotica can stimulate a low sex drive. Men who were impotent and women who had a low sex drive relative to their husbands were treated with 'stimulation' therapy in a series of studies. The idea was to awaken sexual desires by the use of visual and

auditory erotica. In a preliminary study, men listened to exciting music and to tape recordings of women experiencing the
ecstasies of orgasm, watched erotic films such as *Emmanuelle*,
and read erotic books such as *Fanny Hill*. They were also taught
relaxation techniques and encouraged to try oral sex and other
techniques of love play and to develop their sexual fantasies.
Eight out of ten impotent men were judged to have improved as
a result of this treatment.

In the second study, the success of treatment was judged
relative to results from a control group of patients who merely
talked about their problems and were given training in relaxation. Fourteen impotent men and ten frigid women were seen
for six weekly sessions, and those given stimulation therapy
were judged to have improved more than those given 'talking'
therapy. Improvement, as defined in terms of subjective ratings
of the quality of the sexual relationship with their partners, was
apparent immediately after treatment and at follow-up after
one month, as shown in Figure 7. The group presented with
auditory and semantic erotica did slightly, but not significantly, better than the group presented with visual forms of
erotica. Similar results were also obtained using frequency of
sexual intercourse and enjoyment of sex as the criteria for
improvement.

The third study in this series involved a comparison of
stimulation therapy with two fairly conventional procedures in
sex therapy, namely desensitization and 'flooding' (Gillan,
1978b). The patients were twenty-eight women with low libido
who were seen with their partners in six group therapy sessions.
They were assigned to one of four groups involving relaxation
training, stimulation therapy, desensitization and flooding. All
were given relaxation and half were given stimulation therapy
with or without desensitization or flooding. The desensitization
procedure involved touching and massaging, physically examining each other, mutual masturbation, oral sex, female superior
position in sexual intercourse, and finally other 'advanced'
positions. These activities were introduced in turn at each of
the six sessions, and the couples were instructed to imagine
each activity before actually engaging in it at home during the
following week. The 'flooding' procedure involved the same
activities but carried out in the reverse order; that is, proceed-
ing from the most to the least advanced task. The use of a

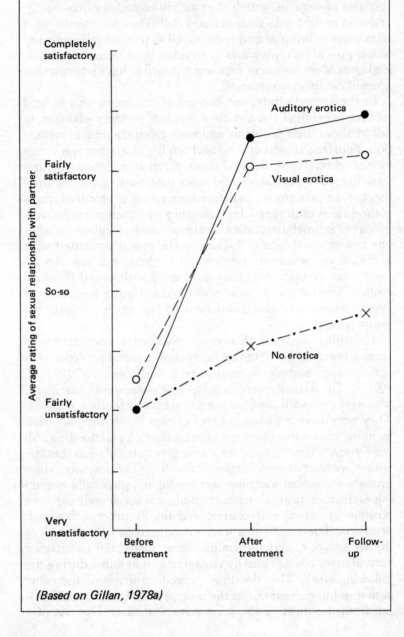

Figure 7. The response of impotent men and frigid women to treatment with erotica

Completely satisfactory

Fairly satisfactory

So-so

Fairly unsatisfactory

Very unsatisfactory

Average rating of sexual relationship with partner

Auditory erotica

Visual erotica

No erotica

Before treatment

After treatment

Follow-up

(Based on Gillan, 1978a)

variety of criteria for improvement, including an assessment interview with a psychiatrist who for any given patient was unaware of which treatment had been administered, indicated stimulation therapy to be the most effective, especially when combined with desensitization or flooding which on their own were of similar and intermediate efficacy. Least effective was a subsequently instituted control condition of relaxation and 'talking' therapy; unfortunately this group was not strictly comparable since it was worse than any of the others to begin with.

In these experiments the erotica may have had a therapeutic effect for any of a variety of reasons. The materials, by being 'exciting', may have directly stimulated sexual desires and testosterone secretion, which in turn could have led to an improvement in sexual and marital satisfaction. Similarly, the 'novelty' value of the erotica may have given the patients ideas on which to model their own sexual activities. Any disinhibiting or desensitizing effects could have led to an improvement in attitude towards their partners, and to a reduction of anxiety or guilt that might have been restricting their enjoyment of sex. It is possible that all these mechanisms played some part in producing the therapeutic effects that were observed. Anyway, these examples may serve to demonstrate that the effects of erotica are not always necessarily 'bad'; indeed a better understanding of the effects means that it will be increasingly possible for erotica to be put to good use.

SUMMARY

Among the psychological theories that are particularly relevant to the effects of media sex and violence is that of desensitization. According to this theory, scenes of violence of gradually increasing severity presented under relaxing conditions should become less and less anxiety-provoking. This effect has been demonstrated in a variety of ways, and could have serious consequences if for some people aggression is held in check by feelings of anxiety and guilt over its expression. Even exposure to a single violent film appears to have the effect of making children temporarily less aware, or less concerned, about aggressive acts in others. Rival theories such as the claim that by watching violence, people may become more rather than less concerned with real-life dangers, have not been supported by carefully designed research. Similarly, the catharsis theory that aggressive urges may find an outlet through vicarious identification with aggressors has not been supported; the very few studies that have indicated such a conclusion are open to alternative interpretations.

Among the theories of the development of sexual deviations, that of conditioning has been experimentally investigated. By associating female boots with normally arousing erotica, male students have been found to respond to the boots with erections. It seems that deviant sexual acts illustrated by pornography could, through fantasy association with sexual excitement and orgasm, become 'conditioned' in this way. However, because of the apparent ease with, and the early age at, which most deviations are acquired it seems likely that some degree of predisposition to respond in this way is also involved. Experimental studies have indicated the effectiveness of treatment involving erotica in reducing inhibitions over sex and in stimulating libido.

9   Discovery of Relevant Variables

Scientists are sometimes called upon to help in arriving at social policy decisions. Belson (1978) warned of the dangers of realistic TV violence, especially when portrayed as being in a good cause; programmes singled out for criticism included *The Sweeney*, *Starsky and Hutch* and *Cannon*. Similarly, after exonerating historical war films and westerns, Noble (1975) wrote:

> Where possible I would try to prevent my young child from watching news violence and violence seen in the neo-realistic police and detective programmes. These latter types of violence, I fear, do show that violence is normal and accepted in everyday life and possibly define the targets at whom aggression can be directed. The sight of children in the news throwing stones at soldiers is for me the worst offender.

If correct, this is the type of information needed by producers, parents and censors alike. But upon exactly what evidence are such recommendations based? Studies have been designed to find the type of violence most effective in leading to acts of aggression, and the type of erotica that is most stimulating which in turn may indicate what is most likely to lead to perversion. This chapter is concerned with the factors that enhance and minimize the effects of exposure to violence and pornography.

Cartoon violence is 'too fantastic or farcical to lend itself to imitation' according to the 1975 annual report of the Independent Broadcasting Authority, but there is little evidence to support this assumption. Bandura *et al.* (1963a) compared the effectiveness of real-life, filmed and cartoon models in leading to aggressive play in children. The cartoon character was played by an adult dressed as a black cat, and filmed in a 'fantasyland' setting. For each condition, the model performed the same acts of novel aggression against a Bobo doll with accompanying verbalizations such as 'Sock him in the nose'.

The total amount of aggression, both imitative and general, subsequently displayed by the children is indicated in Table 30. While all the models induced more aggression than a control condition of nothing, they did not differ significantly from one another. On this evidence, cartoons are just as effective as other films, or even real people, in facilitating later aggression. But since a comparison of cartoon with other types of violence has not been made with respect to disinhibition theory the question is still open.

Table 30   Aggression scores after exposure to different types of model

	Total aggression	
Type of model	*Boys*	*Girls*
Real-life male	132	57
Real-life female	77	66
Filmed male	85	80
Filmed female	115	87
Cartoon cat	117	81
Nothing	72	36

(Based on Bandura et al., 1963a)

Consistent with earlier evidence (Bandura *et al.*, 1961), boys were more aggressive than girls, and a male model was more likely to be *imitated* than a female. Even for nursery-school children, it is somehow inappropriate to see females aggress. Another relevant characteristic may be the age of the model. Kniveton (1973b) found a tendency for an adult model to be more effective than a peer in facilitating aggression. An opposite result was obtained by Hicks (1965), although in a retest for retention after six months only an adult male model was found to have had a lasting influence.

According to Noble (1975), children do not take westerns seriously because the violence is stylized, the setting unfamiliar and the story clearly make-believe. In one of a series of experiments, he compared the effects of realistic and stylistic films on the play of children aged six to seven years (Noble, 1973). Realistic violence was represented by machine-gunning with the victims either at close range or in the distance, and stylistic violence by the burning of a witch or a distant historical battle. Before and after seeing one of the four films, the play of each child was assessed. The average 'before' score for amount of aggressive play was twenty seconds. Against this baseline, Table 31 indicates that aggression was aroused only by the

Table 31 Time spent in destructive play after watching different types of violent film		
	Victim seen	*Victim unseen*
Realistic violence	110 seconds	45 seconds
Stylistic violence	20 seconds	15 seconds
(Based on Noble, 1973)		

realistic films, especially where the victims were in full sight. The realistic nature of the film was interpreted to have aroused anxiety with a consequent 'regression' to earlier forms of play. Similarly, the stylistic film without attention to the plight of the victims was interpreted to have had a beneficial, or 'cathartic', effect in encouraging constructive play. Rather than resorting to psychoanalytic speculations, it is advisable to fully consider more established theories. The realistic films may have given rise to hostile play simply because it is easier for children to imitate machine-gunning than the burning of a witch or the enactment of a historical battle. Similarly, the historical battle may have led to constructive play simply because it was the most enjoyable of the four films and so put the children in good humour. To cover this possibility, it is necessary to include a control condition of a non-violent film. Without such a control, Noble is unjustified in offering the following advice: 'Many boys are aggressive, and I would recommend that these boys work out these feelings by watching fantasy aggression where there is a distance between aggressor and victim, such as westerns, war films and historical violence.'

While it is not yet clear whether stylized and cartoon violence is less 'harmful' than realistic, there is evidence that football arouses aggression. Unfortunately for the Football Association who are concerned with soccer violence and vandalism in Britain, the relevant research has been carried out in the US and so the results apply strictly only to American football. Before and after a football game and a gymnastics competition, Goldstein and Arms (1971) assessed spectators by interview and a self-report scale of hostility. Hostility did not increase for the gymnastics group but it did for the football fans, and this increase occurred regardless of whether their team won or lost. Although this study suffers from limitations, such as subjects not being randomly assigned to the two groups, it does suggest there may be something about football that makes it particularly effective in arousing aggression.

One of the recommendations that the BBC makes to producers is to avoid portraying bad habits, such as smoking, in 'good' characters. This implies acceptance of the theory that we are more likely to be influenced by people with whom we 'identify'. In an attempt to test this theory, Turner and Berkowitz (1972) asked subjects to imagine themselves either as the movie character who wins a fight or as a judge. Half the subjects were also instructed to press a button every time they saw the hero hit his opponent. When tested on the 'aggression machine', it was the subjects who had been told to identify with the hero who tended to deliver the highest electric shocks to a 'victim', especially if they had also been pressing the button. While this result could, conceivably, have been due to greater attention to the film on the part of the 'identifiers', the design of the experiment seems more appropriate for evaluating the effects of the new Death Race game. This game, which is banned in some US cities, involves being at the steering wheel of a simulated racing car and trying to massacre 'pedestrians' who appear on a screen before you. A 'kill', which is accompanied by a convincing electronic scream, is recorded by a tombstone and the official record at the time of writing stands at twenty-nine dead in sixty seconds. On the basis of Turner and Berkowitz's experiment, there do seem to be grounds for fearing that the game will add to the 9,000 deaths recorded annually on American roads.

Other studies have generally failed to find evidence that 'identifying' with an aggressor is likely to cause aggression. But since methodological problems are inherent in most of these studies, no definite conclusions can be drawn; one example will suffice. Howitt and Cumberbatch (1972) showed TV films with aggressive heroes, such as Trampas in *The Virginian*, and asked viewers to rate how much they liked him. Boys who most liked the hero, however, did not differ from the 'low identifiers' in their judgements of the aggressive acts portrayed in the film. But if boys who are inclined to like people are generally peace-loving and friendly, then it may be noted that this experiment was bound to fail. Liking even aggressive heroes may reflect friendliness as much as the inclination to be aggressive oneself. The obvious way round this problem is to experimentally manipulate liking for a model. The manner in which this can be achieved is illustrated in the next experiment.

A basic principle in psychology is that we tend to like others who are similar to us. Baron and Kepner (1970) used this principle in order to experimentally manipulate liking for a model. Seventy-two male students were led to believe that a peer model held attitudes that were either very similar or very dissimilar to their own; the model had ostensibly answered the same twelve-item attitude questionnaire as the subjects. True to prediction, the model was rated as more attractive when he appeared to have given the same answers as the rater. The next step was to see if the subjects were more likely to imitate the 'attractive' than the 'unattractive' model.

After being insulted along with the model, a third of the subjects observed the model acting in an aggressive fashion by apparently administering high-level shocks to the anger instigator. Another third observed the model acting in an unaggressive fashion, while the remainder constituted a 'no model' control group. The subjects were themselves then asked to administer shocks to the person who had insulted them. Contrary to prediction, liking the model did not facilitate imitation; the aggressive model was just as effective in eliciting aggression from subjects who disliked him as from those who liked him. Again, this is evidence failing to support the theory of identification.

Among the other results in this study, it was noted that subjects tended to raise the intensity of the electricity each time they shocked the 'victim'. This is the experimental evidence for the 'overkill' phenomenon mentioned in Chapter 2; other researchers have noted a similar tendency for aggressive expression to increase in severity with each repetition (e.g. Loew, 1967). Baron and Kepner's results also provide evidence of imitation in adults (as opposed to children) since the highest shocks were administered by those subjects who had observed the 'aggressive' model. Moreover, the subjects who had observed the unaggressive model administered lower shocks than the 'no model' controls. This finding that a model, who acts in a restrained fashion in the face of provocation, can inhibit aggression in angered observers has an important implication. It suggests that *TV heroes who overcome trouble in a peaceful fashion are likely to have a calming effect on potentially aggressive viewers.*

The film industry has a moral code whereby it tries to ensure that the 'bad guy' is punished, this being intended to demonstrate that 'crime does not pay'. Although it may be morally desirable for a scoundrel to be caught and receive his 'just deserts', there is evidence that this paradoxically acts to encourage aggression. Berkowitz and Rawlings (1963) introduced a seven-minute fight scene from *The Champion* by giving students the impression that Kirk Douglas was either a scoundrel or not really bad. After seeing him badly beaten, the subjects rated their attitudes towards a confederate of the experimenters. Those who had been led to believe that Douglas deserved his beating felt more aggressive towards the confederate – especially if he had earlier insulted them. A film in which the villain receives a justified beating thus appears particularly effective in facilitating aggressive feelings. This finding was interpreted as suggesting that a student who sees justified aggression is likely to feel justified in expressing his own hostile desires. It is also consistent with the theory that subjects who 'identify' with an aggressor, which they are perhaps inclined to do if they approve of his motives, are themselves likely to feel aggressive. The implication from this experiment is that retribution in films should be in the form of a trial and imprisonment rather than a physical beating up of the culprit. Portrayal of the 'eye for an eye' philosophy probably encourages viewers to take the law into their own hands.

Leifer and Roberts (1972) wanted to see if the above result could be obtained with children. There was a slight tendency for good rather than bad motives for violence to lead to higher aggression scores. But this effect virtually disappeared when full-length TV programmes, such as *McCloud* and *Gunsmoke*, were shown. It was thought that lack of understanding might explain why the results were not clear-cut, and so the children were questioned about the motives for the violence. Consistent with the reduced differences obtained with the longer programmes, understanding was better for the short excerpts. The lack of an effect in the youngest children, aged three years, could be readily explained since they had virtually no understanding of the motives involved. The rather small effect obtained with the oldest, aged thirteen years, could not be explained in this way since they had near perfect understanding. Although it is tempting to offer this as an example of how a laboratory demonstrated effect is reduced when measures are taken to make the experimental conditions closer to real life, it must be noted that the two experiments cannot be directly compared since they involved different assessment procedures and types of subject as well as different films.

Hostility towards an enemy is likely to be increased if we see a film portraying a victim who is similar to our enemy. Berkowitz and Geen (1966) arranged for students to be insulted by an accomplice who was introduced to them as either Kirk or Bob. Aggressive feelings, as assessed on the 'aggression machine', were greater towards Kirk than Bob for the students who saw the film of Kirk Douglas receiving a 'justified' beating. These results together with those for the necessary control groups are presented in Table 32. The finding was

Table 32 Average number of shocks given to accomplice under different conditions

Name of accomplice	Violent film		Track film	
	Angered	*Neutral*	*Angered*	*Neutral*
Kirk	6.1	1.7	4.2	1.5
Bob	4.6	1.5	4.0	1.6

(Based on Berkowitz and Geen, 1966)

interpreted as indicating that the students felt that expressing hostility towards Kirk was justified because they had seen another Kirk receiving his 'just deserts'. Because of the social importance of this finding, it is fortunate that its validity has been checked in various ways; these replications have yielded similar results (e.g. Geen and Berkowitz, 1967). It appears, then, that aggression can be encouraged not just by seeing 'good' heroes being aggressive, but also by seeing what can be done to the 'bad guys'. This finding has the clear implication that public hostility towards minority groups can be increased by the screening of films that portray 'justified' violence against such groups.

Imitation studies have demonstrated that children are more likely to be influenced by models who are rewarded rather than punished. Bandura *et al.* (1963b) exposed children to films of play situations involving two adult models. In one condition, Johnny is playing with some interesting toys and refuses to allow Rocky to join in. Rocky then becomes aggressive in various novel ways, overpowers Johnny, and is soon playing happily with the toys. The film ends with Rocky departing with the toys in a sack, and a commentator announces him as the victor. In another condition, Rocky's efforts are unsuccessful and he ends up being soundly thrashed by Johnny. After seeing one of these films, or being in a control group, the children were observed in a similar situation. Table 33 shows that Rocky was more likely to be imitated by those children who had seen him being successful in taking over the toys. The children were also asked to evaluate the behaviour of the two models, and to say whom they would rather emulate. Even though they evaluated the successful aggressor negatively, seeing him as 'rough and bossy', they preferred to emulate him rather than the successful defender. They rationalized this choice by saying that Johnny was being selfish in not sharing his toys and so deserved what he got. This study thus provides evidence that imitation is partly dependent on consequences, and that successful villainy can outweigh the viewer's value systems. In films where a thief

Table 33	Scores for imitative aggression after watching a model who was either rewarded or punished		
		Boys	*Girls*
Aggressive model rewarded		16	15
Aggressive model punished		8	9
Non-aggressive model		10	4
Nothing		6	5
(Based on Bandura et al., *1963b)*			

gains various rewards and is not caught until the very end, the question arises as to whether his final capture is soon enough to prevent children perceiving him as a successful model.

The design of the above study has been criticized because Rocky may have induced imitation, not because he was a successful thief, but because he was portrayed as happy and the commentator approved of his action by announcing him as the winner. In other words, because relevant variables were confounded the results allow of more than one interpretation. Nevertheless, other studies have generally indicated that imitation of an aggressive model is enhanced if he is rewarded and inhibited if he is punished (e.g. Bandura, 1965). There is also evidence that disinhibition of aggression occurs after seeing a violent model being rewarded (e.g. Albert, 1957). All this adds to the conclusion that exposure to violent TV characters probably strengthens the conviction that aggression is sometimes permissible, especially if it leads to the attainment of desired goals; it also emerges that violent heroes are a particularly potent influence, since, unlike the villains, they do not get punished.

It is a common observation that the presence of an adult can inhibit aggression in a child whereas a peer may actually encourage it. This was demonstrated in a study where 100 children were exposed to a model displaying unusual forms of aggression (Martin *et al.*, 1971). In a free-play situation, the children were then assessed for signs of imitative and general aggression. Relative to a control condition, the presence of a same-sex peer facilitated aggression whereas an adult tended to have an inhibiting influence, although this did depend on the adult's attitude to any aggression. This suggests that, because of their inhibiting influence, some parents may be unaware of any effects that TV violence is having on their children.

Having considered some of the conditions likely to enhance or minimize aggression, we shall now turn briefly to the other side of the coin and consider the type of person who is most likely to be influenced by witnessing violence. Many studies have found that males express more aggression than females after watching a violent film, although this sex difference is reduced when only verbal aggression is considered (e.g. Bandura *et al.*, 1961). Evidence for social class is less clear-cut (e.g. Kniveton and Stephenson, 1972). Similarly there is little evidence for the belief that aggressive or mentally disturbed individuals are more susceptible to the effects of TV violence.

Wolfe and Baron (1971) wanted to see if maximum security prisoners with a long history of violent acts would be more influenced than students by an aggressive model. The subjects were insulted and then half of them were exposed to an aggressive model giving high shocks to a confederate whenever he made a mistake on a learning task. All the subjects were then given the chance to shock the confederate who had earlier made insulting comments about their intelligence and maturity. Table 34 shows that the prisoners tended to administer higher

Table 34   Effects of modelled aggression on adults

	Intensity of shock	
	Aggressive model	*No model*
Students	7.4	4.9
Prisoners	8.5	6.3

Higher shocks were administered to a person who had earlier insulted them by subjects who had been exposed to an aggressive model.

(Based on Wolfe and Baron, 1971)

shocks than the students, thus indicating that the prisoners had weaker inhibitions against the expression of aggression. This study is often quoted as showing that violent offenders are particularly susceptible to modelling effects, but of course it shows nothing of the kind. The prisoners were no more affected by the model than the students – the prisoners were simply more aggressive to begin with. Nevertheless, it does still mean that if impelled to action in real life, the harm inflicted by an aggressive or irresponsible person could well be very serious.

The above study is open to the criticism that the insulting procedure may have had more effect on the prisoners if they were more sensitive about their intelligence than the students. After all, students should feel confident about their cognitive abilities and so be relatively immune to such insults. On the other hand, because intelligence is important to them, the students may have felt more insulted than the prisoners. Either way, it would have helped to include control groups of subjects who were not insulted. Another criticism is that although matched for age, the two groups were not equated for such other characteristics as social class, and so the prisoners may have been more aggressive than the students for reasons other than their violent history. It would have helped to include a control group of non-violent prisoners in case such a group were also more aggressive than the students.

Even with the above control groups, there is still the possibility that the violent prisoners will be more aggressive, not because of their violent history, but because of their personality. While this variable has been neglected in virtually all the studies described in this book, it is almost certainly relevant. Aggression tends to be associated with a personality inclined towards extraversion, neuroticism (emotionality) and psychoticism (tough-mindedness). Each of these variables was associated with a liking for TV violence in a survey of over 1,000 adolescents (Nias, 1975). For boys, highly significant correlations (above 0.15) were obtained for extraversion with a liking for horror films, westerns and war films, for neuroticism with cartoons, and for psychoticism with horror and war films. For girls, similar correlations were obtained for extraversion with cartoons and for psychoticism with horror films. In a similar survey among the parents of these children viewing preferences were associated with social class rather than personality, but a correlation between extraversion and liking war films in men was highly significant. There was also evidence consistent with the observation that aggression tends to 'run in families' since the children tended to like the same programmes as their parents, this applying particularly to war films, westerns and cartoons.

Whether aggressive personality types are particularly likely to be influenced by TV violence is still an open question. It is difficult to investigate since many complicating factors are involved. For example, even if aggressive personalities were shown to be more susceptible to aggressive models or other media influences, then this could be merely on account of their having watched a lot of violence rather than on account of their personality. Similarly, if an opposite result were to be obtained, then this could be explained away in terms of the Law of Initial Value. According to this law, an aggressive person may show less of an increase than his unaggressive colleague because, being already aggressive, he has less scope in which to manifest any further increase in aggressiveness. Because of its importance, we shall return to the issue of individual differences in the next chapter. In terms of social relevance, however, it is not essential to answer the question about relative susceptibilities since, as we have already noted, even a slight increase in the aggressiveness of an already aggressive person could have very serious consequences for his next victim.

The US Commission on Pornography (1970) recommended that restrictions on the availability of pornography be lifted, except for laws protecting children and the sending of unsolicited materials through the mail. This recommendation was based on the claim that no evidence of a clearly harmful nature had been uncovered, and because of the Commission's oft-stated belief that 'interest in sex is normal, healthy, good'. Because no research had been conducted with children, the committee felt that the *status quo* should be maintained. The case for regulating the mailing of pornography was made on the grounds that recipients who might be offended had a right to be protected. The same argument was also applied to the open display of pornography in shop windows and in advertising, but was then overlooked. Many other recommendations have been offered. At one extreme, two dissenting members of the Commission argued that, in the absence of information, existing laws covering children could not be justified and so should be repealed along with all the others. At the other extreme is the argument that materials which are likely to give offence should be censored, unless some counterbalancing advantage can be demonstrated. Between these two extremes are compromise recommendations such as censoring pornography which portrays illegal activities or which involves the exploitation of others; the portrayal of rape, sadism and sex with children and animals usually comes into this category as do films which 'dehumanize' and degrade women of the 'treat them rough and they will get to like it' variety.

If an effect of pornography is to increase sexual behaviour, including pre- and extramarital sex, promiscuity and 'abnormal' activities, then some people will interpret this overall effect as undesirable and others as, on balance, desirable. For this reason, recommendations inevitably involve value judgements as well as *a priori* beliefs concerning the supposed effects of pornography. This point is well illustrated in an experiment by Byrne *et al.* (1974). Students were asked to rate how they felt while looking at erotic themes presented as pictures and stories, and they were later asked whether such materials should be restricted. They were all confident about making this important decision, but their opinions were closely related to their own personal reactions to viewing the materials. Students who responded to the erotic themes with some degree of negative effect thought that there should be censorship, while those who responded with predominantly positive effect were anti-censorship. This prompts the question of how often are political decisions made on the basis of personal feelings rather than on a careful consideration of facts and the feelings of others. The majority of the Commission members viewed sex as being inherently 'good' which, combined with their awareness of the problems of censorship, helps account for their conclusion of 'no harm' and their recommendation against censorship.

Although people are of course welcome to hold viewpoints based on their own feelings and experiences, it is unfortunate when academic arguments confound value judgements with the interpretation of factual information. The issue is very complex, with pornography having a mixture of good, bad and unknown effects. Even if people were in agreement over what was good and bad, it would still be almost impossible to arrive at a satisfactory conclusion in which harmful effects were assessed against those that are beneficial. What we shall do here is to set out some factual evidence relevant to the effects of exposure to erotica and then deal separately with the issue of recommendations in the last chapter. We have already considered some of the effects of pornography in terms of conditioning and imitation theory, and the positive nature of some of the effects was summarized by reference to therapeutic applications. We have also considered the effects of erotica on the facilitation and inhibition of aggression. What remains is to examine the characteristics of erotica that are found to be the most arousing, together with the characteristics of people who are most likely to be affected in this way. This information is directly relevant to conditioning theory. An obvious prediction from this theory would be that the acquisition of new sexual preferences, or the strengthening of existing ones, would be most likely when sexually arousing material is combined with the type of person who is most aroused by it.

A striking aspect of the research on the arousing properties of different types of erotica is the extent to which individuals vary in their sexual preferences. Abel *et al.* (1975) developed a method for investigating such preferences in males. Penile responses are monitored while the subject listens to a tape recording of sexual scenes written specially for him; any scenes that fail to produce an erection are replaced by elaborations of ones that do. It was claimed that erotic cues for people with sexual deviations tended to be highly idiosyncratic, with the person concerned often being unaware of the critical component. For example, one person reported being attracted to female footwear, but erections were found to occur only when a

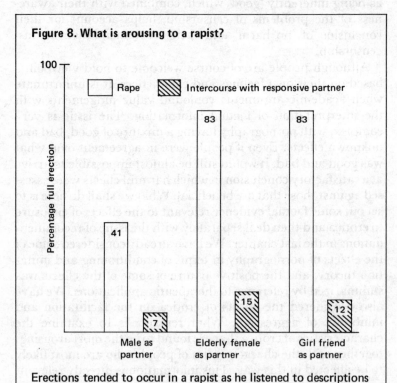

Figure 8. What is arousing to a rapist?

Erections tended to occur in a rapist as he listened to descriptions of intercourse only if his partner was unwilling. *(Based on Abel et al, 1975)*

female was having her foot caressed *and* she was responding with excitement.

A positive response in the female may be a necessary component for arousal in most men, although a judge in Madison became notorious for claiming that women who dress in revealing and provocative clothing are inviting rape, which he saw as 'a normal reaction' of the aroused male. With the method of Abel and his colleagues, it would be possible to test whether a man would continue to be aroused if the woman resisted his attentions. Figure 8 presents some results from a rapist where this was the case. For this young man, the essential characteristic was that his partner be unwilling; the more she resisted, the greater was his arousal and enjoyment. He was aroused only by the theme of forced sex, with the age, race and even sex of his victim being largely immaterial. Although not put to the test, it appears that the clothing of the victim would have made little difference.

Courtship signals play a major role in the sexual behaviour of animals and the same may apply in the human species. Kolářský and Madlafousek (1972) were interested in the extent to which exhibitionists would be aroused by courtship invitations from a female. It was thought that because deviates characteristically leave out the normal courtship niceties – 'flashers' do not usually bother to flirt with their intended victims – they would not be aroused by it. A group of deviates, mostly exhibitionists, were monitored for signs of an erection while viewing various film clips of a bikini-clad girl. In some of the films the girl, a nineteen-year-old student actress dressed only in a bikini and high-heeled shoes, was flirting with the camera by smiling, crossing her legs and caressing herself in a suggestive manner. Other film clips showed her either in static poses or carrying out non-erotic activities such as knitting, sweeping and ironing. Contrary to expectation, the deviates were aroused by the courtship gestures but not the static scenes – in much the same way as a group of non-deviant soldiers. A more refined analysis, however, revealed that relative to the soldiers the deviates were influenced by bodily rather than facial gestures and, most importantly, they were the only ones to be aroused by the non-erotic sequences. Non-erotic movements appeared to have an inhibitory effect on the otherwise arousing effect of the girl's body only for the soldiers. The tendency for exhibitionists to respond to erotic and non-erotic movements alike is of course consistent with their habit of approaching women going about their everyday activities.

A few studies have included an assessment of the arousing qualities of different scenes for the average volunteer. Schmidt *et al.* (1969) found that coitus and petting pictures were rated as most arousing by male students, nudes and oral-genital acts as intermediate, and close-ups of the female genitalia as least arousing. Using a wider range of materials, Levitt and Hinesley (1967) found that coitus, petting and oral sex were rated as most arousing, group sex and female masturbation as intermediate, and male pin-ups and homosexual activity as least arousing. The erotic preferences of females were specifically investigated by Steele and Walker (1976). Short films were presented to single unmarried female students who rated their degree of sexual arousal on a 50-point scale. The results are presented in Table 35, and indicate that heterosexual petting

Table 35 Average ratings of sexual arousal by female students in response to different erotic films

Type of film	Rating of sexual arousal
Heterosexual petting – romantic emphasis	30.5
Heterosexual petting – genital emphasis	28.7
Group sex – two males and one female	29.0
Group sex – three of each sex	28.1
Sadomasochism – rough and forceful	23.9
Sadomasochism – brutal and cruel	12.1
Male homosexuality	4.6
(Based on Steele and Walker, 1976)	

and group sex are about equally arousing, with sadomasochistic scenes intermediate and male homosexuality least arousing. Consistent with previous research, none of the films were rated very highly with most being assigned to the category 'somewhat sexually stimulating'. The question of whether romantic scenes are more arousing than sexual activity without emotion was investigated in two ways. A comparison of romantic and unromantic petting did not give significantly different results. Nevertheless, additional information in the form of interviews suggested a description of the 'ideal' film as follows: 'The cast of the film would consist of one attractive male and one attractive female, displaying affection, "romance", and prolonged foreplay in a bedroom setting. The film would involve a *gradual* process leading to coitus involving a variety of positions. The emotional tone of the film would emphasize the "total" relationship, and not merely genital sexual behavior.'

The above studies on normal volunteers all suffer from the limitation that the ratings were subjective and probably involve distortion in the direction of 'social desirability'. With deviant groups in particular, Abel *et al.* (1975) found that very little reliance could be placed on verbal reports. Often people are unaware as to exactly what arouses them, and a violent sex offender would be naturally reluctant to admit that he is 'turned on' by scenes of violence. In such cases, the occurrence of an erection might betray 'true' feelings. Mavissakalian *et al.* (1975) employed both objective and subjective measures of arousal in assessing the responses of heterosexual and homosexual men to a series of short films. The results, presented in Table 36, are expressed as a percentage of a full erection and as a percentage of maximum subjective arousal. The two sets of results were very similar and could be taken as

Table 36 Average responses of heterosexual and homosexual men to four types of erotic film

	Percentage full erection		Percentage full arousal	
	Hetero-sexuals	Homo-sexuals	Hetero-sexuals	Homo-sexuals
Provocative female	43	22	58	30
Heterosexual intercourse	51	45	68	72
Two lesbians	60	29	69	34
Two male homosexuals	18	55	10	78

(Based on Mavissakalian et al., *1975)*

supporting the claim that, in volunteers at least, subjective reports of arousal are a valid measure. But in order to justify such a conclusion it would be necessary to arrive independently at the two sets of measures. As it stands, the outcome was hardly surprising since a subject could hardly claim low arousal from a film that gave him an erection. More interesting is the finding that the heterosexuals were particularly aroused by the lesbian activities, which contrasts with the very low rating given by females to male homosexuality in the Steele and Walker study. Predictably, the homosexuals were aroused by the films of male homosexuality but they were also aroused by the heterosexual intercourse scenes, presumably because they focused their attention on the man.

A gradual build-up of sexual activity is generally regarded as more exciting than the sudden scenes of passion often portrayed on the screen. Objective evidence for this is provided by Amoroso *et al.* (1971). Using the index of time spent looking at different pictures, it was found that subjects looked for longer when the slides were presented in order of increasing explicitness rather than in a random order. This result was obtained with male students. A related effect was observed in a study involving subjective ratings. Jakobovits (1965) found that both male and female students became progressively more aroused as they read short erotic stories. Presumably a satiation effect did not occur because the stories were short (around 700 words) and varied. The effect appears to be analogous to preliminary 'sex play' having a cumulative effect in increasing arousal.

It is often argued that tempting, partially revealing and suggestive portrayals are more arousing than fully explicit ones. This may be the case with sudden presentations, but with a gradual build-up the opposite may apply. Anyway, what appears to be most important is the opportunity for the viewer to elaborate on the scenes by incorporating his own preferences; this would be especially important for scenes that do not correspond with his personal preferences. We have seen that subjects in an experiment will often spontaneously use their imagination to add to what they are viewing, and that imagining a given theme was rated as more exciting than seeing it in pictorial or written form (Byrne and Lamberth, 1971). A similar experiment, but using an objective measure of arousal, was conducted by Bancroft and Mathews (1971). Erections were monitored in 'normal' volunteers, including psychiatrists, while they looked at a series of erotic slides. Some degree of erection was detected in almost all the subjects, but when the procedure was repeated with the additional instruction of avoiding mental imagery there was little response. As a final stage, they were asked to imagine various sexual scenes and erections were again apparent in most of the subjects. Because the order of conditions was not controlled this can be taken as evidence only suggesting that imagery added to the effect of the slides on the first presentation.

Further evidence for the important role of fantasy comes from research on the effects of censorship. Tannenbaum (1971) was called upon to make a statement about censorship to a local authority which was concerned about a rape scene in a feature film. He answered that the arguments for and against excising the scene were both plausible, but that the question was essentially an empirical one meriting actual research rather than continuing rhetoric. Although the authorities decided nonetheless to censor the scene, Tannenbaum later carried out an experiment involving three versions of the film. Subjects were shown either the original or a censored version in which the rape scene was deleted in a subtle way or in such a way as to make its occurrence obvious. Two days later the subjects were asked to describe what had happened to the girl during this particular scene, and their descriptions were independently assessed for degree of 'erotic vividness'. The censored versions gave rise to the most erotic descriptions, especially the one in which it was obvious that something had been left out. This is evidence that 'suggestion is more enticing than reality'; it also shows that censorship can be self-defeating if not done properly. With obvious censorship, the viewer is stimulated to fill in the missing scene, which he tends to do with heightened vividness. If the aim of censorship is to reduce arousal, then it appears to have the opposite effect.

It is commonly believed that alcohol can facilitate sexual arousal, and it is often blamed as a contributory factor in sex crimes. According to the porter at Macbeth's castle, 'it provokes the desire, but it takes away the performance'. Wilson and Lawson (1976) put the first part of this hypothesis to the test by giving male students a drink before they watched erotic films. In order to prevent the subjects from knowing what they were drinking, various steps were taken to minimize the differences between an alcoholic and a placebo drink. Both drinks were based on tonic water and lime juice, with vodka being added only for the alcohol group. The drinking cup was smeared with alcohol, and a mouthwash given on the pretext that it was necessary before taking a breathalyser test. Moreover, this test was 'rigged' so as to give a reading of 40 mg. per cent (which was the average value obtained by the group given vodka). Irrespective of what they were drinking, half the subjects were told that it was alcoholic. Table 37 gives the

Table 37 Alcohol and sexual arousal		
	Percentage increase in erection	
	Heterosexual film	*Homosexual film*
Expected and received alcohol	27	13
Expected but did not receive alcohol	27	16
Expected tonic but received alcohol	23	9
Expected and received tonic	19	4

Erections were more likely to occur in response to erotic films in subjects led to believe they had consumed an alcoholic drink.

(Based on Wilson and Lawson, 1976)

average percentage increase in erections, which were monitored during the screening of heterosexual and homosexual films, for the different drink conditions. It was found that the effect of the alcohol was only slight, in fact not significant. What mattered was the belief of having taken alcohol. Subjects who believed that they had consumed an alcoholic drink manifested significantly greater sexual arousal than did those believing they had consumed just tonic, regardless of the actual content of their drinks. Apart from failing to support the common belief that alcohol increases arousal, this finding indicates the importance of psychological factors in sexual arousal.

There is very little scientific information on the type of

person who is most responsive to erotica. A model for investigating the effects of past experience on attitudes to sex is suggested by an experiment on cheating by Mills (1958). He was interested in changes in moral attitudes following temptation. Children were assessed for their attitudes to cheating, and later they were put in a situation which tempted them to cheat. Some resisted the temptation and others did not. Following this experience, those who had cheated became more lenient in their attitudes while those who had resisted adopted a harsher attitude. Probably for ethical reasons (cheating is considered permissible for the purposes of an experiment whereas sexual activity would be out of the question!), this classic experiment has not been used as a basis for investigating attitudes towards sex and censorship. If we allow ourselves to generalize the finding to the present case, then people who are most outraged by promiscuity and sexual variations, and who are most zealous in wanting to crack down on this behaviour, would tend to be those who were tempted, came dangerously close to giving in, but who finally resisted. People who almost decided to live in glass houses may be the ones who are most prone to throw stones.

Several studies have included an attempt to relate previous sexual experience with response to erotica (Athanasiou and Shauer, 1971; Brady and Levitt, 1965; Griffitt, 1975). It is usually found that people with little sexual experience are likely to be aroused, at least by mild erotica, but to have a tendency to regard it as pornographic, disgusting and offensive. In contrast, people with extensive sexual experience are more likely to be aroused by strong erotica and to have favourable attitudes towards it. Unfortunately, such results are of limited value since it is impossible to tell whether it is sexual experience which leads to a positive attitude or whether it is simply people with a positive attitude towards erotica who are most likely to seek out sexual experiences. Slightly more fruitful has been the research on sex differences in response to erotica.

It is usually assumed that men are more aroused than women by erotica; this was the conclusion reached in the Kinsey *et al.* (1953) interview survey. Recent research, however, has provided grounds for questioning this conclusion, although a definite conclusion is not possible because only volunteers have been studied. Women who volunteer for this type of study may be more atypical than the men who do; it is quite possible for a 'biased' sample of females who are very interested in erotica to be attracted to the study. Anyway, taking the research findings at face value, it seems that any sex difference in response to erotica is only slight and for some types of erotica women are more aroused than men. Three examples will suffice. It was noted in the original German studies that, although men reported being more aroused than women by much of erotica, there was considerable overlap. For example, although seventeen of twenty-four themes were rated as significantly more arousing by men than women, about one-third of the women gave higher ratings than the average man for scenes of coitus and petting (Sigusch *et al.*, 1970). As regards sex differences over content, men were relatively more aroused by nudes of the opposite sex and by unusual practices, while women were relatively more aroused by scenes involving kissing and affection.

Table 38   Self-ratings of sexual arousal in response to erotica presented in different ways

	Average sexual arousal	
	Males	*Females*
Photographic	22.7	19.5
Literary	23.1	25.6
Imaginary	41.2	45.1

The highest degree of sexual arousal was obtained by imagining rather than seeing erotic scenes.

(Based on Byrne and Lamberth, 1971)

Byrne and Lamberth (1971) asked married couples to rate their degree of sexual arousal to each of nineteen erotic themes presented in the form of photographs, or short passages from books, or, as an instruction, to imagine each theme. Table 38 presents the results. Overall, there was no sex difference, but there was a significant interaction, with photographs being relatively preferred by men and stories and imaginary forms by women. A similar experiment was conducted by Gillan and Frith (1978). Stories were written to match the themes of five erotic films and then tape-recorded. The tapes and films were presented to students who were asked to rate their degree of sexual arousal. Table 39 shows that the films tended to be more arousing than the stories, but again there was a statistical interaction, with the films being relatively preferred by men and the stories by women. Another interesting interaction concerns the theme of female masturbation; men preferred this on film and women as a story. Perhaps the women tended to identify with the girl, which was probably easier while listening to the tape, whereas the men may have imagined themselves participating with the girl, which was probably easier with the film. It was also noted in this experiment that the male and female groups were similar for degree of sexual experience and, since male students are on average more experienced than females, this supports the suspicion that it is the more experienced females who volunteer for this type of experiment.

Table 39 Average ratings of sexual arousal on a seven-point scale for erotica presented on film and tape

	Films		Stories	
	Males	*Females*	*Males*	*Females*
Sexual intercourse	5.7	5.2	3.7	3.5
Lesbians	5.1	4.9	3.8	4.0
Female masturbation	5.0	3.9	3.6	4.7
Fellatio	4.9	4.2	4.0	4.0
Threesome	4.7	4.9	3.1	4.3

(Based on Gillan and Frith, 1978)

This survey of the factors that determine sexual arousal may serve to illustrate a number of points. Clearly, not all that much is known about exactly what is arousing and still less about what makes one person excited by erotica, another indifferent, and yet another 'turned off'. This lack of knowledge is unfortunate since it limits our ability to predict what is likely to modify sexual preferences and in whom. Nevertheless, the findings so far seem to point in directions that are consistent with relatively well established psychological theories such as conditioning. People obviously vary in their sexual preferences, although this has only been researched by reference to groups such as males versus females. In extreme cases, sexual preferences are so circumscribed as to qualify as a fetish with the person being 'turned on' only by a specific object or set of circumstances. In a very similar way, the responses of sex offenders may be specific to the type of activity for which they have been convicted. They probably feel compelled to commit their offences because nothing else meets their requirements for obtaining satisfaction. If such people are virtually unresponsive to all other stimuli, then much of erotica will have little interest to them. Contrary to popular opinion, it may be these people who are most likely to be immune to pornography, and even for their 'speciality' they may prefer action to fantasy. In such cases, exposure to erotica, by encouraging the development of new preferences, may act in a normalizing direction. Indeed, as we have seen, this is one of the ways in which pornography is used in therapy.

Evidence consistent with the specific nature of arousing stimuli is apparent in an important series of studies by Thorne and Haupt (1966). They administered the *Sex Inventory* to criminal and control groups and found that rapists and murderers, in particular, reported having little interest in sex. 86 per cent of those convicted of sex crimes against females denied obtaining pleasure from self-stimulation; pornography-aided masturbation as a 'substitute' for such men would not seem to be a very promising solution. This research also provides an illustration of the need for careful interpretation of questionnaire data. Cline (1974) relates how in response to the statement 'I have never had a sexual orgasm', 30 per cent of the rapists answered 'true'. This might be taken as evidence of deprived sexuality but since 40 per cent of the murderers gave the same answer, it seems that a more likely explanation is to be found in the observation that most of the prisoners did not know the meaning of the word 'orgasm'.

Research has indicated the types of erotica that are most arousing for the average person. In general, this does not correspond with the types of material that are commercially available. In particular, the evidence that imagining erotic scenes is more arousing than looking at pictures or films suggests that presenting a scene too explicitly, or catering for too specialized an interest, makes it difficult for the viewer to modify the scene in accordance with his personal preferences. Direct attempts to make something arousing are usually self-defeating. The principles of 'leaving something to the imagination' and 'anticipation being better than realization' are generally overlooked by the producers of 'blue' movies and the designers of pornographic advertisements.

SUMMARY

In assessing the impact of sex and violence in the media, it is important to consider the context within which the offending material is presented. Is realistic or fantasy violence more likely to affect viewers, for instance? No very clear answer emerges from the evidence, although effects have been shown to exist for both types of material. Does 'identifying' with an aggressor lead to violence? Again no definite conclusions can be drawn. But violence used in a righteous cause does seem to increase viewer aggression more than violence used in a bad cause, contrary to much TV and cinema preaching. The nature of the enemy in the portrayal of violence may also be of importance; this finding has implications for minority groups. Successful violence may be the most likely to be imitated, providing vicarious rewards, as it were. Arousal produced by erotic films can be shown to depend on the types of scenes shown, coitus and petting, for instance, being more arousing than close-ups of the genitals. A gradual build-up of sexual activity is generally regarded as more arousing than the sudden scenes of sexual activity so frequently shown on pornographic films. Censored scenes may become more arousing through the activation of fantasy; thus even censorship has its dangers. Altogether, oddly enough, the erotic and pornographic material commercially available does not correspond with what is known to be most sexually arousing. These are generalizations which apply to groups; there are considerable individual differences as to what turns people on. The existence of such individual differences, partly no doubt innate, partly acquired through the mechanism of conditioning, makes generalizations hazardous.

10 Individual Differences and Personality

Nothing is more obvious in reading the literature on the pornography and violence debate than the tremendous differences which emerge in beliefs and attitudes between the permissive 'libertarians' and the restrictive 'puritans'. We have already noted, in relation to the experimental and field studies carried out in attempts to discover the effects of pornography on various types of subject, that sex plays an important role; in this chapter we shall be concerned primarily with the role played by personality, although, for reasons which will become obvious, differences between males and females will also have to be discussed in some detail. Curiously enough, individual differences, particularly those related to personality, have not attracted much research interest; this is all the more puzzling as not only are they so obvious as to defy anyone not to notice them, but in addition they clearly make it impossible to come to any clear-cut decision which would have universal relevance about the portrayal of pornographic and violent scenes in the media. Puritans and libertarians both have the right to have their preferences considered; it would seem to be an important task for the psychologist to discover the why and wherefore of the divergent attitudes manifested by different people.

Let us first of all define in broad outline what is meant by personality here. Human behaviour is part consistent, part inconsistent; observation discloses large areas in which a given person's activities seem to indicate some latent traits which make him behave in a similar fashion when confronted with a series of different situations. Thus we call a person 'sociable' who likes going to parties, to have many friends, to chat up people, who dislikes sitting quietly at home reading by himself, and so forth. There is a consistency to his behaviour which we designate with the trait label 'sociability'; this trait label does not of course *explain* why he behaves in this manner, but it does serve to *describe* what he does. Furthermore, we can grade people from one extreme to the other, ending up with a continuum on which the most sociable, say, has a score of 100, the least sociable a score of 0. Many such traits have been isolated by psychologists, and can be measured in various ways – by questionnaire, by ratings of actual observed life conduct, by experiment, or in various other ways, such as the analysis of imaginative products. Personality may be defined as the sum of consistent patterns, measured with reasonable reliability and validity; the causes of such consistency are, of course, an important part of the psychologist's theory of personality, but this usually comes later on, i.e. after the major aspects of personality have been identified and measured.

Before turning to a brief discussion of these causal factors, we must look at an important feature of the very extensive work done so far in this field, namely the fact that most of the traits discovered and measured so far tend to correlate together. Thus for instance sociability and impulsiveness, although logically quite distinct, are correlated in actual fact; i.e. when both are measured in a random group of people, we find that those who are impulsive also tend to be sociable, and vice versa. Correlations of this kind give rise to higher order concepts such as Extraversion; typically, the extravert is sociable, impulsive, care-free, active, playful and easygoing, while the introvert is serious, thoughtful, unsociable, controlled, introspective, and in every way the opposite of the extravert. Not everyone is either an introvert or an extravert; this too is a continuum ranging from one extreme to the other, with the majority of people somewhere in between. Higher order concepts like extraversion–introversion are sometimes called 'types', or 'dimensions of personality'; they are based on statistical evidence collected from large-scale studies of trait measurements of many people (Eysenck and Eysenck, 1969). There are three major 'type' concepts which emerge again and again from empirical studies, not only in the Western countries, but also in other cultures – Japan, India, Nigeria, Yugoslavia, and many others. Extraversion–introversion (often abbreviated to 'E') is one of these concepts; Emotionality and Psychoticism are the other two.

Some people differ from others by being overly emotional; their feelings are easily aroused, strong, and lasting. They tend to worry too much, are often anxious and depressed, quickly aroused and slow to cool down. Such people are often liable to develop overt signs of neurotic behaviour, and consequently emotionality has often been referred to as 'neuroticism' (abbreviated 'N') – implying that here we have a personality dimension, a high standing on which predisposes a person to the development of neurosis, although whether this does or does not take place is in large part a function of the stresses imposed on the individual (Eysenck and Rachman, 1965).

The third, major 'type' factor has been called various names (as indeed have the others); it arose from the observed correlations between several rather tough-minded behaviour patterns and attitudes. Thus people high on this dimension would be egocentric, aggressive, suspicious, impersonal, not worried about cruelty to animals, children, and other people, cold, and generally somewhat anti-social. People scoring high on tests of this dimension were often found among criminals, psychopaths ('moral imbeciles'), and psychotics; hence this factor has been labelled 'P' (for psychoticism, psychopathy, and paranoia). The term psychoticism suggests that here we have a personality dimension which predisposes a person to psychosis, and the associated disturbances of psychopathy, criminality, alcoholism, drug-taking, etc., without implying an actual clinical diagnosis – here too, as in the case of neuroticism, predisposition is not enough by itself to produce the disorder, and an external stress is required (Eysenck and Eysenck, 1976).

P, E and N describe a large slice of an individual's personality; can we say anything about the causal factors involved? The first point to note is that heredity plays an important part; twin studies, studies of adopted children, and familial studies all point to the conclusion that well over half of all the factors which make for individual differences along these three dimensions are genetic in origin (Eysenck, 1976a). Recent studies by Plomin and Rowe (1977) demonstrate that even in very young children (average age $3\frac{1}{2}$) genetic factors are pronounced, and Thomas and Chess (1977) have shown remarkable consistency of behaviour in a follow-up study of babies over a twenty-year period. It would be foolish to play down environmental influences, of course, but it would be even more foolish to disregard genetic factors, or the interplay between these two sets of causal factors.

Genetics, of course, cannot determine behaviour directly; it must act through physiological and anatomical mechanisms. These have been identified, with some degree of success, for E and N, and some suggestive evidence exists for such identification in the case of P. As far as N is concerned, individual differences in emotionality are almost certainly connected with the autonomic nervous system, which governs bodily processes concerned with the expression of the emotions, and the limbic system, which controls the autonomic and coordinates its workings. As far as E is concerned, this appears to be connected with individual differences in the level of cortical arousal, which in turn is mediated by the ascending reticular formation – extraverts have low arousal levels, introverts high ones. This, as we shall see, produces a number of behavioural reactions very relevant to our main topic (Eysenck, 1967).

As far as P is concerned, a major clue to its nature is the fact that men have much higher scores on this factor than do women; indeed, it will be clear from looking at the traits which are characteristic of P that these are typically masculine rather than feminine. Furthermore, we may remember the association of P with criminality and psychopathy; both are very largely male prerogatives. It seems likely that P is connected with maleness, i.e. with the hormonal balance of the individual (Eysenck and Eysenck, 1976). Thus P links up with the sex differences so often observed in the reactions of people to pornographic material, and with their attitudes to it. As this is such an important factor in connection with our main theme, a few words may be said about the biological basis of maleness and femaleness, particularly as in recent years adherents of 'women's lib' have denied such biological differentiation (apart from primary sex characteristics) and have suggested that socially imposed 'sex roles' are responsible for the observed differences. This is not so. Maleness and femaleness are first programmed when the child is conceived, in a very obvious manner; it is less well known that there is a secondary push given towards maleness in boys by hormonal (androgen) secretions during the foetal stage. (Androgens are male hormones.) Failure of this secretion to occur would leave a very effeminate boy anatomically undoubtedly male. Femaleness biologically appears to be the norm; maleness requires an extra push. This foetal masculinization through hormone secretion can occur in girl foetuses when the mother, either through genetic defect or because of drugs, secretes androgen-like substances which masculinize the unborn girl. The so-called adrenogenital syndrome is a type of genetic defect, in which the mother's suprarenal glands fail to produce cortisol, but rather produce an androgenic variant. Girls who inherit this disease are exposed to this intra-uterine masculinizing hormone, and grow up with typically masculine mannerisms and behaviour patterns – including not only dominant and aggressive modes of conduct, but even preference for male toys, such as tin soldiers. Such tomboyish behaviour can also be found in girls whose mothers took progestin-type fertility pills, which, too, have an androgenic effect. Compared with control groups of normal girls, these victims of drug therapy showed more interest in careers and less interest in marriage, as well as toy preferences typical of boys. There is by now a large literature on such androgen-producing and masculinizing drugs, and their effects on behaviour, and the results are as outlined – behaviour of girls so affected becomes distinctly more 'masculine', in the ordinary, old-fashioned meaning of this term. The result is, of course, not unaffected by social precepts and teaching; nobody has ever suggested that social factors are completely powerless to influence conduct. All that is said is that there is a strong biological determinant which predisposes individuals in the direction of greater or lesser 'maleness'.

Some of the strongest evidence for this point of view comes from the work of Dr Willhart Schlegel, a Hamburg physician who made an exhaustive study of the shape of the pelvis in men and women. In men, typically, the pelvis is shaped like a funnel, tapering down to a narrow outlet; in women, the pelvis is shaped more like a tube, with a broad outlet. There is much variety within each sex; thus there are men with tube-shaped pelvis structures, and women with funnel-shaped ones. But on the average there is a considerable difference. What made Schlegel interested in the pelvic outlet is that its shape is apparently determined at the foetal stage by precisely the kind of hormonal burst already described; if such androgenic material is supplied, the pelvic shape will be masculine; if not, feminine. This led Schlegel to study in detail the social and sexual behaviour of men and women having typical and atypical pelvic shapes, using over a thousand men and women in his researches. What he found was that pelvic shape within a given sex correlated in a predictable manner with behaviour; thus men and women with funnel-shaped pelvises tended to behave in a masculine manner, while men and women with tube-shaped pelvises tended to behave in a feminine manner. Masculine-type pelvis correlated with leadership, an active sexual role, dominance and preference for a younger sex partner, in men and women alike. Feminine-type pelvis correlated with empathy, suggestibility, and compliance. In other words, behaviour in both sexes seemed to be determined by the same hormonal factors which originally produced skeletal features of the pelvis, namely androgen secretion at the foetal stage. Schlegel even studied cows (whose pelvic outlets are more easily observed than are those of human subjects) and found that cows with narrow outlets, i.e. funnel-shaped pelvises, tended to mount other cows and generally behave in a more masculine manner. Truly, the ways of nature are wondrous to behold.

It is interesting to note that Schlegel found two further correlates of pelvic shape. Homosexual males tended to have feminine-type pelvises; this is perhaps not entirely unexpected, in view of the fact that a genetic component has been demonstrated to exist in predisposition to homosexual conduct. He also found that men and women concordant for pelvis shape (i.e. men with masculine-type pelvis, women with feminine-type pelvis) were much less likely to be divorced than men and women discordant for pelvis shape (i.e. men with feminine-type pelvis, women with masculine-type pelvis). This finding suggests fascinating vistas of computer-dating organizations and marriage guidance officials adding pelvic shape to their other data, and advising clients accordingly. To do this would certainly not decrease the accuracy of their predictions, nor lower the value of their advice.

There is, of course, much additional evidence to support the view that maleness and femaleness are not just roles which boys and girls are taught in infancy, and play out in adult life. It would appear, rather, that these 'roles' are predetermined by biological factors, some of which we are now beginning to understand and measure, and that society emphasizes the direction of the push given us by these hormonal factors, by undertaking to prepare us in our infancy for the roles nature

intended us to play – although, as the discordant pelvis structures of some men and women indicate, agreement is not
perfect by any means. All of this, as well as carefully established
personality differences (such as the greater anxiety proneness of
women, and the more impersonal approach of men to sex) with
their demonstrable genetic determination, makes perfectly
good sense in terms of evolution. The female has to bear, bring
up and protect her children; the male has to hunt and fight.
Both are biologically suitable for these roles by virtue of their
physical make-up; it is only sensible for nature to complement
this suitability by appropriate mental and temperamental
qualities. The fact that other mammals show similar differentiation in sex roles strongly supports some such explanation.

We must now turn to the data to be discussed. These are
derived from a series of questionnaire investigations of normal
student, normal adult and psychiatrically ill adult populations.
The samples used were quite large; for instance, in the student
sample there were some 800 subjects, and in the adult sample
some 850. A questionnaire of sexual attitudes was used which
contained about 100 questions for the student sample, and
some 150 for the adult sample. The results are analysed and
discussed in great detail by Eysenck (1976b); here we are only
concerned with those items which deal with pornography (in its
widest sense) and aggression/violence. The questionnaire was
also administered to about 500 twins, in order to study the
genetic basis of sexual attitudes. In addition to these sex questionnaires, personality inventories and social attitude inventories were administered, as well as various other measuring
instruments which will not concern us here.

In view of the importance of sex differences, it may be useful
to begin by looking at the actual percentage endorsement differences between male and female students on the most dis-
criminating items; Table 40 shows the actual items, as well as
the difference in percentage endorsements between the male
and female students. The figures are derived by subtracting the
percentage of female endorsements from that of male endorsements. For the first item, referring to readiness to take part in
an orgy, we find that 61 per cent of the men would do so, as
compared with 4 per cent of the women; thus the difference
noted in the table is 57 per cent. Where the difference is
preceded by a minus sign the women agree more with the item

Table 40   Percentage differences between men and women in endorsements of items in a sex inventory

	Percentage differences
If you were invited to take part in an orgy, would you: (a) accept? (b) refuse?	57
I like to look at pictures of nudes	53
I like to look at sexy pictures	53
The thought of a sex orgy is disgusting to me	−47
If you were invited to see a 'blue' film, would you: (a) accept? (b) refuse?	43
It is all right to seduce a person who is old enough to know what they are doing	38
I believe in taking my pleasures where I find them	37
If you were offered a highly pornographic book, would you: (a) accept it? (b) refuse it?	36
It doesn't take much to get me excited sexually	35
Buttocks excite me	34
I get excited sexually very easily	33
I think about sex almost every day	32
Seeing a person nude does not interest me	−32
Sex without love ('impersonal sex') is highly unsatisfactory	−31
I do not need to respect a woman, or love her, in order to enjoy petting and/or intercourse with her	31
Prostitution should be legally permitted	30
If you had a chance to see people making love, without being seen, would you take it?	29
Pornographic writings should be freely allowed to be published	27
It is better not to have sexual relations until you are married	−25
Sometimes the woman should be sexually aggressive	24
I get pleasant feelings from touching my sexual parts	24
Something is lacking in my sex life	24
There should be no censorship, on sexual grounds, of plays and films	34
Conditions have to be just right to get me excited sexually	−22
I find the thought of a coloured sex partner particularly exciting	21
The opposite sex will respect you more if you are not too familiar with them	−21
All in all I am satisfied with my sex life	−20

(Based on Eysenck, 1976b)

than do the men. It will be clear that this list of most differentiating items contains a number of statements dealing with pornography; on each of them males are far more 'permissive' than females. There is some overlap between the sexes; this is brought out quite well by giving each person a score on the most diagnostic items in the whole questionnaire, using 40 items altogether; thus the lowest (most feminine) score would be 0, the highest (most masculine) score 40. Fig 9 shows the distribution of these scores; it is quite clear that the men have much higher scores than the women, but also that there is much overlap, particularly in the middle.

Results for the adult sample are very similar. Outstanding among items giving marked differences between the sexes are items relating to pornography, orgies, voyeurism, and prostitution, closely followed by impersonal sex. Other items refer to sexual excitement, premarital sex and promiscuity; on all these items men give a more positive response than do women. Men are also less prudish in general, and feel less guilt associated with sexual behaviour. All these differences are not unex-

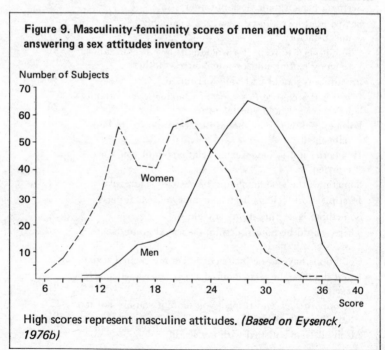

Figure 9. Masculinity-femininity scores of men and women answering a sex attitudes inventory

Number of Subjects

High scores represent masculine attitudes. *(Based on Eysenck, 1976b)*

pected, of course; they are well in line with the traditional male and female stereotypes with which we are all familiar. In part, it is possible that they merely reflect the values and roles which our educational system imprints on boys and girls, but this is clearly not everything; as we have seen, hormonal factors also play an important and probably decisive part. As we shall see later, our own twin data support this view.

We can now turn to a consideration of the relationship between personality and items which may be connected with pornography and/or violence. The detailed quantitative findings are contained in Eysenck (1976b); here we shall merely indicate the general line of the results. First let us look at hostile, violent and aggressive feelings in relation to sex. These are all correlated with N; this is in good accord with clinical evidence linking neurosis and sexual dysfunctions of various kinds. Thus for both sexes there is a positive correlation between neuroticism and the item 'I have sometimes felt hostile to my sex partner'. There is also a somewhat lower correlation of this item with P; in other words, these are psychiatrically somewhat abnormal feelings. The item 'My sexual fantasies often involve flogging' also correlates with N, as does 'I usually feel aggressive with my sexual partner'. The last item of this kind, 'I sometimes feel like scratching and biting my partner during intercourse', again correlates with both N and P; there is also a correlation with E, however, which suggests that this may be a more normal reaction. These data are from the adult sample; for the students relevant questions were not included.

Coming now to the questions relating to pornography, we shall begin with the student sample. 'Seeing a person nude doesn't interest me' correlates negatively with P and N; in other words, high P and high N scorers do find it interesting. There is a positive correlation between P and N, and the item 'I like to look at pictures of nudes'. The same correlation is found for the item 'If you had the chance to see people making love, without being seen, would you take it?' The next item, 'Pornographic writings should be freely allowed to be published', correlates positively with P, as does the item 'There should be no censorship, on sexual grounds, of plays and films'. This agrees with the findings of a negative correlation between P and the item 'There are too many immoral plays on TV'. Last, there are three items of the form 'If you were invited to see a "blue" film;

to read a highly pornographic book; to take part in an orgy; would you accept?' On all three, the high P scorers would tend to accept; correlations with E are also positive, but lower, as are those with N. If one had to summarize these findings, one could say that attitudes in favour of pornographic films, pictures, writings, actions, etc. are positively related to the two psychiatrically abnormal factors, P and N; in other words, persons favourable to open displays of pornography tend towards the 'abnormal' pole on these two dimensions of personality. High P scorers are particularly opposed to legal restrictions on pornographic displays of one kind or another.

Results from the adult sample support this view on the whole. High N scorers 'like to look at sexy pictures', and like 'to look at pictures of nudes'. They would 'take a chance to see people making love', and agree, as do high P scorers, that 'pornographic writings should be freely allowed to be published'. High P scorers disagree with the proposition that 'there are too many immoral plays on TV', and say that 'there should be no censorship, on sexual grounds, of plays and films'. At the same time, high N scorers are 'disturbed when looking at sexy photographs'. High P scorers do not 'object to four letter swear-words being used in mixed company'. On the three items relating to seeing a 'blue' film, reading a highly pornographic book, and taking part in an orgy, positive correlations are again found for both P and N. The results for the adults thus bear out those for the students; there is a tendency for psychiatrically abnormal personality patterns to be related to liking for pornography, and toleration for pornographic exhibitions. In some cases extraverts show a similar tendency, but to a much less marked extent.

So far, we have looked at results for single items from the questionnaire; psychologists prefer to work with scales, i.e. sets of items, because this increases the reliability of the measurement – single questions invariably are somewhat unreliable, and hence do not correlate very highly with personality and other traits. Scales are constructed by paying attention to statistical considerations; items are put together which are found to correlate together, i.e. where a person answers 'Yes' to one item, he also tends to say 'Yes' to the other. Thus all the items in a scale tend to measure the same quality or trait, and the nature of that quality or trait can be identified by close study of the items which do, and those which do not, form part of this set of intercorrelated items. Eleven such sets were in fact identified in the questionnaire, as given to the adult population; these sets were similar for men and women, and can be identified quite clearly by the names given to the traits. Pornography is one of these; others are permissiveness, impersonal sex, aggressive sex, prudishness, sexual shyness, sexual disgust, neurotic sex, satisfaction, physical sex, and sexual excitement. These traits themselves are, of course, not independent; thus permissiveness and pornography are quite highly correlated, as are disgust and prudishness, or physical sex and sexual excitement. When these intercorrelations between scales are analysed in turn, it is found that two major concepts emerge which present a very clear and meaningful picture; a very similar picture emerged from the analysis of the student results, and also from that of other groups.

The two factors which emerge are quite independent, i.e. they are not correlated with each other. One is libido; this may be defined as strong, outgoing sexual interests, seeking physical satisfaction and disregarding social and moral considerations. Figure 10 shows the relative positions of the various traits in relation to this factor, and to the second factor, 'satisfaction', which may be defined as contentment with one's sexual life, one's adjustment in the sexual sphere, and one's sexual partner. The traits which best characterize high libido are liking for pornography, permissiveness, and impersonal sex; the low end of the libido factor is characterized by prudishness, sexual disgust and sexual shyness. Note the importance of pornography in this picture; it very well defines the high end of the libido factor, and shows no correlation with the satisfaction factor – in other words, whether a person does or does not like pornography is irrelevant to his satisfaction with his sex life. A person satisfied with his sex life may or may not like pornography, may or may not be permissive, and may or may not like 'impersonal sex'. This finding goes counter to two extreme views often voiced by puritans and advocates of permissiveness alike, namely that satisfaction can only be achieved by following their particular recommendations. Puritans advocate sexual restraint, and believe, and often state, that permissive and impersonal sex are unsatisfactory and lead to unhappiness; there is no evidence in our data that this is so. Advocates of

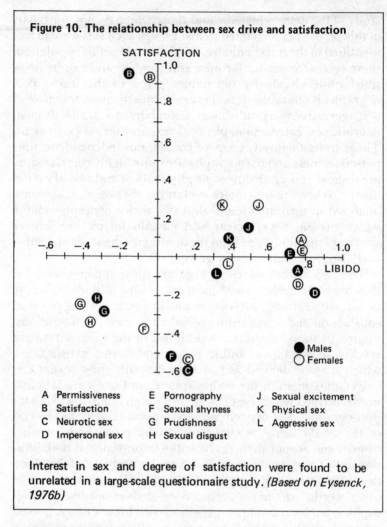

Figure 10. The relationship between sex drive and satisfaction

A Permissiveness	E Pornography	J Sexual excitement
B Satisfaction	F Sexual shyness	K Physical sex
C Neurotic sex	G Prudishness	L Aggressive sex
D Impersonal sex	H Sexual disgust	

Interest in sex and degree of satisfaction were found to be unrelated in a large-scale questionnaire study. *(Based on Eysenck, 1976b)*

permissiveness believe, and often state, that sexual inhibition leads to dissatisfaction and unhappiness, and is ultimately unsatisfactory; there is no evidence in our data that this is so. Extreme statements of this kind, whether by puritans or by libertarians, are simply projections of their particular attitudes; they have no evidential value. It is possible to achieve a satisfactory sexual adjustment either by choosing a 'high libido' or a 'low libido' approach – or indeed by choosing a middle way;

there is no guarantee of either a satisfying or a dissatisfying life associated with either choice. A liking for pornography certainly does not make for a satisfactory or an unsatisfactory sex life – both outcomes are equally likely, and obviously depend on other factors. If the banning, or the promotion, of pornography is to be favoured, it will have to be on grounds other than its effects on sexual happiness and adjustment.

Further analysis of the data reveals some interesting and relevant points. High libido is correlated with masculinity, low libido with femininity. Men have higher scores on a scale of libido, women tend to have a low score. There is much overlap, but the distinction is clear, and indeed very similar to that found in Fig. 9; it is almost the same items which discriminate between men and women, and which go to make up the libido scale. This strongly supports the traditional view of men as more highly 'sexed' than women, although this is no absolute distinction, in view of the overlap between the sexes. Schlegel's work, already mentioned, on pelvic measurement leaves little doubt that hormonal and other physical factors play a causal role in this differentiation, and hence in the differential attitudes of men and women towards pornography. (It is interesting that women claim slightly more satisfaction with their sex lives than do men; this may come as a surprise to supporters of an extreme 'women's lib' position.)

In general, dissatisfaction is correlated with the psychiatric 'abnormality' associated with high N (Neuroticism) and high P (Psychoticism) scores. High N scorers are often found to show the signs of prudishness, disgust, and shyness; this is sometimes combined with prurient attitudes, and with a strong interest in things sexual. High P scorers tend to show a 'Don Juan' complex, i.e. attitudes of hostility towards their sex partners, which, combined with very impersonal and purely biological views of sex, often leads them to dissatisfaction with their sex lives. There appear to be two equally satisfactory and happy methods of sexual adjustment; the low-libido, introverted one, and the high-libido, extraverted one. When either the high- or the low-libido approach shows sign of psychiatric abnormality, whether quasi-neurotic or quasi-psychotic, satisfaction tends to disappear. This suggests that there may be a healthy, acceptable kind of extraverted pornography, i.e. pornography which looks upon sexual functions as normal, enjoyable, and acceptable; equally, there may be an unhealthy, unacceptable kind of P/N pornography, i.e. pornography which looks upon sexual functions in a perverted, unsatisfying manner. Such a distinction is, of course, commonly made by those who distinguish between 'erotica' and 'pornography'; unfortunately there is not all that much agreement between different judges as to the allocation of specific items in either of these categories. Probably it would sometimes be more useful to look upon them as the end-points of a continuum, ranging from one extreme to the other. A nude young man kissing a nude young woman passionately would probably be allocated by most people to the 'healthy' end; a girl of five being raped by an elderly male would probably be allocated by most people to the 'unhealthy' end. Differences between people would lie, not so much in ordering a given set of items (pictures, films, live shows) along this dimension, but rather in deciding at what point the division lay between 'erotica' and 'pornography'.

Eysenck (1972a) has analysed responses to a questionnaire which illustrates this point. The questionnaire itself is reproduced below (Table 41). It lists sixteen activities of a sexual nature, and also five different kinds of women with whom each activity might be undertaken. An attempt was made to get clear what the legal terms 'deprave and corrupt' mean to different people; which of these activities would they look upon as depraved and corrupt? If 'obscenity' is defined as that which tends to deprave and corrupt, then we must obviously have some idea of what this depravity and corruption consist of – otherwise, how could we ever show that a particular item of pornography had this particular, undefined, effect?

Several hundred intelligent and co-operative students took part in the experiment; some people – mostly introverts – sprinkled ticks liberally over the surface of the inventory; seemingly they disapproved of all sexual activities outside the marital union. Even within that union, anything going beyond the 'missionary position' was condemned. Others – mostly extraverts – had only a few marks, indicating that as far as they were concerned 'anything goes', provided it is within the law; rape and the seduction of a minor tended to be frowned upon even by the most 'enlightened'. Most respondents tended to come in between these two extremes, but their notions of depravity were clearly not identical either; indeed, the spectrum of opinion goes right across the board, from one extreme of permissiveness to the other extreme of puritanism, without a break anywhere. There is no evidence here of that substratum of reasonable agreement on which the law seems to rely; the only degree of agreement is upon those behaviours which are indeed frowned upon by the law, and made the explicit target of its wrath.

Why is it that extraverts are more permissive than introverts? As regards males compared with females, there is no real problem, as we have seen, the difference being in large part due to hormonal influences. Similarly low and high P scorers share so many characteristics with the female and the male sex respectively that an explanation seems fairly obvious. For high N scorers again the strong anxiety and fear reactions to which they are genetically prone can account for their curious sexual behaviours, as well as their sexual difficulties – we found that high N scorers suffered significantly more frequently than low N scorers from impotence, premature ejaculation, frigidity and orgasm difficulties (Eysenck, 1976b). For extraversion there is no such obvious explanation, but fortunately the fact that extraverts show low cortical arousal, while introverts show high cortical arousal, makes it possible to make predictions, and to explain the respective behaviour of these two extreme types. We must note first of all that there appears to exist an optimum level of cortical arousal – too little leads to boredom, too much leads to over-excitement and exhaustion. As a consequence, we would expect the low-arousal extraverts to seek excitement (in order to raise their too-low arousal level), while introverts would seek to avoid excitement (in order to lower their too-high arousal level). This is, of course, much too over-simplified an account to do justice to the complex underlying physiological and psychological reality, but it gives an idea at least of the line of argument which we are following.

Based on some such reasoning as this, Eysenck predicted a number of consequences that should follow from his theory. Among these predictions were the following: extraverts will have intercourse earlier in life than introverts; they will have intercourse more frequently than introverts; they will have intercourse with more different partners; they will have intercourse in more different positions; they will indulge in more varied sexual behaviour outside intercourse; they will indulge

Table 41 The Pornography Scale

ACTIVITY (of adult male) towards FEMALE TYPE

	A 15-year-old virgin	A 25-year-old virgin	An un-married non-virgin	(Husband) to married woman	(Man other than husband) to married woman
Kiss on the mouth	☐	☐	☐	☐	☐
Seduce	☐	☐	☐	☐	☐
Have intercourse normal fashion	☐	☐	☐	☐	☐
Lend pornographic books	☐	☐	☐	☐	☐
Touch and kiss sexual parts	☐	☐	☐	☐	☐
Initiate into prostitution and live on immoral earnings	☐	☐	☐	☐	☐
Take to strip-tease show	☐	☐	☐	☐	☐
Take to watch couple having intercourse	☐	☐	☐	☐	☐
Take to see 'blue' films	☐	☐	☐	☐	☐
Vigorous petting	☐	☐	☐	☐	☐
Take to theatre in which nude actors simulate intercourse	☐	☐	☐	☐	☐
Exhibit sexual parts to female	☐	☐	☐	☐	☐
Make female dress up in male clothes	☐	☐	☐	☐	☐
Take to an orgiastic party	☐	☐	☐	☐	☐
Use four-letter words	☐	☐	☐	☐	☐
Rape; force to have intercourse	☐	☐	☐	☐	☐

(Based on Eysenck, 1972a)

in longer pre-coital love play than introverts. Studies in Germany, England and the USA have since given ample confirmation of these predictions (Eysenck, 1976b). Consider just a few results from a large-scale German study, using students as subjects. These were divided into extraverts, ambiverts (i.e. intermediate) and introverts on the basis of a personality questionnaire, and then asked to give an account of their sexual conduct. It was found that for the males, 47 per cent, 70 per cent and 77 per cent of introverts, ambiverts and extraverts had had intercourse; for the females the figures were 42 per cent, 57 per cent and 71 per cent. Frequency of coitus was about double for extraverts compared with introverts, with ambiverts in between. Number of coitus partners during the last year increased dramatically from introverts, through ambiverts, to extraverts; those who had four or more sex partners in that time included 7 per cent of the introvert group, 12 per cent of the ambivert, and 25 per cent of the extravert group. These figures are for males; for females they are 4 per cent, 6 per cent and 17 per cent. *Cunnilingus, fellatio*, and use of many different coital positions all showed extraverts superior to introverts. These and many other similar results show that extraverts are in fact high on the libido factor, in behaviour as well as in attitudes.

This difference also extends to sexual preferences. Thus Eysenck (1972a) predicted that extraverted males would like big-breasted women better than did introverted males; this was indeed found to be so. Presumably the arousal produced by big-breasted women was too much for the already over-aroused introverts! (Freudian theory predicts what is essentially the opposite, but, as Scodel (1957) has shown, empirical results are exactly the opposite to what Freud predicted. His paper is reprinted in Eysenck and Wilson's (1973) book, *The Experimen-*

Opposite are listed a number of activities of adult males towards different types of females. For each female type please place a tick in the appropriate box IF YOU CONSIDER THAT THE ACTIVITY TOWARDS THAT PARTICULAR FEMALE TYPE IS EITHER DEPRAVED OR CORRUPT.

N.B. There are *five* female types to be rated for each activity.

Do not make any mark if you do not consider the activity to be depraved or corrupt.

tal Study of Freudian Theories, together with a discussion of the reasons for this disconfirmation.)

These data all deal with verbal statements of the people questioned, and it might be argued that what people say and what people do are two quite different things. There are reasons for believing that what was stated in these questionnaires was in fact an accurate portrayal of the habitual sexual reactions of the persons involved, but there is also strictly objective, experimental evidence which points in the same direction. We have already had occasion to mention the importance of habituation in dealing with pornographic films, i.e. the fact that repeated showing of such films lowers the reactions of viewers. Habituation is related to arousal (negatively), and there is much evidence that extraverts habituate more quickly than introverts to simple acoustic and visual stimuli, repeated a number of times. Nelson (1978) carried out an experiment to test whether the same effect would be found with pornographic films. He chose a sample of 40 male subjects, selecting them on the basis of a personality questionnaire such that 10 each fell into the four possible combinations of high and low extraversion, and high and low neuroticism. Nine films were prepared, each lasting for four minutes, and each portraying one particular type of sexual activity (*fellatio, cunnilingus*, intercourse from behind, *soixante-neuf*, etc.); the films were prepared by cutting up and splicing together excerpts from very explicit pornographic films. Subjects were tested on three occasions, separated by at least twenty-four hours; they were shown three films on each occasion, separated by four minutes of rest. What was measured as an index of the individual's reaction was his penile erection, using a penis plethysmograph which gave an accurate measure of the increase in the size of the penis. There are three measures of habituation in this design. (1) There is habituation within each film, i.e. from beginning to end; (2) there is habituation from film to film within each session; and (3) there is habituation from occasion to occasion, i.e. from day to day. All three measures of hábituation showed that extraverts habituated more quickly and more thoroughly than did introverts, thus verifying on an experimental basis the prediction from theory.

There is also experimental evidence from the differential conditioning effects of erotic pictures on introverts and extraverts. Kantorowitz (1978) has reported on a study in which he tried to verify certain extensions of Eysenck's personality theory made by Gray (1972). Gray had suggested that introverts condition better to stimuli associated with anxiety, guilt, frustrative non-reward, etc., while extraverts condition better to potential rewards, and appetitive contexts. In a similar way, Eysenck and Levey (1972) had suggested that introverts would condition better to weak unconditioned stimuli, extraverts to strong unconditioned stimuli. Kantorowitz used pictures of nude women as his conditioned stimuli, and measured the strength of the penile response before and after conditioning. Conditioning consisted of pairing certain of these pictures either with tumescence (build-up of orgasm through masturbation), or with detumescence (post-orgasm period). He found that pictures paired with tumescence *gained* in erotic effect (i.e. produced greater penile erection after the experiment), while pictures paired with detumescence *lost* in erotic effect (i.e. produced smaller penile erection after the experiment). The former effect was much stronger in extraverts, as predicted, while the latter effect was much stronger in introverts. Thus pleasant consequences produce quick conditioning in extraverts, unpleasant ones in introverts. The relevance of these findings of the conditioning situation presented by the showing of erotic and pornographic material on the screen will be clear; extraverts are likely to be turned on, and conditioned to respond positively to the situations and activities shown in the film, much more strongly than introverts. Introverts, in so far as they respond with disgust and other negative emotions, are likely to be turned off, and conditioned not to respond sexually, or to respond in a negative manner, to the situations and activities shown in the film. A long history of such conditioning may be largely responsible for the differences in attitudes and behaviour we found between extraverts and introverts.

One further point may be of interest, partly because it deals with some possible consequences of pornographic portrayals of certain sexual behaviours. These often include oral sex, and the likely consequence of this is that those viewing many of these films are likely to wish to experiment with *cunnilingus* and *fellatio*, and try out the delights of '69'. Puritans will likely view oral sex as 'perversion', and condemn its showing as pornographic and 'obscene'; libertarians will likely view it rather as a liberating act which shows many people what they have been missing. What has been found in some actual studies of sexual behaviour of male and female respondents has been that when we ask separately whether the person in question has indulged in a particular type of activity, and whether he/she has enjoyed it, great differences are found between men and women. Men nearly always enjoyed whatever it was that they had done; women in nearly half the cases said that they had not enjoyed various activities, including *fellatio* and '69', although they had participated in them. Thus if showing oral sex in films has the effect of making this type of activity more popular among males (who after all constitute the majority of viewers of pornographic material) it would also have the effect of forcing many women to take part in *fellatio*, say, in order to please their men, while in reality disliking it. This point would repay more detailed study; most writers seem to assume that what people do in the sexual sphere, they enjoy. Clearly this is not so; we must distinguish between *doing* and *liking,* and this suggests that much of the material surveyed in earlier studies needs to be looked at again from this point of view. Men's higher libido pushes them towards activities that many low-libido women do not like, although they may acquiesce and take part (Eysenck, 1976b).

This completes our survey of individual differences in attitudes towards pornography; inevitably there is more material available here than in relation to violence. Here we have two major sources of information, namely political association (some parties are more committed to violence than others), and criminality (some crimes are associated with violence, others are not). Taking the political side first, Eysenck (1954) showed that the usual manner of thinking of different political attitudes and parties, i.e. in terms of a right–left continuum, with conservatives on the right, socialists on the left, and liberals in the middle, is over-simplified. There are in fact two major dimensions involved, of which one is indeed the right–left axis. However, quite independent of this we have a second axis which was called toughmindedness vs. tendermindedness. At the toughminded end were found individuals who were members of the communist and fascist parties; at the tenderminded end individuals who were members of the liberal party. Members of the toughminded parties were studied in detail, with respect to their personalities, and they were indeed found to be highly aggressive and dominant (Eysenck and Coulter, 1972). Further study of toughminded attitudes showed that these were much more pronounced in males than in females, and in addition were correlated with the personality factor of P (psychoticism); in the same study it was found that there was a strong genetic component to this attitude dimension (Eaves and Eysenck, 1974). Toughminded people tended to have very anti-marriage, and pro-premarital and extramarital sex attitudes, linked with a strong dislike of censorship of sexual material; this agrees well, of course, with the predominantly male and high P nature of the group. We thus have a fairly broad association of maleness, high P personality test scores, a high libido, strong aggressive and dominant behaviour patterns, toughminded political and social attitudes, and a liking for pornography and sexual indulgence outside the confines of marriage. While obviously influenced by environmental factors, these various attitudes and behaviours were found to have a firm genetic basis which makes it unlikely that they would be easily changed into more socially approved types of behaviour; it is also possible that they may be exacerbated by pornography and by explicit teaching of more 'advanced' sexual mores and behaviours.

A last addition to this group of behaviours and attitudes is overtly anti-social and indeed criminal behaviour. Maleness has always been known to be associated with criminality, there being about ten male criminals in our prisons for every single woman. The personality factor P has also been found to be associated with maleness, as we have already seen, and with antisocial behaviour and criminality (Eysenck, 1977b). There are thus links between anti-social behaviour, violence, and permissive sexual attitudes, including a liking for pornography, in the personalities of men and women; furthermore, these links are at least in part genetic in origin, possibly based on hormonal secretions. It seems extremely unlikely that the presentation of explicit scenes of sex and violence would have identical effects on persons showing this combination of characteristics, and on those showing exactly the opposite combination. We would therefore argue that any satisfactory experiment into the effects of sex and violence in the media should always incorporate separate measures of the most relevant personality traits of the subjects taking part in the experiment, and should explicitly formulate differential predictions about the reactions of different personality types. To treat everyone alike, and expect all subjects to react similarly to these experimental stimuli, is unreasonable, and out of line with the empirical evidence.

Mention of a genetic basis for sexual attitudes and behaviour, as well as for social attitudes like 'toughmindedness', and for anti-social conduct, requires at least a brief look at the evidence for these statements. The relevant work (Eysenck, 1976a, 1976b) used the twin paradigm, i.e. compared similarities between identical twins with similarities between fraternal same-sexed twins. If a given trait or behaviour pattern has a strong genetic basis, then identical twins, sharing 100 per cent identical heredity, should be more alike than fraternal twins, who only share on the average 50 per cent identical heredity. This rather simple scheme can be used very effectively to test models of genetic and environmental causation, interaction, and also the influence of non-additive genetic variables, such as dominance or assortative mating. (There is some assortative mating (i.e. men marrying women having similar attitudes or behaviour patterns) for libido (correlation for 239 spouses = 0.51), for satisfaction ($r = 0.46$), and for pornography ($r = 0.36$). As far as sexual attitudes are compared, like marries like – at least to some extent.) It would take us too far afield to go into details of the many studies done, and reviewed in the references given above; the major outcome has been a demonstration that genetic factors account for much if not most of the observed differences between people in respect of personality, sexual attitudes and behaviour, social attitudes, anti-social behaviour, etc. It is sometimes objected that the assumption of much of this twin work, namely that the environmental pressures of identical twins are similar to those on fraternal twins, is incorrect, and that parents and others treat identical twins more alike than they do fraternal twins. Special studies to investigate this point have shown that there is some truth in it, but the greater similarities in the treatment of identical twins tend to be in relation to unimportant issues, such as wearing similar clothes, and do not affect important personality aspects; indeed, if anything the effect may be in the opposite direction. Identical twins often attempt to assert their individuality by deliberately going in different directions; it is possibly for this reason that when identical twins are separated early in life, their personalities are found to be somewhat more alike than those of identical twins brought up together.

The suggestion which emerges from this review of individual differences studies is that there is a common source for sexual and aggressive/violent behaviour, and this connection has often been suggested before (see Chapter 7). There is a biological basis for such a link in a number of brain stimulation and endocrinological studies with animals. MacLean (1965), for instance, found evidence that the neural systems for sexual and aggressive behaviour are located in close proximity to each other within the limbic system of the brain, and it seems likely that they partly overlap, or are directly linked. It has also been shown that injections of male sex hormone into female mice and rats produced an *aggressive* effect. Similarly, it has been shown in animals that painful stimulation can evoke sexual as well as aggressive responses, suggesting that these two kinds of behaviour may somehow be intimately linked to each other. Thus there was a greatly increased incidence of copulation in response to electric shock applied to the tails of rats (Caggiula and Eibergen, 1969); it is well known that such stimulation usually issues in aggressive behaviour.

At the human level, too, there is some evidence to suggest a close connection between aggression and sex. Jaffe *et al.* (1974) review some of the earlier work, showing that erotic fantasies are elicited by picture stimuli to a greater extent after exposure to anger-producing situations, and that exposure to sexual stimuli increases aggressive as well as sexual fantasy. Inhibition of aggression also seems to inhibit sexual responsiveness. In their actual experiment, Jaffe *et al.* had half their subjects read sexually arousing passages, while the other half read neutral passages. All subjects were given an opportunity to (apparently) give shocks to an experimental confederate as 'punishment' for incorrect responses in an experiment. Sexually aroused males and females delivered more intense shocks than non-aroused subjects, regardless of the sex of the confederate or experimenter – although, of course, as usual, no real shocks were given.

There are many such studies, showing that strong erotica, including films depicting pre-coital and coital behaviour, can intensify or produce aggressive behaviour; a list of these studies is given by Zillmann and Sapolsky (1977). There seems to be no doubt that exposure to explicit sexual material increases aggressiveness – although there is the curious fact that mild erotic material may have the opposite effect, reducing aggressive feelings and behaviours even below the level produced by neutral material. The association between aggression and sex, originally suggested by the frequency with which prostitutes are murdered, or attacked, and which has strong psychiatric support from individual case studies of rape, thus finds support in the experimental literature. This result is of considerable importance. Many critics have argued that while violence in the media should be curbed (provided we agree that the showing of violence does in fact have an observable effect on viewers), there is no reason to curb erotic presentations because the effects, if any, would not be socially undesirable, as the effects of violence undoubtedly are. But if the effects of viewing overtly sexual behaviour are in fact to increase aggressive and violent behaviour, as the literature suggests, then this defence falls to the ground. Attempts to reduce violence should be concerned with a reduction of both violent and sexual behaviour on the screen.

The studies mentioned, and those to which reference will be found in the papers already cited, have uniformly failed to look at the important role undoubtedly played by personality in mediating violent and aggressive reactions to sexually explicit stimuli. This seems unfortunate; here too it is unlikely that all men and women react uniformly to the stimuli presented, and it could be of considerable importance to discover which personality types are more likely to be incited to aggression by sexual stimuli. The theory underlying the personality dimensions of P, E and N suggests answers to this problem, but only empirical research can be counted upon to tell us just what the facts are. For the moment, this particular refinement must be left for the future; all that is clear is that in many people sex and aggression are intimately linked, and stimulation along one dimension can easily lead to stimulation in the other. In this the work described in the earlier part of this chapter, and that described in the last few paragraphs, seems to lead to much the same conclusion.

SUMMARY

It has been observed throughout this volume that there are great dangers in averaging results over groups, in view of the marked individual differences in reaction which are seen constantly. This chapter demonstrates that these differences are not haphazard, but are consistently related to personality, and to sex. Men and women differ in their sexual behaviour and their attitudes, not only in obvious ways, but also in many details which accord with popular stereotypes. Personality differences are related particularly to the extraversion–introversion dimension, to neurotic emotionality, and to tough-mindedness, in predictable and testable ways. Extraverts, for instance, indulge in intercourse earlier than introverts, do so more frequently, with more different partners, in more different positions, and use more unorthodox methods of love-making. Highly emotional people tend to have strong guilt feelings, suffer more from impotence, lack of orgasm, premature ejaculation, and frigidity. The tough-minded tend to go for impersonal sex, aggressive sex, and to look down upon marriage as an institution. All these differences have a strong genetic component, although environmental factors are not lacking. Direct experimental studies have shown that these behaviour patterns have a physiological basis; thus extraverts show much greater habituation to repeated sexual stimuli, and condition quickly to stimuli paired with sexually exciting and stimulating events, such as orgasm. Introverts do not habituate readily to sexual stimuli, but condition quickly to sexual stimuli characterized by negative emotional reactions. *Individual differences are so marked and universal, and conform so closely to scientific laws that any empirical study which neglects to pay attention to their existence is likely to miss the most important part of the evidence.* The calculation of averages which disguise the existence of individual differences is often misleading, and may account for the frequency with which experimental results are found not to be replicable by other workers.

11 Conclusions and Recommendations

In this chapter we shall briefly recapitulate the major findings and conclusions; these will then be followed by some discussion, and our recommendations. We shall begin with the portrayal of acts of violence in the media, and the effects this portrayal may have on viewers. The evidence is fairly unanimous that *aggressive acts new to the subject's repertoire of responses, as well as acts already well established, can be evoked by the viewing of violent scenes portrayed on film, TV or in the theatre*. There is ample evidence that media violence increases viewer aggression, and may also increase viewer sexual libido. To say that TV has such effects is not to say that these are the only, or even the most important, influences which lead to violence and aggression; TV is just one of a number of such influences, but withal a powerful and omnipresent one. It is particularly convincing, in our view, that different methods of investigation all point to an association between viewing violence and subsequent aggression. Admittedly many studies have major or minor methodological faults, but these tend to cancel out in view of the fact that different studies have different strengths and different weaknesses. This conclusion that media presentation of violence does have an effect is of some social importance; it provides a factual framework within which to plan social action.

Clearly there are still many lacunae in our knowledge. We do not know in any detail just what aspects of the violent scenes are responsible for producing strong or weak effects; suggestions that what is clearly fantasy material (cartoons) may not be harmful, or that justified aggression may not be harmful, have not been borne out by empirical studies. Much work remains to be done in this field. Similarly we know very little about the differential effects of violent material on different personality types; future research will clearly have to bear this variable in mind more carefully than has been done in the past. It is as important in science to know what the gaps in one's knowledge are, as to know what has already been ascertained; these gaps must be filled to give us a proper model to work with.

As regards the effects of pornography, clearly the differential effects are even more pronounced than in the case of violence. *That pornography has effects on viewers and readers can no longer be disputed, but these effects can be quite variable.* It may produce titillation in some, in others it may elicit feelings of guilt or revulsion, while in yet others it may provoke anti-social sexual behaviour, or help condition them into deviancy. It may lead to marital maladjustment and sex problems, and have all manner of subtle effects, such as modifying fantasies and attitudes to one's sex partner. There is even evidence that it may lead to aggression and violence. On the other hand, used in conjunction with behaviour therapy, pornographic material may be of help in solving some deep-seated sexual problems, although there is no evidence that it can do so without the help of a therapist. A good deal, then, is known about the effects of pornography, but here too there are large areas of ignorance.

Researchers have not looked very much at the effect that pornography may have on feelings and attitudes to sex, although anti-pornography crusaders have stressed the possibility that it is precisely in relation to such attitudes that pornography may do the worst damage. Reactions of children have, for obvious reasons, not been looked at experimentally; this is of particular concern because they would appear to be the most vulnerable. Perhaps empirical work could be begun using the so-called sex education classes which are held in many schools; these are regarded by many parents (and children) as pornographic, even though the intention is of course quite different; it might be possible to discover differential effects of differing emphases on biological and social factors, libido vs. love, physical attraction vs. emotional involvement, etc. It seems likely that whatever effects pornography may have, these effects will be strongest in children, but evidence for this belief is lacking.

The tentative way in which researchers often speak of their findings, and the general refusal of scientists to express certainty about their conclusions, have given rise in politicians and laymen not used to this self-effacing and modest way of presenting data to the illusion that 'nothing is really known', or that 'it is impossible to come to any conclusions'. This is not so. All scientific judgements are probabilistic, i.e. they are never certain, but only probable. This is as true of conclusions reached in physics, astronomy and chemistry, as it is in psychology. Philosophers of science have pondered the nature of scientific induction since the days of Hume, if not earlier; how can we ever draw general inferences from limited knowledge? The self-denying ordinance following upon such philosophical doubts serves scientists well, in reminding them of the nemesis of disregarding the limitations their methodology imposes on them, but it may give altogether wrong notions to non-scientists who read these conclusions. Our theories concerning gravitation may not be certain, but our deductions from these theories are accurate enough to land a man on the moon.

In the same way, to profess certainty about our theories of desensitization, evaluative conditioning, modelling, identification or socialization would be absurd; nevertheless, these theories clearly possess a kernel of truth, and give rise to predictions many of which have been verified in the laboratory, or in real life. These theories can be, and have been, applied to the field of sex and violence, and have been tested directly in a variety of situations, with positive results. All this does not give us the right to claim certainty for far-reaching conclusions, but it does enable us to claim that the notions that 'nothing is known', or that 'all is disagreement' are no longer tenable. We do know something about the effectiveness of the media in these fields, and we do know something about just how this effectiveness is mediated. Much remains to be known, but a good beginning has been made which can be used to make certain recommendations, albeit with considerable caution. These recommendations inevitably imply certain social value judgements; in this the present chapter differs from those that precede it. However, an effort will be made wherever possible to link these value judgements with the factual evidence.

Our first recommendation will not come as a surprise to anyone who has read thus far; it is to the effect that *makers of films and TV programmes, producers of theatre plays and others concerned with the portrayal of violence should show more social responsibility than they have done so far*. This means that they should be required to familiarize themselves with the literature reviewed in this book, and take seriously the findings which show that viewing violence does, for many people and in many instances, act to increase the chances of aggression occurring. By itself, of course, this would not be enough; producers of such films, documentaries and shows often work under orders from businessmen, advertisers and others whose concern is to produce the maximum viewing figures, and who may not be impressed by requests for social responsibility. This means, necessarily, that some form of censorship may be essential. Such censorship already exists, to some extent, but it needs to be strengthened, and those acting as censors should also be made familiar with the facts outlined in this book.

Any mention of censorship immediately calls forth protests on the part of those concerned with individual liberty and freedom of speech, and such protests deserve a respectful hearing. We would like to call attention to the similarity of the situation, in respect of violence, to that obtaining in relation to the law concerning incitement to racial hatred and violence. Most people feel, quite rightly, that such laws are essential for the preservation of racial harmony; their absence in Hitler's Germany, and in the Weimar Republic immediately preceding Hitler's take-over, give an awful warning of the dangers of unlimited licence, and the need for some form of censorship. (It is debatable whether the existing laws of the Weimar Republic were insufficient, or whether it was their application that was at fault; the point is not material to our argument.) If we forbid the use of words and actions which may lead to violence directed at certain minority groups, are we not justified in forbidding the use of words and actions which may lead to violence directed at random members of the nation as a whole? The argument seems a strong one to us, and to justify the use of censorship, *given that it has been established that the portrayal of violence in the media can incite some viewers to violence.*

We shall discuss presently the ways in which prohibitions could be worded to avoid the absurd situation which has arisen in relation to the laws about pornography; here let us first consider which would be the best locus for such censorship. Laws administered by the courts would seem to be the last resort in this connection; as far as TV and the films are concerned some form of self-censorship might be preferable.

Indeed, some such form of censorship already exists, but is presumably too weak to be very effective. This weakness may in part be a function of the lack of knowledge (or rather the presumed lack of knowledge) which enemies of censorship in this field have always pleaded as giving film and TV producers the unlimited right to introduce as much sex and violence into their products as the market would bear. Now that this excuse has been removed by the large body of research here reviewed it may be hoped that internal censorship may be more effective. It might also be suggested that the persons and bodies concerned should be instructed to pay more attention to the views of ordinary viewers, rather than to those of a self-styled intellectual and artistic 'elite' whose ideas are quite alien to those of the great majority. (It would, of course, be counter-productive if these 'bodies of ordinary viewers' were to be made up of groups as far removed from the broad consensus in the censorious direction as the trendy 'elite' is in the direction of permissiveness.) But above all they must be instructed to become familiar with the facts of the case; ignorance may be bliss, but such bliss can be bought at too high a price. No one ignorant of the facts should be allowed to pass judgement in matters of this kind; the present situation of the blind leading the blind has gone on too long to be tolerable.

In saying that there should be censorship of violence in the media, we would not wish to exclude all violence; this would clearly be impossible, as well as undesirable. We have reviewed the kinds of violence which have the greatest likelihood of being imitated, and which should be drastically reduced; we have also discussed the kinds of context within which violence is particularly dangerous. We have no wish to lay down a code of practice here; this would be inappropriate. But we do feel that such a code of practice should be drawn up, and that there is now sufficient empirical evidence to make at least a beginning.

Our second recommendation will also not come as a surprise; it is that *the kind of censorship we have suggested for violence should also apply to the portrayal of perverted sexual behaviour.* (By perversions we do not mean to refer to unusual positions in intercourse, but to extreme forms of sadism, rape, incest, and other demonstrably harmful types of behaviour.) However, even more than in the case of violence, we feel that this is a two-dimensional problem; there is the degree of sexual activity to be tolerated on the screen, and there is the context of this sexual activity. It is often suggested that the viewing of sexual intercourse on the screen should be the free right of all adults, and that no one has the right to interfere with this. Even if this were to be accepted, there would clearly be a number of restrictions to this universal right. The wording of the sentence above automatically rules out viewing by children, but to provide shows on the screen which would definitely exclude children is a difficult task in the cinema, and an impossible one on TV. This automatically differentiates cinema and TV entertainment, with much tougher rules for the latter. The need not to offend viewers who find such displays disgusting, but who for various reasons may have them brought to their (unwilling) attention if TV were to follow the cinema in its degree of permissiveness reinforces this point. Advertising in the press, and on posters outside cinemas, also requires close attention from these two points of view; rules seem to be rather lax in respect to these points, particularly in so far as the access of children to the offending material is concerned.

We shall return to the measurement of the degree of sexual activity a little later; here let us go back to the problem of context. It seems clear to us that there are certain areas of sexual behaviour which should be completely excluded from the list of permitted activities; sex involving children is one such area, rape and other forms of sexual violence, vividly and explicitly presented, are others. Sex involving animals would probably also come into this category, although there is too little evidence to make it safe to say anything much about this. Torture, bondage and sado-masochistic acts involving sex may also be mentioned here. Such films may perhaps be shown on psychiatric prescription to patients addicted to such perversions, but they are not safe for public showing. There are minor perversions, such as rubber fetishism, which do not seem to present any great danger, and which could be freely permitted in cinemas, though perhaps not on TV.

We now come to the crux of our recommendations in relation to pornography; the suggestions made so far are little more than common sense, and are in fact pretty well in line with ordinary practice. What we are suggesting next is that *the content of a presentation should be judged in relation to the prevailing tone of the presentation*. An example may make this point clear. John Cleland's *Fanny Hill* is perhaps as erotic a book as one could wish to read; it contains detailed descriptions of sexual intercourse in a great variety of positions, pre- and extramarital sex, promiscuity, prostitution and 'unnatural' sexual behaviours. Yet the tone is one of enjoyment, women are not degraded by the men they consort with, and there is no violence to destroy this sense of good humour and enjoyment. For adult viewers and given the precautions named above, we cannot see any reason why such a work should not be shown on film, for adult audiences, however explicit the sexual scenes might be. Such a film would undoubtedly have certain effects on the people who chose to view it, but none of the effects could be said to be socially undesirable – unless we regard sexual behaviour outside marriage as undesirable in itself. The film might lead to an increase in sexual activity, and it might lead to greater variety in sexual activity, but it is difficult to see that the censor would have any right to interfere with the freedom of the adult citizen to choose such material for viewing should he or she so desire.

We are aware that many people would disagree with this suggestion, but we know of no evidence that such a presentation would do harm, and indeed there is evidence, as we have pointed out, that the effect on attitudes towards the other sex might be positive. From a Christian position such a film would portray values unacceptable to believers, and would possibly lead to consequences (such as an increase in premarital sex) unacceptable to them. But our civilization is not predominantly a Christian one any longer, and non-Christians have a right to their own value systems; it would be impossible to enforce a minority set of values on the majority, even if there were any evidence regarding the superiority of such values.

However, many if not most of the commercially available pornographic films are not of this 'wholesome', hedonistic character. Even when they do not overtly depict scenes of violence and degradation of women at the hands of men, such as rape, beatings, and subordination, the tone is consistently anti-feminist, with women only serving to act as sexual slaves to men, being made use of, and ultimately being deprived of their right to a sexual climax – in the majority of such films, the portrayal ends with the men spraying their semen over the faces and breasts of the women. This is clearly not done because it is sexually appealing to men; our subjects in a series of unpublished experiments were questioned about their attitudes to different parts of the pornographic films they were shown, and they almost universally regarded this bit as 'silly', 'stupid', and 'uninteresting'.[1] The intention would seem to be simply to degrade women, and it is noteworthy that in many cases of rape the men involved either act in the same manner, or else urinate all over the women involved, a type of behaviour very similar in intention.

It is this sort of thing we mean by saying that actions of a sexual character should be judged in terms of the context; where the context is hostile to women, as most pornographic films are, we feel that such films should fall under the category of 'incitement to violence towards minority groups' – even though women are not a minority group. Nevertheless such films do constitute a clear case of incitement to maltreat women, downgrade them to a lower status, regard them as mere sex objects, and elevate male *machismo* to a superior position in the scale of values. Evaluative conditioning, modelling, and desensitization all point to the same conclusion, namely that such presentations have effects on men's attitudes which are detrimental to women; in fairness to more than one half of the population, such incitements should be proscribed. The amount of overt sex in such films may not differ in any way from that shown in our hypothetical *Fanny Hill* film; what is important in marking the difference is the context, which is pro-love, pro-sex, and pro-women, in the one case, but anti-women, anti-love, and even anti-sex (in the sense of gentle, pleasant, co-operative sex) in the other.

[1] We have found, rather surprisingly, that many if not most of the pornographic films available for private viewing, and mostly imported from Denmark, Sweden and Germany, do not emphasize erotic arousal to anything like the degree one might have expected. Judging by the comments and ratings of our subjects, and also by interviews with some of the makers of such films, the aim is often rather to shock, and some vague *avant-garde* notion of departure from acknowledged standards, rather than to please. Long-continued close-up shots of intercourse have little erotic appeal to most viewers, and the failure to use establishing shots often makes it almost impossible to even guess who is doing what to whom; the piston-like movements shown soon become boring, and lose all sexual meaning. Most viewers seem to like a pleasant story, told in sequence; pornographic films of the commercial kind seldom have much of a story, and what there is is often filmed in so hurried and perfunctory a fashion as to be meaningless. Whole chunks are left out; thus a couple is often seen kissing, fully clothed, and naked in bed in the next shot. One consequence of greater permissiveness of 'nice' pornography might be an improvement in the standard of such films. Film makers might with advantage seek psychological advice on what may 'turn on' their customers; they clearly only succeed at a very low level at the moment.

It is odd that present-day laws of censorship seem to work in exactly the opposite direction. Pleasant, simple, enjoyable love-making is actively discouraged in its portrayal in films and on TV; instead we have *A Clockwork Orange*, *Straw Dogs*, and the like. The anti-censorship warriors seem to have a strong point in suggesting that puritanism dies hard, and that much of the censoriousness which bedevils discussions of this issue is due to a determined desire on the part of the censors that no one should enjoy sex and its portrayal in the media. Our suggestion, based as it is on the existing evidence, goes clearly counter to this trend; we would apply censorship to sexual material only when it is joined with undesirable secondary matter, such as violence, anti-female sentiments, or the celebration of male *machismo*. Women have as much right to be protected in this respect as do racial minorities; the rules of censorship should be changed accordingly.

We believe that the trend of jury decisions in prosecutions under the obscenity laws points this way; it has become very difficult to get anything but an acquittal where pornographic material is concerned. These acquittals are accompanied by obvious unease; this unease seems to be equally attributable to two causes. One is that while the simple portrayal of sexual acts does not seem to the juries to be actionable, the tone or context within which the sexual acts occur does seem to introduce doubt. The other cause is the absurd way in which the law is framed; to succeed, the prosecution has to prove a tendency to deprave and corrupt, terms which are too imprecise to carry much meaning.

It is curious that while few people would dispute that violence presents much more of a problem than does pornography, yet laws and restrictions are much more concerned with the latter than with the former. We have suggested that this point of view should be reversed, and that violence should be made the prime target of censorship, with pornography being censored mainly in terms of its 'context'. How can this best be accomplished? It is one of the great difficulties of all censorship that it tends to appear subjective, capricious, and far removed from the putative certainty of other types of law; there is constant argument about phrases such as 'tending to deprave and corrupt'. It is virtually impossible, as we have seen, to attribute any agreed meaning to such a phrase, and to express the intention of a law in such almost meaningless language is to make certain that the law will be brought into disrepute.

Is it possible to bring greater certainty into such a field as this? Eysenck (1972a) has suggested (if with tongue partly in cheek) a way of doing so, in relation to verbal erotica. Starting with evidence from several studies about the degree of 'explicitness' or 'severity' of a number of sexual behaviours, he derived a scale which is reproduced below, as Table 42. This scale ranges from behaviour having no sexual content (social talking – rating 0 points), through groping and intercourse to *soixante-neuf* (rating 15 points). Other items could be included, after suitable research on their proper position on this scale.

Given this table as a guide-line, Eysenck went on to construct a rating scale for the measurement, objectively and with reasonable accuracy, of the amount of erotic content of a given passage of prose. Points were given for specific mention of parts of the body, and specific erotic activities; Table 43 sets out

Table 42 Scale of sexual activity	
	Points
Social talking	0
One minute continuous lip kissing	3.0
Manual manipulation of female breast, over clothes	4.5
Manual manipulation of female breast, under clothes	5.3
Kissing nipples of female breast	6.3
Manual manipulation of female genitals	6.5
Manual manipulation of male genitals	7.2
Mutual manual manipulation of genitals	7.3
Sexual intercourse, face to face	8.3
Manual manipulation of male genitals to ejaculation	8.6
Oral manipulation of female genitals	10.3
Oral manipulation of male genitals	10.8
Sexual intercourse, man behind woman	12.2
Mutual oral-genital manipulation	12.5
Oral manipulation of male genitals to ejaculation	12.8
Mutual oral manipulation of genitals to mutual orgasm	15.0
(Based on Eysenck, 1972a)	

points for mention of specific parts of the body, and Table 42 was used to fix the number of points given for specific actions. The details of the procedure are not important here; suffice it to say that when a number of subjects were asked to rate a variety of erotic and pornographic passages according to their salaciousness or obscenity, the order agreed over 90 per cent with that given by the formula. The method would of course have to be extended to include more clearly 'pornographic' acts, such as sex with children, rape, etc.; there is no difficulty in that.

Much the same could be done, of course, with visual presentations; we have drawn up a similar list, and made up a similar formula, which has been applied to pornographic films and also agrees well with overall judgements made by viewers. Nothing would prevent the construction of such a formula for acts of violence, going from pushing someone to gouging out of eyes, flaying, or impaling. It would be necessary to state duration of each act, distancing of shots, and other variables, but in principle such a formula presents the only possibility of making the law what it ought to be – certain, objective, and predictable. The function of a jury would not be that of experts in psychology, psychiatry, and sociology, interpreting the Delphic overtones of meaningless jargon, but simply to assess the factual evidence concerned with the application of the formula to a given piece of film.

Obviously this method would need some research before it could be properly evaluated; nevertheless we believe that if there is to be censorship, something of this kind is necessary in order to remove the huge aura of uncertainty which bedevils all present attempts to frame laws involving censorship. It will be objected that such a formula leaves out of account the intention of the whole work of art, does not concern itself with the artistic value of the product, and is altogether too mechanical and atomistic to be acceptable. We believe that these are not defects, but rather advantages.[1] Many readers of such books as

[1] Scientific measurement is concerned with measuring one thing at a time; it is confusing when a single measurement combines two or more entirely different concepts. Early thermometers left the top open, thus measuring a mixture of temperature and atmospheric pressure; this confusion was ended when the top was closed, and we now have thermometers which measure temperature, and barometers which measure atmospheric pressure separately. In the same way, the erotic or pornographic potential of a film or a book is one thing; its artistic merit is another. Any scientific measurement of the former should be quite without regard to the latter; if we wish to take into account artistic merit, this should be separately assessed.

Table 43 The Erotic Index

Nouns	Points			
lips, mouth	1	*Adjectives*		
shoulders	1	favourable	+1 ⎱	up to two adjectives
body	2	unfavourable	−2 ⎰	for one noun
back, stomach	2	*Verbs*		
legs	2	signifying manual	2 ⎱	multiple appropriate
breasts	4	manipulation		nouns
nipples	5	signifying oral	4 ⎰	
buttocks	5	manipulation		
thighs	5	*Adverbs*		
sexual parts	8	favourable	1 ⎱	up to two adverbs
		unfavourable	−2 ⎰	for one verb

(Based on Eysenck, 1972a)

Lady Chatterley's Lover are not concerned with its artistic merits; their attitude is much closer to that of the kind reader who, in the copy available at our Public Library, had obligingly written on the front page of the book the numbers of the pages on which the most sexy events occurred.

Our point would be, not only that art does not need the explicit portrayal of sex and violence (to the degree which we would like to suggest as subject to censorship), but that such portrayal is entirely counter-productive, destroying whatever artistic intentions the author may have had. Nudity, extreme violence and cruelty, and extreme suggestiveness of sexual conduct are so arousing in themselves that they draw attention away from the artistic integrity of the film or drama, and reduce its aesthetic impact. To show Lady Macbeth, to take but one example, sleep-walking in the nude (because in her time people slept in the nude) does not add to the artistic impact of Shakespeare's play; it simply sidetracks viewers' attention, and instead of being absorbed by the play they begin to wonder about the size and shape of the particular actress's breasts and buttocks. Similarly, the film production of *Macbeth* in cinemas we attended at first held the audience spellbound, and then completely lost it, and produced helpless laughter, when Macbeth had his head cut off at the end, and it rolled down from the battlements like a football. Realism in these matters is much less gripping and artistic than the use of poetic imagination, and we have already considered some empirical evidence for this point of view.

In any case, we would query the argument that much of what is presented in the cinema and on TV nowadays is motivated by artistic and creative motives, particularly as far as the portrayal of violence and explicit sex is concerned. Artistic integrity is a useful cover for all sorts of motives – commercial, revolutionary, desire to shock; to judge by the final product artistic considerations do not seem to play a very large part in these 'shocking' portrayals. It is obviously dangerous to argue about motives on the sole evidence of the finished product, but a good deal is known about the commercial drives behind much of TV and film violence, and one would have to be very naive to believe in the importance of the 'artistic' defence of the vast majority of pornographic and violent productions.

Our fourth recommendation is so obvious, and is made so

frequently at the end of a discussion of almost any psychological problem, that we hesitate to put it down in print. However, we have to offer some qualifications to our recommendation which may make a discussion worthwhile. The recommendation is the time-honoured one that *more research is required*; clearly we have only scratched the surface of the problem, and much more remains to be known. This much will be obvious to everyone who has looked at the evidence, and indeed almost all writers on the topic have said as much. We have considered the problems arising from this recommendation rather carefully, and we feel that simply to say: 'More research!' is not enough. Research cannot be bought like so many pounds of potatoes, although the view that it can is often held by Government agencies commissioning research. (We have held research contracts with US agencies which asked for a contract to be signed which in fact was identical with the form of contract used for buying potatoes and other supplies.) To ask for more research often means to get research of the same redundant, poor quality as that already in existence; there would clearly be very little benefit in that. To commission research under the same constraints operating against discovery of the truth, e.g. banning certain researchers because they might obtain results unacceptable to the US television networks, would be useless and worse. It is obviously necessary to specify the conditions under which research can be of value, and this is a difficult and complex task.

We might approach this end by first of all enquiring why the existing research is of such poor quality, and why so much of it is subject to criticism which ought to have been anticipated and avoided. One or two of these reasons we have already discussed. Much work has been done by sociologists unaware of the psychological complexities of the topic, and ignorant of the psychological literature; the consequent lack of attention to relevant psychological theories, to well-known psychological facts, and to proper designs and research paradigms has made this whole literature rebarbative, and has severely limited its usefulness. Research, to be useful, must build on what is already known; it cannot start *de novo*, rising like Athene from the head of Zeus. Non-psychologists may have a supportive role to play in research of this kind, particularly when there is concern about institutional problems and policies, but without the necessary training in statistics, methodology and especially psychological theory they should never be asked to design or control the research project.

Psychological studies have often suffered from lack of time, lack of funds, and lack of imagination. The US Commission work was farmed out, and had to be finished, in a great hurry; this is not the way to get good results. Financing always underestimated the need for follow-ups and other vital aspects of a proper research design; finance was also lacking to elaborate designs by introducing experts in psychophysiological recording, for instance, leading to reliance on subjective assessments. Lack of imagination was probably the worst fault, aggravating the others mentioned. Research in science begins with an idea, not with funds; if funding precedes individual research ideas, the work done is likely to be shoddy, meretricious, and of low scientific value. It is instructive to note how repetitive much of the work commissioned at various times has been; simply doing again what others have done before is unlikely to generate new insights.

Another aspect of the work here reviewed which has militated against success is the individual nature of much of the experimentation. Continuity and team work are essential marks of successful research. The sudden influx of money into this field took a number of research workers away from their proper research sphere, kept them busy for two or three years, and then released them back to their previous careers. This mode of working almost guarantees poor research; it takes that long just to become properly acquainted with the problems involved, to get to know previous research in depth, and to start thinking creatively about what could be done to obviate the many obstacles that stand in one's way. It would be silly to blame the research workers concerned; the blame must attach to those doling out the money, in abject ignorance of what scientific research is all about.

We have just mentioned the need for team work; this is apparent whenever a particular problem (often of an applied kind) involves many diverse aspects, each of which demands a specialized skill for its solution. Our discussions throughout the book will have illustrated the complexity of the problem in question; experts in social psychology, clinical psychology, psychophysiology, personality, psychometrics, conditioning and learning theory are all involved with its many aspects. Thus a team approach is needed; individual workers, however brilliant, will be frustrated if their work does not have the back-up of a well-chosen team.

The simplest solution would thus appear to be the setting up of a research team, on a semi-permanent basis, to carry out research into the problems raised by the possibly anti-social effects of sex and violence in the media; financed perhaps by the Government, or by the TV authorities and the cinema companies. There is some precedent for such action. The drug companies are obliged by law to provide strong evidence of the non-harmful nature of any new drugs they seek to market, and this has led to the setting up by the drug companies of large, permanent research facilities. The analogy may be closer than is at first apparent; should we not demand of TV companies and film producers that they should provide evidence for the harmless nature of their wares, rather than insist that critics should prove their harmful nature? A small percentage of the licence fees, or the advertisement revenues, or the profits of such companies would serve to set up a Research Institute of sufficient magnitude to give us answers, in time, to most of the questions raised. This, then, would be our fourth recommendation; however, we would like to point out some serious dangers involved in the process.

The history of research in this field has left us entirely disenchanted with the activities of either governments and their nominees, or commercial undertakings and their representatives, in relation to scientific research. Neither group seems to be concerned with the facts, with truth, or with the possible consequences of coming to a wrong decision. Political and commercial expediency seems to take precedence over scientific requirements; we have amply documented these strictures in previous chapters, and will not do so again here. If such an institute as that mentioned above were to be set up, either by the Government or by the commercial groups involved, we have no doubt that every effort would be made to nominate for leading positions psychologists known to be favourable to whatever views might be held by the interests concerned, while those not holding these views, or suspected to be impartial, would be blackballed; the memory of Albert Bandura, a highly respected professor of psychology, a former president of the

American Psychological Association, and a pioneer of experimental work in modelling, being blackballed and prevented from sitting on the US Presidential Commission on Violence by the veto of the TV companies will take a lot of living down.

There are ways and means of reducing such a threat. Thus a committee could be formed by one of the Research Councils, or by the British Psychological Society, or the American Psychological Association, or by some other non-partisan, scientific organization, such as the Royal Society, or by some combination of these; such a committee might then consider the details of the setting up of such an institute, its finances, its manning, and its policy. Unless research is completely divorced from both politics and commerce there is little hope that research money, even if handed out in abundance, will produce worth-while results. The best research workers are already concerned with their own particular problems, and are unlikely to abandon these for a short-term research grant of the usual kind; even if they are willing to accept the money, they will require most of the time just to become familiar with the background knowledge, with the specific research problems, and with the needed know-how. By the time such research workers are beginning to have original ideas, and to become really able to do useful work, the grant is finished, and they have to return to their previous work.

In any case, what worth-while research worker will accept money for research when his independence is not guaranteed? Freedom to follow wherever the facts lead is indispensable to scientific research; to be hamstrung by political or commercial interference, or to have time and other limits placed on one's work because of such considerations, is intolerable. One realizes that large sums of money are at stake for film producers and TV companies, but social interest and scientific integrity must take precedence.

Our next recommendation is rather difficult to implement, but is also of some importance. We suggest that *the many absurd and often ludicrous suggestions for censorship of what is obviously acceptable material should cease, as they only bring the whole notion of censorship into disrepute.* Psychoanalysts have suggested that Lewis Carroll's books should be removed from the public libraries, on the grounds that *Alice's Adventures in Wonderland* contain many symbolic acts of aggression, and various sexual symbolisms. Similarly some sociologists have suggested removing Enid Blyton's *Little Noddy* because of the occasional pranks played by the Gollywog, a black doll; this was supposed to produce racial hatred. The decision by some Finnish librarians to ban Donald Duck (because he is naked, and because he gives a bad and bourgeois example of a one-parent family) is equally difficult to understand, unless it was done to bring all censorship into disrepute. Not far removed from these inanities was the attempt to have Linda Lovelace's book *Inside Linda Lovelace* banned; this gave enormous publicity to the book at the expense of the British taxpayer. The book is comical in its absurdity, rather than obscene. We doubt if the famous judge of whom it was once said that the proof of obscenity in a book was that it produced an erection in him, would have obliged in the case of Linda's silly frolic.

A further recommendation, or perhaps we should call it a plea, is to *cease to regard the battle between puritans and libertarians as one between political right and left.* There is no meaningful relation between opposing pornography and wishing to lower income tax, or between a belief that the portrayal of violence in the media will cause violence in the streets and dislike of nationalization. In fact, it is obvious that there is far more pornography, obscenity and violence in the media of the capitalist countries than there is in the communist countries – we have seen practically none in the Soviet Union, Poland, or the DDR, and from all accounts there are no such programmes in communist China. The impression of some political link has probably come about because the cause of pornography is featured by some youngish intellectuals connected with the media who also show anti-establishment attitudes in political and other fields; it seems likely that should the revolution they advocate ever happen, they would be among the first of its sons to be devoured. This is what happened in the USSR and in China, and quite generally the old, somewhat tolerant establishment is replaced by a new, quite intolerant one. Right-wing and left-wing politics do not enter into the subject to any extent, and to argue the case in these political terms is irrelevant. On these issues left-wing voters have never been shown to differ in any marked way from right-wing voters.

Beyond all the points discussed in this book there is one which concerns many of the people who are opposed to the

present permissiveness in the media, and which is often neglected in the arguments so far reviewed. It also does not feature
much in the experimental literature. A given country, at a given
time, has a certain moral climate; this climate can easily be
disrupted by propaganda in the media and elsewhere. Plato
was already fully aware of this possibility, and argued vehe-
mently against the influence of poets and musicians in his
Republic, to the extent of wanting to banish them all. It is this
disruption of the moral tone which obtained when many people
now living grew up, rather than specific acts of sexual immoral-
ity and violence, which concerns them. They would argue that
it is quite wrong to say that they are bent on a process of
indoctrination, with their opponents wishing only to set people
free to follow their inclinations. The propaganda of the libertarians also constitutes a process of indoctrination; children as
they grow up are bound to become conditioned, indoctrinated
and brainwashed in some direction by the prevailing tone set
by the writers, film-makers and TV producers. Many youngsters now bow to the tyranny of those who consider chastity an
outgrown shibboleth, and against their better judgement ape
the models appearing in the cinema or on TV. *Freedom to embrace
promiscuity should also mean freedom to embrace marital fidelity*; it is
this freedom that is denied the average person when all the
pressure in the media is in the other direction. It is small
wonder that this pressure is interpreted, perhaps rightly, as an
assault on established values, and resented accordingly.

Such a view is supported by much of the work here reviewed,
and in particular the well-established facts of modelling, desensitization and evaluative conditioning suggest that something
of the kind must be happening. If it could be shown that the
majority of the population had been consulted on the point, and
had unambiguously voted in favour of such a change in the
value system of society, then one might argue that the democratic process had validated the change in emphasis. But this has
not happened, and indeed population surveys show quite strik-
ingly that the great majority still believe in such issues as the
sanctity of the family, and the importance of its preservation.
Given that modern trends in the cinema and on TV threaten
this survival, it is not perhaps unreasonable that many people
should feel tempted to protest vigorously against what they see
as a threat to their value system. If there were an opposing

value system, well articulated and meaningfully presented, then one could allow the two systems to battle it out between them, as the Christian and the Roman religious systems did 2,000 years ago.

This, however, is not the position. Many who oppose the traditional value system have in fact nothing to put in its place; as we have seen, acceptance of the communist value system would if anything strengthen the emphasis on family life, chastity, and spiritual aspects of the sexual relation. Thus the emphasis in the media on pornography and violence is purely destructive, similar in many ways to the decadence apparent in the later years of the Roman Empire. There is little doubt that critics have a strong point here; however, it is not clear that censorship is the answer. Censorship of extreme deviations from the norm, particularly when these can be shown empirically to have particular unwanted consequences (unwanted by the majority of the population), is one thing; censorship of something as amorphous as the destructive critique of a whole system of values is quite another. It does not seem possible to counter the present obsession with sex and violence by prohibition, and indeed it does not seem desirable. What is needed instead is a more positive assertion of traditional values, if those who hold these values wish to overcome the challenge presented by their critics. Our last recommendation, therefore, would be *not to demand or expect too much from censorship*; we should not use censorship to keep criticism quiet and impotent, however much that criticism may hurt. Nothing should be banned because it is new, uncomfortable, or different; it is only when there is some evidence that it causes actual harm to individuals within society, in some measurable way, that such action becomes advisable.

One last point may deserve examination. Those in favour of some form of censorship often claim that people need to be protected from themselves; they may quote the example of enforced safety belt wearing regulations in some countries, laws regarding advertising for tobacco and alcoholic beverages, and other similar examples. The answer, predictably enough, is that people must be left to themselves to choose how to live their lives, even though we may not approve of the way in which they do so. Paternalism, with its implied sense of superiority, is rightly resented by those whose activities are restricted, even though the restriction may be imposed with the best of motives. Should we prevent people from harming themselves? Actually it is an oversimplification to say that the person who drinks or smokes to excess is harming no one but himself, an objection often made to any form of action that would discourage these habits. The person who becomes an alcoholic certainly harms his family; the person who drinks and drives may (and only too frequently does) injure and kill innocent victims. The person who smokes too much may cost society a great deal of money in medical costs, hospital charges, and other hidden costs such as unemployment benefit. Heroin addicts are an even better example; while apparently only harming themselves, many also commit serious crimes in order to get enough money to satisfy their need for the drug. Society has a right to concern itself with such matters, although the experience of prohibition has shown the difficulties involved in discharging this social duty.

Note that it is not a question of taking away from people something nice and enjoyable, in the name of some spoil-sport nanny who does not like them to have fun. The argument is entirely based on the point that *the portrayal of pornography and violence has effects on many people which cause them to interfere with the lives, health and happiness of other people.* We have to weigh the amusement, enjoyment and delight viewers may derive from such presentations against the injuries, degradation and even deaths which may be caused to innocent victims who become subject to the perverted sexual and violent urges in part produced or increased by these portrayals. In so far as we judge that we would not like to be exposed to such films and shows, and that consequently others too should be prevented from seeing them, we are on very poor ground. However, that is not the burden of our argument; the argument is fairly and squarely based on the demonstration that presentations of the kind mentioned do have effects on the actions, beliefs and attitudes of viewers which affect other people, and that these effects are serious enough to demand consideration. It is understood that these arguments come into conflict with equally cogent arguments for free speech, and other freedoms which may have to be curtailed to some extent. We have made certain recommendations, but these reflect to some extent our own value system, as well as being based on the factual evidence. As such, they are subject to argument, criticism, and rejection.

However, there is a subtle difference between enforcing a rule which restrains a person from following his natural bent (such as not wearing a safety belt) and laying down rules which make it more difficult for one group of people to 'lead others into temptation' – e.g. by appropriate advertising of tobacco or alcohol, promising eternal youth, sexual omnipotence, and other wonderful things. Proscribing certain types of obscene publications, pornographic films and TV shows, and portrayals of violence would seem to fall into the second category; many of our subjects have stated that they would not have considered going to see pornographic films had it not been for tempting advertisements, and that they often regretted having succumbed to temptation. Furthermore, this may be an acquired taste (like smoking); *l'appetit vient en mangeant*. Removal of the temptation, while leaving the goods in question accessible to those really intent on securing them, is one method of compromise, half-way between censorship and complete permissiveness. Rules about advertising of shows of pornography and violence, out-of-house showing of enticing pictures, and other similar measures are available to reduce the temptation without removing the essential freedom of showing films in the 'grey' area between permissible and definitely impermissible. Film clubs constitute another such half-way house. The solution is rather similar to that proposed by the Wolfenden Committee for street prostitution; prostitution was permitted to continue, but street soliciting was abolished. Sweeping vice under the carpet may not seem an occupation worthy of the brave new world we are supposed to be building, but it may resolve difficult conflict into widely acceptable compromise.

When all is said and done, pornography and violence in the media are only symptoms of a much more widespread disease, namely a general loss of values, Christian, moral, or social. Being born of this general loss of values, it in turn feeds into it in a kind of positive feedback cycle. No great changes in social well-being should be expected even if the proposals here reviewed should be carried into effect, and no great disaster should be expected should nothing in fact be done. Clearly this is but one of many areas where changes are required; violence in the streets is much more likely to be encouraged by the general permissiveness which has now engulfed both the lawmakers and the law-enforcers, than by the much less important effects that screen presentations and portrayal may have (Eysenck, 1977b). But every little helps; if we cannot turn the tide in one go we may have to be content with attacking the many different manifestations of our social malaise piecemeal. A society which cannot guarantee its citizens a fair degree of safety from arbitrary violence, rape, vandalism and sheer destructiveness ceases to deserve the name of civilization; it must fight back or go under. The overt, exciting, and tempting portrayal of violence in the media is one target which lends itself to attack; given the factual knowledge which we now possess and granted all the qualifications we have noted, one cannot but agree with those who have expressed concern over the years that indeed some at least of the burden of guilt for our present position must be laid at the door of those who for mainly commercial reasons have been responsible for this type of titillation. Pornography, although probably less serious in its effects, cannot escape blame entirely. Society must take action, soon, to redress the balance.

SUMMARY

Our major conclusions are that the evidence strongly indicates that the portrayal of sex and violence in the media does affect the attitudes and behaviour of viewers; that these effects are variable, depending on the details of presentation and the personality of the viewers; and that recommendations for action depend in part on a person's value system. Aggressive acts new to the subject's repertoire of responses, as well as acts already well established, can be evoked by violent scenes portrayed on film, TV, or in the theatre. Pornography, too, affects many viewers, but its effects are likely to be much more variable. Variability of reaction is associated with such factors as the sex of the viewer, or his personality; genetic as well as environmental factors operate here. Conditioning has been shown to play a large part in determining a person's reactions to such presentations, but conditioning itself is closely related to personality, and follows certain innate patterns. The great variability of attitudes and reactions make it clearly impossible for recommendations to be universally acceptable; compromise is inevitable, and compromise pleases nobody. It also has the virtue that it displeases nobody sufficiently to provoke public disorder. Our recommendations, which are clearly subject to debate, disagreement and argument to a degree that our factual findings are not, suggest a closer watch on the portrayal of violence in the media, and also certain restrictions on the portrayal of pornography, though not of erotica. We also recommend a greater objectivity in the wording of rules and laws in this context; present laws are impossible to enforce because of the subjectivity of interpretation of the terms employed. It can no longer be said that the evidence is ambiguous, or too contradictory to allow any conclusions to be drawn; the evidence is remarkably consistent, and congruent in its major aspects. Much still clearly remains to be discovered, but our major conclusions are unlikely to be changed by such future work.

Bibliography

Abel, G. C., Blanchard, E. B., Barlow, D. H. and Mavissakalian, M. (1975). Identifying specific erotic cues in sexual deviations by audiotaped descriptions. *Journal of Applied Behaviour Analysis*, 8, 247–60.

Abelson, H., Cohen, R., Heaton, E. and Suder, C. (1971). National survey of public attitudes toward and experience with erotic materials: Findings. In *Technical Report of the Commission on Obscenity and Pornography* (Vol. 6). Washington, DC: US Government Printing Office.

Albert, R.S. (1957). The role of mass media and the effect of aggressive film content upon children's aggressive responses and identification choices. *Genetic Psychology Monographs*, 55, 221–85.

Amoroso, D. M., Brown, M., Pruesse, M., Ware, E. E. and Pilkey, D. W. (1971). An investigation of behavioral, psychological, and physiological reactions to pornographic stimuli. In *Technical Report of the Commission on Obscenity and Pornography* (Vol. 8). Washington, DC: US Government Printing Office.

Athanasiou, R. and Shauer, P. (1971). Correlates of heterosexuals' reactions to pornography. *Journal of Sex Research*, 7, 298–311.

Averill, J. R., Malmstrom, E. J., Koriat, A. and Lazarus, R. S. (1972). Habituation to complex emotional stimuli. *Journal of Abnormal Psychology*, 80, 20–8.

Bailyn, L. (1959). Mass media and children: A study of exposure habits and cognitive effects. *Psychological Monographs*, 73 (Whole No. 471).

Baker, R. K. and Ball, S. J. (Eds) (1969). *Violence and the Media: A Staff Report to the National Commission on the Causes and Prevention of Violence* (Vol. 9). Washington, DC: US Government Printing Office.

Baldwin, T. F. and Lewis, C. (1972). Violence in television: The industry looks at itself. In *T.V. and Social Behavior* (Vol. 1). Washington, DC: US Government Printing Office.

Bancroft, J. and Mathews, A. (1971). Autonomic correlates of penile erection. *Journal of Psychosomatic Research*, 15, 159–67.

Bandura, A. (1965). Influence of models' reinforcement contingencies on the acquisition of imitative responses. *Journal of Personality and Social Psychology*, 1, 589–95.

Bandura, A. (1973). *Aggression: A Social Learning Analysis*. Englewood Cliffs, New Jersey: Prentice-Hall.

Bandura, A. and Menlove, F. L. (1968). Factors determining vicarious extinction of avoidance behavior through symbolic modeling. *Journal of Personality and Social Psychology*, 8, 99–108.

Bandura, A., Ross, D. and Ross, S. A. (1961). Transmission of aggression through imitation of aggressive models. *Journal of Abnormal and Social Psychology*, 63, 575–82.

Bandura, A., Ross, D. and Ross, S. A. (1963a). Imitation of film-mediated aggressive models. *Journal of Abnormal and Social Psychology*, 66, 3–11.

Bandura, A., Ross, D. and Ross, S. A. (1963b). Vicarious reinforcement and imitative learning. *Journal of Abnormal and Social Psychology*, 67, 601–7.

Barclay, A. M. (1969). The effect of hostility on physiological and fantasy responses. *Journal of Personality*, 37, 651–67.

Barclay, A. M. (1970). The effect of female aggressiveness on aggressive and sexual fantasies. *Journal of Projective Techniques and Personality Assessment*, 34, 19–26.

Barclay, A. M. and Haber, R. N. (1965). The relation of aggressive to sexual motivation. *Journal of Personality*, 33, 462–75.

Baron, R. A. and Bell, P. A. (1977). Sexual arousal and aggression by males: Effects of type of erotic stimuli and prior provocation. *Journal of Personality and Social Psychology*, 35, 79–87.

Baron, R. A. and Kepner, C. R. (1970). Model's behavior and attraction toward the model as determinants of adult aggressive behavior. *Journal of Personality and Social Psychology*, 14, 335–44.

Bartell, G. D. (1970). Group sex among mid-Americans. *Journal of Sex Research*, 6, 113–30.

Belson, W. A. (1978). *Television Violence and the Adolescent Boy*. Farnborough: Teakfield.

Ben-Veniste, R. (1971). Pornography and sex crime: The Danish experience. In *Technical Report of the Commission on Obscenity and Pornography* (Vol. 7). Washington, DC: US Government Printing Office.

Berger, S. M. (1962). Conditioning through vicarious instigation. *Psychological Review*, 69, 450–66.

Bergin, A. E. and Garfield, S. L. (Eds) (1971). *Handbook of Psychotherapy and Behavior Change*. London: Wiley.

Berkowitz, L. (1962). *Aggression: A Social Psychological Analysis*. New York: McGraw-Hill.

Berkowitz, L. and Geen, R. G. (1966). Film violence and the cue properties of available targets. *Journal of Personality and Social Psychology*, 3, 525–30.

Berkowitz, L. and Rawlings, E. (1963). Effects of film violence on inhibitions against subsequent aggression. *Journal of Abnormal and Social Psychology*, 66, 405–12.

Boffey, P. M. and Walsh, J. (1970). Study of TV violence: Seven top researchers blackballed from panel. *Science*, 168, 949–52.

Bogart, L. (1972). Warning: The Surgeon General has determined that TV violence is moderately dangerous to your child's mental health. *Public Opinion Quarterly*, 36, 491–521.

Brady, J. P. and Levitt, E. E. (1965). The relation of sexual preferences to sexual experiences. *Psychological Record*, 15, 377–84.

Briand, P. L. (Ed.) (1969). *Mass Media Hearings: A Staff Report to the National Commission on the Causes and Prevention of Violence* (Vol. 9A). Washington, DC: US Government Printing Office.

Brown, M., Amoroso, D. M. and Ware, E. E. (1976). Behavioral effects of viewing pornography. *Journal of Social Psychology*, 98, 235–45.

Byrne, D., Fisher, J. D., Lamberth, J. and Mitchell, H. E. (1974). Evaluations of erotica: Facts or feelings? *Journal of Personality and Social Psychology*, 29, 111–16.

Byrne, D. and Lamberth, J. (1971). The effect of erotic stimuli on sex arousal, evaluative responses, and subsequent behaviour. In *Technical Report of the Commission on Obscenity and Pornography* (Vol. 8). Washington, DC: US Government Printing Office.

Caggiula, A. R. and Eibergen, R. (1969). Copulation of virgin male rats evoked by painful peripheral stimulation. *Journal of Comparative and Physiological Psychology*, 69, 414–19.

Carruthers, M. and Taggart, P. (1973). Vagotonicity of violence: Biochemical and cardiac responses to violent films and television programmes. *British Medical Journal*, 3, 384–9.

Cater, D. and Strickland, S. (1975). *TV Violence and the Child: The Evolution and Fate of the Surgeon General's Report*. New York: Russell Sage Foundation.

Chaffee, S. H. (1972). Television and adolescent aggressiveness (Overview). In *T.V. and Social Behavior* (Vol. 3). Washington, DC: US Government Printing Office.

Cline, V. B. (Ed.) (1974). *Where do you Draw the Line? An Exploration into Media Violence, Pornography, and Censorship*. Provo, Utah: Brigham Young University Press.

Cline, V. B., Croft, R. G. and Courrier, S. (1973). Desensitization of children to television violence. *Journal of Personality and Social Psychology*, 27, 360–5.

Comstock, G. and Lindsey, G. (1975). *Television and Human Behavior: The Research Horizon, Future and Present*. Santa Monica: Rand Corporation.

Cook, R. F. and Fosen, R. H. (1971). Pornography and the sex offender: Patterns of exposure and immediate arousal effects of pornographic stimuli. In *Technical Report of the Commission on Obscenity and Pornography* (Vol. 7). Washington, DC: US Government Printing Office.

Court, J. H. (1977). Pornography and sex-crimes: A re-evaluation in the light of recent trends around the world. *International Journal of Criminality and Penology*, 5, 129–57.

Cressey, P. G. and Thrasher, F. M. (1933). *Boys, Movies and City Streets*. New York: Macmillan.

Davis, K. E. and Braucht, G. N. (1971a). Exposure to pornography, character, and sexual deviance: A retrospective survey. In *Technical Report of the Commission on Obscenity and Pornography* (Vol. 7). Washington, DC: US Government Printing Office.

Davis, K. E. and Braucht, G. N. (1971b). Reactions to viewing films of erotically realistic heterosexual behavior. In *Technical Report of the Commission on Obscenity and Pornography* (Vol. 8). Washington, DC: US Government Printing Office.

Dominick, J. R. and Greenberg, B. S. (1972). Attitudes toward violence: The interaction of television exposure, family attitudes, and social class. In *T.V. and Social Behavior* (Vol. 3). Washington, DC: US Government Printing Office.

Donnerstein, E., Donnerstein, M. and Evans, R. (1975). Erotic stimuli and aggression: Facilitation or inhibition. *Journal of Personality and Social Psychology*, 32, 237–44.

Drabman, R. S. and Thomas, M. H. (1974). Does media violence increase children's tolerance of real-life aggression? *Developmental Psychology*, 10, 418–21.

Eaves, L. J. and Eysenck, H. J. (1974). Genetics and the development of social attitudes. *Nature*, 249, 288–9.

Ekman, P., Liebert, R. M., Friesen, W. V., Harrison, R., Zlatchin, C., Malmstrom, E. J. and Baron, R. A. (1972). Facial expressions of emotion while watching televised violence as predictors of subsequent aggression. In *T.V. and Social Behavior* (Vol. 5). Washington, DC: US Government Printing Office.

Eron, L. D. (1963). Relationship of T.V. viewing habits and aggressive behavior in children. *Journal of Abnormal and Social Psychology*, 67, 193–6.

Eron, L. D., Lefkowitz, M. M., Huesmann, L. R. and Walder, L. O. (1972). Does television violence cause aggression? *American Psychologist*, 27, 253–63.

Eysenck, H. J. (1954). *The Psychology of Politics*. London: Routledge & Kegan Paul.

Eysenck, H. J. (1961). Television and the problem of violence. *New Scientist*, 12, 606–7.

Eysenck, H. J. (1967). *The Biological Basis of Personality*. Springfield: Thomas.

Eysenck, H. J. (1972a). *Psychology is about people*. London: Allen Lane.

Eysenck, H. J. (1972b). Obscenity – officially speaking. *Penthouse*, 4, 69–76.

Eysenck, H. J. (1973). Personality, learning, and 'anxiety'. In H. J. Eysenck (Ed.), *Handbook of Abnormal Psychology*. London: Pitman.

Eysenck, H. J. (Ed.) (1974). *Case Histories in Behaviour Therapy*. London: Routledge & Kegan Paul.

Eysenck, H. J. (1976a). Genetic Factors in Personality Development. In A. R. Kaplan (Ed.), *Human Behavior Genetics*. Springfield: Thomas.

Eysenck, H. J. (1976b). *Sex and Personality*. London: Open Books.

Eysenck, H. J. (1977a). *You and Neurosis*. London: Temple Smith.

Eysenck, H. J. (1977b). *Crime and Personality* (3rd Edition). London: Routledge & Kegan Paul.

Eysenck, H. J. and Coulter, T. (1972). The personality and attitudes of working-class British Communists and Fascists. *Journal of Social Psychology*, 87, 59–73.

Eysenck, H. J. and Eysenck, S. B. G. (1969). *Personality Structure and Measurement*. London: Routledge & Kegan Paul.

Eysenck, H. J. and Eysenck, S. B. G. (1976). *Psychoticism as a Dimension of Personality*. London: Hodder & Stoughton.

Eysenck, H. J. and Levey, A. (1972). Conditioning, introversion–extraversion and the strength of the nervous system. In V. D. Nebylitsyn and J. A. Gray (Eds), *Biological Bases of Individual Behavior*. New York: Academic Press.

Eysenck, H. J. and Rachman, S. (1965). *Causes and Cures of Neurosis*. London: Routledge & Kegan Paul.

Eysenck, H. J. and Wilson, G. D. (1973). *The Experimental Study of Freudian Theories*. London: Methuen.

Feldman, M. P. and MacCulloch, M. J. (1971). *Homosexual Behaviour, Therapy and Assessment*. Oxford: Pergamon.

Feshbach, S. (1955). The drive-reducing function of fantasy behavior. *Journal of Abnormal and Social Psychology*, 50, 3–11.

Feshbach, S. (1961). The stimulating versus cathartic effects of a vicarious aggressive activity. *Journal of Abnormal and Social Psychology*, 63, 381–5.

Feshbach, S. and Singer, R. D. (1971). *Television and Aggression: An Experimental Field Study*. San Francisco: Jossey-Bass.

Foulkes, D., Belvedere, E. and Brubaker, T. (1972). Televised violence and dream content. In *T.V. and Social Behavior* (Vol. 5). Washington, DC: US Government Printing Office.

Gebhard, P. H., Gagnon, J. H., Pomeroy, W. B. and Christenson, C. V. (1965). *Sex Offenders: An Analysis of Types*. London: Heinemann.

Geen, R. G. (1978). Some effects of observing violence upon the behavior of the observer. In B. Maher (Ed.), *Progress in Experimental Personality Research* (Vol. 8). New York: Academic Press.

Geen, R. G. and Berkowitz, L. (1967). Some conditions facilitating the occurrence of aggression after the observation of violence. *Journal of Personality*, 35, 666–76.

Geen, R. G. and Quanty, M. B. (1977). The catharsis of aggression: An evaluation of a hypothesis. In L. Berkowitz (Ed.), *Advances in Experimental Social Psychology* (Vol. 10). New York: Academic Press.

Gerbner, G. (1972). Violence in television drama: Trends and symbolic functions. In *T.V. and Social Behavior* (Vol. 1). Washington, DC: US Government Printing Office.

Gerbner, G. and Gross, L. (1976). Living with television: The violence profile. *Journal of Communication*, 26, 173–99.

Gillan, P. (1978a). Therapeutic uses of obscenity. In R. Dhavan and C. Davis (Eds), *Censorship and Obscenity*. London: M. Robertson.

Gillan, P. (1978b). Group therapy for increasing the sexual interest of female patients and their partners. In M. Cook and G. D. Wilson (Eds), *Love and Attraction: An International Conference*. Oxford: Pergamon.

Gillan, P. and Frith, C. (1978). Male–female differences in response to erotica. In M. Cook and G. D. Wilson (Eds), *Love and Attraction: An International Conference*. Oxford: Pergamon.

Goldstein, J. H. and Arms, R. L. (1971). Effects of observing athletic contests on hostility. *Sociometry*, 34, 83–90.

Goldstein, M. J. and Kant, H. S. (1973). *Pornography and Sexual Deviance*. Berkeley: University of California Press.

Goldstein, M. J., Kant, H. S., Judd, L. L., Rice, C. J. and Green, R. (1971). Exposure to pornography and sexual behavior in deviant and normal groups. In *Technical Report of the Commission on Obscenity and Pornography* (Vol. 7). Washington, DC: US Government Printing Office.

Gorman, G. F. (1964). Fetishism occurring in identical twins. *British Journal of Psychiatry*, 110, 255–6.

Gosselin, C. (1978). Personality attributes of the average rubber fetishist. In M. Cook and G. D. Wilson (Eds), *Love and Attraction: An International Conference*. Oxford: Pergamon.

Gray, J. (1972). The psychophysiological nature of introversion–extraversion: A modification of Eysenck's theory. In V. D. Nebylitsyn and J. A. Gray (Eds), *Biological Bases of Individual Behavior*. New York: Academic Press.

Griffitt, W. (1975). Sexual experience and sexual responsiveness: Sex differences. *Archives of Sexual Behavior*, 4, 529–40.

Halloran, J. D. and Croll, P. (1972). Television programs in Great Britain: Content and control. In *T.V. and Social Behavior* (Vol. 1). Washington, DC: US Government Printing Office.

Hanratty, M. A., Liebert, R. M., Morris, L. W. and Fernandez, L. E. (1969). Imitation of film-mediated aggression against live and inanimate victims. *Proceedings of the 77th Annual Convention of the American Psychological Association*, 457–8.

Hanratty, M. A., O'Neal, E. and Sulzer, J. L. (1972). Effect of frustration upon imitation of aggression. *Journal of Personality and Social Psychology*, 21, 30–4.

Hapkiewicz, W. and Roden, A. H. (1971). The effect of aggressive cartoons on children's interpersonal play. *Child Development*, 42, 1583–5.

Hicks, D. J. (1965). Imitation and retention of film-mediated aggressive peer and adult models. *Journal of Personality and Social Psychology*, 2, 97–100.

Hicks, D. J. (1968). Short- and long-term retention of affectively varied modeled behavior. *Psychonomic Science*, 11, 369–70.

Himmelweit, H. T., Oppenheim, A. N. and Vince, P. (1958). *Television and the Child: An Empirical Study of the Effect of Television on the Young*. London: Oxford University Press.

Hoult, T. B. (1949). Comic books and juvenile delingquency. *Sociology and Social Research*, 33, 779-84.

Howard, J. L., Reifler, C. B. and Liptzin, M. B. (1971). Effects of exposure to pornography. In *Technical Report of the Commission on Obscenity and Pornography* (Vol. 8). Washington, DC: US Government Printing Office.

Howitt, D. and Cumberbatch, G. (1972). Affective feeling for a film character and evaluation of an anti-social act. *British Journal of Social and Clinical Psychology*, 11, 102–8.

Howitt, D. and Cumberbatch, G. (1975). *Mass Media Violence and Society*. New York: Halstead.

Hurwood, B. J. (1969). *Torture Through the Ages*. New York: Paperback Library.

Jaffe, Y., Malamuth, N., Feingold, J. and Feshbach, S. (1974). Sexual arousal and behavioral aggression. *Journal of Personality and Social Psychology*, 30, 759–64.

Jakobovits, L. A. (1965). Evaluational reactions to erotic literature. *Psychological Reports*, 16, 985–94.

Johnson, W. T., Kupperstein, L. R. and Peters, J. J. (1971). Sex offenders' experience with erotica. In *Technical Report of the Commission on Obscenity and Pornography* (Vol. 7). Washington, DC: US Government Printing Office.

Kantorowitz, D. A. (1978). Personality and conditioning of tumescence and detumescence. *Behaviour Research and Therapy*, in press.

Kinsey, A. C., Pomeroy, W. B., Martin, C. E. and Gebhard, P. H. (1953). *Sexual Behavior in the Human Female*. Philadelphia: Saunders.

Kniveton, B. H. (1973a). The effect of rehearsal delay on long-term imitation of filmed aggression. *British Journal of Psychology*, 64, 259–65.

Kniveton, B. H. (1973b). Social class and imitation of aggressive adult and peer models. *Journal of Social Psychology*, 89, 311–12.

Kniveton, B. H. and Stephenson, G. M. (1970). The effect of pre-experience on imitation of an aggressive film model. *British Journal of Social and Clinical Psychology*, 9, 31–6.

Kniveton, B. H. and Stephenson, G. M. (1972). The effect of social class on imitation in a pre-experience situation. *British Journal of Social and Clinical Psychology*, 11, 225–34.

Kobasigawa, A. (1966). Observationally induced disinhibition of inappropriately sex-typed responses in young children. *Japanese Journal of Educational Psychology*, 14, 9–14.

Kobasigawa, A. (1967). Avoidance of inappropriately sex-typed objects by kindergarten children through modeling. *Japanese Journal of Educational Psychology*, 15, 34–41.

Kolářský, A. and Madlafousek, J. (1972). Female behavior and sexual arousal in heterosexual male deviant offenders: An experimental study. *Journal of Nervous and Mental Disease*, 155, 110–18.

Krech, D., Crutchfield, R. S. and Livson, N. (1974). *Elements of Psychology* (3rd Edition). New York: Knopf.

Kupperstein, L. R. and Wilson, W. C. (1971). Erotica and antisocial behavior: An analysis of selected indicator statistics. In *Technical Report of the Commission on Obscenity and Pornography* (Vol. 7). Washington, DC: US Government Printing Office.

Kutschinsky, B. (1971a). Towards an explanation of the decrease in registered sex crimes in Copenhagen. In *Technical Report of the Commission on Obscenity and Pornography* (Vol. 7). Washington, DC: US Government Printing Office.

Kutschinsky, B. (1971b). The effect of pornography: A pilot experiment on perception, behavior and attitudes. In *Technical Report of the Commission on Obscenity and Pornography* (Vol. 8). Washington, DC: US Government Printing Office.

Langevin, R. and Martin, M. (1975). Can erotic responses be classically conditioned? *Behavior Therapy*, 6, 350–5.

Laws, D. R. and Rubin, H. B. (1969). Instructional control of an autonomic sexual response. *Journal of Applied Behaviour Analysis*, 2, 93–9.

Lazarus, R. S., Speisman, J. C., Mordkoff, A. M. and Davison, L. A. (1962). A laboratory study of psychological stress produced by a motion picture film. *Psychological Monographs*, 76 (Whole No. 553).

Lefkowitz, M. M., Eron, L. D., Walder, L. O. and Huesmann, L. R. (1972). Television violence and child aggression: A follow-up study. In *T.V. and Social Behavior* (Vol. 3). Washington, DC: US Government Printing Office.

Leifer, A. D. and Roberts, D. F. (1972). Children's responses to television violence. In *T.V. and Social Behavior* (Vol. 2). Washington, DC: US Government Printing Office.

Levitt, E. E. and Hinesley, R. K. (1967). Some factors in the valences of erotic visual stimuli. *Journal of Sex Research*, 3, 63–8.

Leyens, J. P., Camino, L., Parke, R. D. and Berkowitz, L. (1975). The effects of movie violence on aggression in a field setting as a function of group dominance and cohesion. *Journal of Personality and Social Psychology*, 32, 346–60.

Liebert, R. M. and Baron, R. A. (1972). Short-term effects of televised aggression on children's aggressive behavior. In *T.V. and Social Behavior* (Vol. 2). Washington, DC: US Government Printing Office.

Loew, C. A. (1967). Acquisition of a hostile attitude and its relationship to aggressive behavior. *Journal of Personality and Social Psychology*, 5, 335–41.

Lövaas, O. I. (1961). Effect of exposure to symbolic aggression on aggressive behavior. *Child Development*, 32, 37–44.

Lyle, J. and Hoffman, H. R. (1972). Children's use of television and other media. In *T.V. and Social Behavior* (Vol. 4). Washington, DC: US Government Printing Office.

McConaghy, N. (1967). Penile volume change to moving pictures of male and female nudes in heterosexual and homosexual males. *Behaviour Research and Therapy*, 5, 43–8.

McGuire, R. J., Carlisle, J. M. and Young, B. G. (1965). Sexual deviations as conditioned behavior: A hypothesis. *Behaviour Research and Therapy*, 2, 185–90.

McIntyre, J. J. and Teevan, J. J. (1972). Television violence and deviant behavior. In *T.V. and Social Behavior* (Vol. 3). Washington, DC: US Government Printing Office.

MacLean, P. D. (1965). New findings relevant to the evolution of psycho-sexual functions of the brain. In J. Money (Ed.), *Sex Research: New Developments*. New York: Holt, Rinehart & Winston.

McLeod, J. M., Atkin, C. K. and Chaffee, S. H. (1972). Adolescents, parents and television use: Self-report and other-report measures from the Wisconsin sample. In *T.V. and Social Behavior* (Vol. 3). Washington, DC: US Government Printing Office.

McMullen, S. (1978). The use of film or manual for anorgasmic women. In M. Cook and G. D. Wilson (Eds), *Love and Attraction: An International Conference*. Oxford: Pergamon.

Mann, J., Berkowitz, L., Sidman, J., Starr, S. and West, S. (1974). Satiation of the transient stimulating effect of erotic films. *Journal of Personality and Social Psychology*, 30, 729–35.

Mann, J., Sidman, J. and Starr, S. (1971). Effects of erotic films on sexual behavior of married couples. In *Technical Report of the Com-*

mission on Obscenity and Pornography (Vol. 8). Washington, DC: US Government Printing Office.

Marshall, W. L. (1973). The modification of sexual fantasies: A combined treatment approach to the reduction of deviant sexual behaviour. *Behaviour Research and Therapy*, 11, 557–64.

Martin, M. F., Gelfand, D. M. and Hartmann, D. P. (1971). Effects of adult and peer observers on boys' and girls' responses to an aggressive model. *Child Development*, 42, 1271–5.

Martin, I. and Levey, A. B. (1978). Evaluative conditioning. *Advances in Behaviour Research and Therapy*, 1, 57–104.

Masters, W. H. and Johnson, V. E. (1966). *Human Sexual Response*. Boston: Little, Brown.

Mavissakalian, M., Blanchard, E. B., Abel, G. C. and Barlow, D. H. (1975). Responses to complex erotic stimuli in homosexual and heterosexual males. *British Journal of Psychiatry*, 126, 252–7.

Milgram, S. and Shotland, R. L. (1973). *Television and Antisocial Behavior: Field Experiments*. New York: Academic Press.

Mills, J. (1958). Changes in moral attitudes following temptation. *Journal of Personality*, 26, 517–31.

Morgan, P. (1978). *Delinquent Fantasies*. London: Temple Smith.

Mosher, D. L. (1971). Psychological reactions to pornographic films. In *Technical Report of the Commission on Obscenity and Pornography* (Vol. 8). Washington, DC: US Government Printing Office.

Mosher, D. L. and Katz, H. (1971). Pornographic films, male verbal aggression against women, and guilt. In *Technical Report of the Commission on Obscenity and Pornography* (Vol. 8). Washington, DC: US Government Printing Office.

Mussen, P. and Rutherford, E. (1961). Effects of aggressive cartoons on children's aggressive play. *Journal of Abnormal and Social Psychology*, 62, 461–4.

National Commission on the Causes and Prevention of Violence (1969). *To Establish Justice, to Insure Domestic Tranquility: Final report of the National Commission on the Causes and Prevention of Violence*. Washington, DC: US Government Printing Office.

Nelson, E. (1978). Habituation to sexual stimuli of extraverts and introverts. *Advances in Behaviour Research and Therapy*, in press.

Nias, A. H. W. and Kay, H. (1954). Immediate memory of a broadcast feature programme. *British Journal of Educational Psychology*, 24, 154–60.

Nias, D. K. B. (1975). Personality and other factors determining the recreational interests of children and adults. Ph.D. Thesis: University of London.

Noble, G. (1973). Effects of different forms of filmed aggression on children's constructive and destructive play. *Journal of Personality and Social Psychology*, 26, 54–59.

Noble, G. (1975). *Children in Front of the Small Screen.* London: Constable.

Paisley, M. B. (1972). Social policy research and the realities of the system: Violence done to T.V. research. Unpublished manuscript. Institute for Communication Research: Stanford University.

Parke, R. D., Berkowitz, L., Leyens, J. P., West, S. G. and Sebastian, R. J. (1977). Some effects of violent and nonviolent movies on the behavior of juvenile delinquents. In L. Berkowitz (Ed.), *Advances in Experimental Social Psychology* (Vol. 10). New York: Academic Press.

Plomin, R. and Rowe, D. C. (1977). A twin study of temperament in young children. *Journal of Psychology*, 97, 107–13.

Poser, E. G. (1977). *Behaviour Therapy in Clinical Practice.* Springfield: Thomas.

Prince, V. and Bentler, P. M. (1972). Survey of 504 cases of transvestism. *Psychological Reports*, 31, 903–17.

Propper, M. M. (1972). Exposure to sexually oriented materials among young male prisoners. In *Technical Report of the Commission on Obscenity and Pornography* (Vol. 9). Washington, DC: US Government Printing Office.

Rabinovitch, M. S., McLean, M. S., Markham, J. W. and Talbot, A. D. (1972). Children's violence perception as a function of television violence. In *T.V. and Social Behavior* (Vol. 5). Washington, DC: US Government Printing Office.

Rachman, S. (1966). Sexual fetishism: An experimental analogue. *Psychological Record*, 16, 293–6.

Rachman, S. and Hodgson, R. J. (1968). Experimentally-induced 'sexual fetishism': Replication and development. *Psychological Record*, 18, 25–7.

Reifler, C. B., Howard, J., Lipton, M. A., Liptzin, M. B. and Widmann, D. E. (1971). Pornography: An experimental study of effects. *American Journal of Psychiatry*, 128, 575–82.

Reisinger, J. J. (1974). Masturbatory training in the treatment of primary orgasmic dysfunction. *Journal of Behaviour Therapy and Experimental Psychiatry*, 5, 179–83.

Robinson, J. P. and Bachman, J. G. (1972). Television viewing habits and aggression. In *T.V. and Social Behavior* (Vol. 3). Washington, DC: US Government Printing Office.

Savitsky, J. C., Rogers, R. W., Izard, C. E. and Liebert, R. M. (1971). Role of frustration and anger in the imitation of filmed aggression against a human victim. *Psychological Reports*, 29, 807–10.

Schmidt, G. and Sigusch, V. (1970). Sex differences in responses to psychosexual stimulation by films and slides. *Journal of Sex Research*, 6, 268–83.

Schmidt, G., Sigusch, V. and Meyberg, U. (1969). Psychosexual stimulation in men: Emotional reactions, changes of sex behavior, and measures of conservative attitudes. *Journal of Sex Research*, 5, 199–217.

Schmidt, G., Sigusch, V. and Schäfer, S. (1973). Responses to reading erotic stories: Male–female differences. *Archives of Sexual Behavior*, 2, 181–99.

Schramm, W., Lyle, J. and Parker, E. B. (1961). *Television in the Lives of our Children*. Stanford: Stanford University Press.

Scodel, A. (1957). Heterosexual somatic preference and fantasy dependency. *Journal of Consulting Psychology*, 21, 371–4.

Seligman, M. E. P. (1971). Phobias and preparedness. *Behavior Therapy*, 2, 307–20.

Shemberg, K. M., Leventhal, D. B. and Allman, L. (1968). Aggression machine performance and rated aggression. *Journal of Experimental Research in Personality*, 3, 117–19.

Siegel, A. E. (1956). Film-mediated fantasy aggression and strength of aggressive drive. *Child Development*, 27, 365–78.

Sigusch, V., Schmidt, G., Reinfeld, A. and Wiedemann-Sutor, I. (1970). Psychosexual stimulation: Sex differences. *Journal of Sex Research*, 6, 10–24.

Spence, J. T. and Spence, K. W. (1966). The motivational components of manifest anxiety: Drive and drive stimuli. In C. D. Spielberger (Ed.), *Anxiety and Behavior*. London: Academic Press.

Spengler, A. (1977). Manifest sadomasochism of males: Results of an empirical study. *Archives of Sexual Behavior*, 6, 441–56.

Sprafkin, J. N., Liebert, R. M. and Poulos, R. W. (1975). Effects of a prosocial televised example on children's helping. *Journal of Experimental Child Psychology*, 20, 119–26.

Steele, D. G. and Walker, C. E. (1976). Female responsiveness to erotic films and the 'ideal' erotic film from a feminine perspective. *Journal of Nervous and Mental Disease*, 162, 266–73.

Stein, A. H. and Friedrich, L. K. (1972). Television content and young children's behavior. In *T.V. and Social Behavior* (Vol. 2). Washington, DC: US Government Printing Office.

Stein, A. H. and Friedrich, L. K. (1975). The effects of television content on young children. In A. D. Pick (Ed.), *Minnesota Symposia on Child Psychology* (Vol. 9). Minneapolis: University of Minnesota Press.

Steuer, F. B., Applefield, J. M. and Smith, R. (1971). Televised aggression and the interpersonal aggression of preschool children. *Journal of Experimental Child Psychology*, 11, 442–7.

Surgeon General's Scientific Advisory Committee on Television and Social Behavior (1972). *Television and Growing Up: The Impact of Televised Violence*. Washington, DC: US Government Printing Office.

Tannenbaum, P. H. (1971). Emotional arousal as a mediator of erotic communication effects. In *Technical Report of the Commission on Obscenity and Pornography* (Vol. 8). Washington, DC: US Government Printing Office.

Thomas, A. and Chess, S. (1977). *Temperament and Development*. New York: Brunner/Mazel.

Thomas, M. H. and Drabman, R. S. (1975). Toleration of real life aggression as a function of exposure to televised violence and age of subject. *Merrill-Palmer Quarterly*, 21, 227–32.

Thomas, M. H., Horton, R. W., Lippincott, E. C. and Drabman, R. S. (1977). Desensitization to portrayals of real-life aggression as a function of exposure to television violence. *Journal of Personality and Social Psychology*, 35, 450–8.

Thorne, F. C. and Haupt, T. D. (1966). The objective measurement of sex attitudes and behavior in adult males. *Journal of Clinical Psychology*, 22, 395–403.

Thouless, R. H. (1935). The tendency to certainty in religious belief. *British Journal of Psychology*, 26, 16–31.

Turner, C. W. and Berkowitz, L. (1972). Identification with film aggressor (covert role taking) and reactions to film violence. *Journal of Personality and Social Psychology*, 21, 256–64.

US Commission on Obscenity and Pornography (1970). *The Report of the Commission on Obscenity and Pornography*. New York: Bantam.

Walker, C. E. (1971). Erotic stimuli and the aggressive sexual offender. In *Technical Report of the Commission on Obscenity and Pornography* (Vol. 7). Washington, DC: US Government Printing Office.

Walters, R. H., Bowen, N. V. and Parke, R. D. (1964). Influence of looking behavior of a social model on subsequent looking behavior of observers of the model. *Perceptual and Motor Skills*, 18, 469–83.

Walters, R. H. and Thomas, E. L. (1963). Enhancement of punitiveness by visual and audiovisual displays. *Canadian Journal of Psychology*, 17, 244–55.

Walters, R. H., Thomas, E. L. and Acker, C. W. (1962). Enhancement of punitive behavior by audio-visual displays. *Science*, 136, 872–3.

Wells, W. D. (1973). Television and aggression: Replication of an experimental field study. Unpublished manuscript. Graduate School of Business: University of Chicago.

West, S. G., Berkowitz, L., Sebastian, R. J. and Parke, R. D. (1975). The effect of viewing physical aggression on verbal aggression in delinquent girls. Unpublished manuscript. Florida State University.

Whitehouse, M. (1977). *Whatever happened to sex?* London: Wayland.

Wilson, G. D. and Nias, D. K. B. (1973). The need for a new approach to attitude measurement. In G. D. Wilson (Ed.), *The Psychology of Conservatism*. London: Academic Press.

Wilson, G. T. and Lawson, D. M. (1976). Expectancies, alcohol, and sexual arousal in male social drinkers. *Journal of Abnormal Psychology*, 85, 587–94.

Winick, C. (1971). Some observations on characteristics of patrons of adult theatres and bookstores. In *Technical Report of the Commission on Obscenity and Pornography* (Vol. 4). Washington, DC: US Government Printing Office.

Wober, M. and Dannheisser, P. (1977). Does televised violence provoke paranoid perception? Gerbner's theory explored. *Bulletin of the British Psychological Society*, 30, 188–9.

Wolfe, B. M. and Baron, R. A. (1971). Laboratory aggression related to aggression in naturalistic social situations: Effects of an aggressive model on the behavior of college student and prisoner observers. *Psychonomic Science*, 24, 193–4.

Woodrick, C., Chissom, B. and Smith, D. (1977). Television-viewing habits and parent-observed behaviors of third-grade children. *Psychological Reports*, 40, 830.

Yaffé, M. (1972). Research survey. In Lord Longford (Ed.), *Pornography: The Longford Report*. London: Coronet.

Zillmann, D. (1971). Excitation transfer in communication-mediated aggressive behavior. *Journal of Experimental and Social Psychology*, 7, 419–34.

Zillmann, D. and Sapolsky, B. S. (1977). What mediates the effect of mild erotica on annoyance and hostile behavior in males? *Journal of Personality and Social Psychology*, 35, 587–96.

Zuckerman, M. (1971). Physiological measures of sexual arousal in the human. *Psychological Bulletin*, 75, 297–339.

Selected works that were consulted but not referred to in the text

Aronson, E. and Carlsmith, J. M. (1969). Experimentation in social psychology. In G. Lindzey and E. Aronson, *Handbook of Social Psychology* (Vol. 2), (2nd Edition). Reading, Massachusetts: Addison-Wesley.

Bandura, A. (1969). *Principles of Behavior Modification*. New York: Holt, Rinehart & Winston.

Baron, R. A. (1974). The aggression-inhibiting influence of heightened sexual arousal. *Journal of Personality and Social Psychology*, 30, 318–22.

Baron, R. A. (1978). Aggression-inhibiting influence of sexual humor. *Journal of Personality and Social Psychology*, 36, 189–97.

Brown, R. (Ed.) (1976). *Children and Television*. London: Collier Macmillan.

Bryan, J. H. and Schwartz, T. (1971). Effects of film material upon children's behavior. *Psychological Bulletin*, 75, 50–9.

Byrne, D., Cherry, F., Lamberth, J. and Mitchell, H. E. (1973). Husband–wife similarity in response to erotic stimuli. *Journal of Personality*, 41, 385–94.

Carlson, E. R. and Coleman, C. E. H. (1977). Experiential and motivational determinants of the richness of an induced sexual fantasy. *Journal of Personality*, 45, 528–42.

Collins, W. A. and Zimmermann, S. A. (1975). Convergent and divergent social cues: Effects of televised aggression on children. *Communication Research*, 2, 331–46.

Cook, R. F., Fosen, R. H. and Pacht, A. (1971). Pornography and the sex offender: Patterns of previous exposure and arousal effects of pornographic stimuli. *Journal of Applied Psychology*, 55, 503–11.

Daniels, D. N., Gilula, M. F. and Ochberg, F. M. (Eds) (1970). *Violence and the Struggle for Existence*. Boston: Little, Brown.

Davis, K. E. and Braucht, G. N. (1973). Exposure to pornography, character and sexual deviance: A retrospective study. *Journal of Social Issues*, 29, 183–96.

Diener, E. and DeFour, D. (1978). Does television violence enhance program popularity? *Journal of Personality and Social Psychology*, 36, 333–41.

Donnerstein, E. and Barrett, G. Effects of erotic stimuli on male aggression towards females. *Journal of Personality and Social Psychology*, 36, 180–8.

Fisher, W. A. and Byrne, D. (1978). Sex differences in response to erotica? Love versus lust. *Journal of Personality and Social Psychology*, 36, 117–25.

Friedrich, L. K. and Stein, A. H. (1973). Aggressive and prosocial television programs and the natural behavior of preschool children. *Monographs of the Society for Research in Child Development*, 38 (Whole No. 151).

Frodi, A. (1977). Sexual arousal, situational restrictiveness, and aggressive behavior. *Journal of Research in Personality*, 11, 48–58.

Geen, R. G. and O'Neal, E. C. (Eds) (1976). *Perspectives on Aggression*. New York: Academic Press.

Goldstein, M., Kant, H., Judd, L., Rice, C. and Green, R. (1971). Experience with pornography: Rapists, pedophiles, homosexuals, transsexuals, and controls. *Archives of Sexual Behavior*, 1, 1–17.

Gunn, J. (1973). *Violence in Human Society*. Newton Abbot: David & Charles.

Halloran, J. D., Brown, R. L. and Chaney, D. (1970). *Television and Delinquency*. Leicester: Leicester University Press.

Hartnagel, T. F., Teevan, J. J. and McIntyre, J. J. (1975). Television violence and violent behavior. *Social Forces*, 54, 341–51.

Howe, M. J. A. (1977). *Television and Children*. London: New University Education.

Hyde, H. M. (1964). *A History of Pornography*. London: Heinemann.

Jaffe, Y. and Berger, A. (1977). Cultural generality of the relationship between sex and aggression. *Psychological Reports*, 41, 335–6.

Johnson, M. C. (1976). Viewer aggression, self-esteem and television character preference as variables influencing social normative judgments of television violence. Ph.D. Thesis: Univeristy of Massachusetts.

Kniveton, B. H. (1972). Nursery school as an inhibitor of working-class aggressive imitation. *British Journal of Social and Clinical Psychology*, 11, 295–6.

Kniveton, B. H. and Stephenson, G. M. (1975). The effects of an aggressive film model on social interaction in groups of middle-class and working-class boys. *Journal of Child Psychology and Psychiatry*, 16, 301–13.

Kronhausen, E. and Kronhausen, P. (1959). *Pornography and the Law: The Psychology of Erotic Realism and Pornography*. New York: Ballantine.

Krus, D. J., Sherman, J. L. and Krus, P. H. (1977). Changing values over the last half-century: The story of Thurstone's crime scales. *Psychological Reports*, 40, 207–11.

Kutschinsky, B. (1977). *Pornography and Sex Crimes in Denmark: Early Research Findings*. London: Martin Robertson.

Lefkowitz, M. M., Eron, L. D., Walder, L. O. and Huesmann, L. R. (1977). *Growing up to be Violent: A Longitudinal Study of the Development of Aggression*. New York: Pergamon.

Liebert, R. M. and Baron, R. A. (1972). Some immediate effects of televised violence on children's behavior. *Development Psychology*, 6, 469–75.

Liebert, R. M., Neale, J. M. and Davidson, E. S. (1973). *The Early Window: Effects of Television on Children and Youth*. New York: Pergamon.

Liebert, R. M. and Schwartzberg, N. S. (1977). Effects of mass media. *Annual Review of Psychology*, 28, 141–73.

Malumuth, N. M., Feshbach, S. and Jaffe, Y. (1977). Sexual arousal and aggression: Recent experiments and theoretical issues. *Journal of Social Issues*, 33, 110–33.

Meyer, T. P. (1972). Effects of viewing justified and unjustified real film violence on aggressive behavior. *Journal of Personality and Social Psychology*, 23, 21–9.

Mulvihill, D. J., Tumin, M. M. and Curts, L. A. (1969). *Crimes of Violence: A Staff Report to the National Commission on the Causes and Prevention of Violence* (Vol. 13). Washington, DC: US Government Printing Office.

Murray, J. P. (1973). Television and violence: Implications of the Surgeon General's research program. *American Psychologist*, 28, 472–8.

Noble, G. (1970). Film-mediated aggressive and creative play. *British Journal of Social and Clinical Psychology*, 9, 1–7.

Siegman, A. W. and Dintzer, L. (1977). The catharsis of aggression and hostility. *Psychological Reports*, 41, 399–410.

Storr, A. (1968). *Human Aggression*. London: Allen Lane.

Tannenbaum, P. H. and Zillmann, D. (1975). Emotional arousal in the facilitation of aggression through communication. In L. Berkowitz (Ed.), *Advances in Experimental Social Psychology* (Vol. 8). New York: Academic Press.

Thomas, M. H. and Drabman, R. S. (1978). Effects of television violence on expectations of other's aggression. *Personality and Social Psychology Bulletin*, 4, 73–6.

Wilson, G. D. (1978). *The Secrets of Sexual Fantasy*. London: Dent.

Zillmann, D., Hoyt, J. L. and Day, K. D. (1974). Strength and duration of the effect of aggressive, violent, and erotic communications on subsequent aggressive behavior. *Communication Research*, 1, 286–306.

Index

Page numbers in *italic* type refer to tables or figures.